POETRY AND REFORM

POETRY AND REFORM

Periodical Verse from the English Democratic Press 1792-1824

MICHAEL SCRIVENER

 WAYNE STATE UNIVERSITY PRESS   DETROIT

Copyright © 1992 by Wayne State University Press,
Detroit, Michigan 48202. All rights are reserved.
No part of this book may be reproduced
without formal permission.
Manufactured in the United States of America.
99 98 97 96 95 94 93 92   5 4 3 2 1

Library of Congress
Cataloging-in-Publication Data

Poetry and reform : periodical verse from the
English democratic press, 1792–1824 /
[edited by] Michael Scrivener.
p. cm.
Includes bibliographical references and index.
ISBN 0-8143-2378-2 (alk. paper)
1. Great Britain—Politics and government—
1789–1820—Poetry.
2. Great Britain. Parliament—Reform—History—
Poetry.   3. Radicalism—Great Britain—History—
Poetry.   4. Working class writings,
English.   5. English poetry—19th century.
6. English poetry—18th century.   7. Romanticism—
Great Britain.   8. Political poetry, English.
9. Protest poetry, English.   I. Scrivener,
Michael Henry, 1948–
PR1195.H5P64   1992
821'.7080358—dc20   92-15136

Designer: Mary Krzewinski

TO
**KATHERINE
AND SARAH**

Contents

PREFACE 7
ABBREVIATIONS 9
INTRODUCTION 11

PART ONE
THE REVOLUTIONARY DECADE AND ITS REPRESSIVE AFTERMATH, 1792–1809

NEWSPAPERS

1. *Morning Chronicle*, 1792–1796 37

SENSIBILITY (1792) 37
ODE ON LIBERTY (1792) 38
TO LIBERTY (1792)
   J. A. 40
STANZAS TO T. PAINE (1792)
   J. T. R[utt]. 41
THE MAID'S ENIGMA (1792) 42
THE GENIUS OF FRANCE (1792) 43
HYMN ON THE FAST (1793)
   George Dyer 44
SEDITION ACT (1796)
   A Lady 45

2. *Manchester Herald*, 1792 47

ON SUGAR (1792)
   A Citizen of the World 47
THE REFORM.
BY THE RIGHT HON. WILLIAM PITT
   (1792) 48
TO THE ENGLISH FRIENDS
OF FRENCH FREEDOM
   (1792) 49
A SONG, COMPOSED FOR THE
ANNIVERSARY OF THE FRENCH
REVOLUTION . . . (1792)
   Mr. Scott (of Dromore) 50
EPIGRAM (1792)
   Sam Sly 52
SONG. THE FIRE OF LIBERTY
   (1792) 52

3. *Cambridge Intelligencer*, 1793–1799 53

THE WRONGS OF POVERTY (1793)
   J. T. R[utt]. 54
SONG. INVOCATION TO LIBERTY
   (1793) 56
SOLILOQUY (1794)
   T. R. 57
THE WISH (1794)
   Renege *Trin. Coll.* 57
DOMESTIC FELICITY (1795)
   C. V. L. 58
SONNET (1799) 59
SONNET (1799) 60

Contents

LONDON POLITICAL JOURNALS

1. *The Patriot*, 1793 61
THE PRESENT WAR (1793)
Tell *61*

2. *Pig's Meat*, 1793–1795 62
[JUBILEE HYMN] FROM SPENCE'S
RIGHTS OF MAN . . . (1793)
[Thomas Spence] *63*
BURKE'S ADDRESS TO THE "SWINISH
MULTITUDE!" (1793)
[Thomas Spence] *65*
ALTERATION (1794)
[Thomas Spence] *67*
EXAMPLES OF SAFE PRINTING (1794)
[Thomas Spence] *68*
TRIBUTE TO LIBERTY (1794)
W. D. Grant *69*
EDMUND BURKE'S ADDRESS TO THE
SWINISH MULTITUDE (1794)
[Thomas Spence] *69*
THE RIGHTS OF MAN
FOR ME . . . (1794)
[Thomas Spence] *72*
THE DOWNFALL OF FEUDAL
TYRANNY . . . (1795)
[Thomas Spence] *73*

3. *Politics for the People*, 1793–1794 75
WHAT MAKES A LIBEL?
A FABLE (1793) *76*
TWO WAYS . . . (1793–1794)
No Work *76*
1694 (1794) *77*
LOGS, STORKS, AND ASSES
(1794) *78*
THE GOITRE. A FABLE (1794) *79*
HYMN TO LIBERTY (1794) *82*

INDEPENDENCE (1794) *83*
EFFECTS OF WAR (1794)
Philanthropos *84*
A PARALLEL BETWEEN RICHES AND
POVERTY. FROM THE GREEK
OF RHIANUS (1794) *86*
A TALE (1794)
Tommy Pindar *87*
AN HYMN FOR THE FAST DAY,
TO BE SUNG BY THE FRIENDS
OF MANKIND (1794) *88*
ON ABUSES (1794) *90*

4. *The Philanthropist*, 1795–1796 91
ADDRESS TO POVERTY (1795) *92*
SONNET (1795)
Sylvanus Amicus *93*
CATO'S SOLILOQUY PARODIED
(1795)
M. [W.] H. Green *93*
A NEW SONG (1795) *94*
SONG (1795)
T. Best *95*
POLITICAL CONUNDRUMS (1795)
W. H. Green *96*
THE CARMAGNOLE (1795) *97*
AN ODE TO KENTUCKY (1795)
An Emigrant *98*
THE ATTRIBUTES OF LIBERTY (1795)
W. H. Green *100*
FOR THE TENTH OF AUGUST, 1795
(1795) *102*
THE REPUBLICAN CROP. A NEW
SONG (1796)
W. H. Green *103*
EVERY INCH A PATRIOT, A NEW
SONG (1796)
R. M. *104*
ODE TO FREEDOM (1796) *105*

Contents

5. *The Tribune*, 1795   108

ODE ON THE DESTRUCTION OF THE BASTILLE (1795)
John Thelwall   *109*

NEWS FROM TOULON . . . (1795)
John Thelwall   *113*

A SHEEPSHEERING SONG (1795)
John Thelwall   *115*

A PATRIOT'S FEELING; OR THE CALL OF DUTY . . . (1795)
[John Thelwall?]   *119*

LINES WRITTEN BY A FEMALE CITIZEN! (1795)
F. A. C.   *122*

PROVINCIAL POLITICAL JOURNALS

1. *The Cabinet*, 1795 (Norwich)   124

SONNET TO WINTER (1795)
N. [Amelia Alderson]   *124*

2. *The Oeconomist*, 1798 (Newcastle)   125

THE COTTAGE. A COMPETENCE AND NOT RICHES THE SOURCE OF HAPPINESS (1798)
[Z.]   *125*

THE HARVEST MOON (1798)   *126*

MONTHLIES

1. *Moral and Political Magazine*, 1796–1797   127

SONG (1796)
George Dyer   *127*

SONNET: THE LION (1796)
Joshua   *128*

INVOCATION TO THE GENIUS OF BRITAIN (1796)
A Female Citizen F. A. C.   *129*

SONNET (1797)   *130*

FABLE. THE ASS AND THE DRIVER (1797)   *130*

2. *Monthly Magazine*, 1796–1809   131

ADDRESS TO POVERTY (1796)
L.   *131*

BALLAD (1796)   *132*

GLEE (*GLORIOUS APOLLO*) (1796)
J[ohn]. T[helwall].   *134*

STANZAS, TO THE MEMORY OF ROBERT BURNS (1797)   *134*

TO STELLA, ON HER BIRTH-DAY . . . (1797)
John Thelwall   *138*

EFFUSION ON THE APPROACHING FAST-DAY (1797)
T. S. S.   *139*

ODE TO TERROR (1797)
S. W.   *140*

CONSCIENCE THE WORST OF TORTURES (1798)
Miss [Fanny] Holcroft   *143*

ON MISS LINWOOD'S ADMIRABLE PICTURES IN NEEDLE-WORK (1798)
L[ucy]. A[ikin].   *145*

OWEN PARFET (1799)   *146*

FEMALE EDUCATION AT TWO PERIODS (1799)   *150*

HORACE, BOOK I. EPIST. 18 VERSE 96. TO THE END (1800)
Gilbert Wakefield   *154*

TO GILBERT WAKEFIELD, A.B. ON HIS LIBERATION FROM PRISON (1801)
J[ohn]. Aikin   *155*

TO JOHN AIKIN, M.D. (1801)
Gilbert Wakefield   *157*

TO THE MEMORY OF THE

Contents

Rev. G. Wakefield (1801)
L[ucy]. A[ikin]. *158*

The Condemned Sailor (1801)
Fanny Holcroft *159*

Part of an Inscription Designed for a Garden (1801)
J[ohn]. T. R[utt]. *160*

A Picture and a Prophecy (1803)
A.R. *160*

[Burdett!] (1809)
Anthocles *162*

3. *Athenaeum*, 1808 163

Necessity (1808) *163*

4. *Flower's Political Review*, 1807–1808 165

Monday's News, at Bath . . . (1807)
T. P. *165*

To the Memory of the Right Honourable Charles James Fox (1807)
S. W. *168*

Holy Anticipation; For a Future Thanksgiving Day (1808) *171*

Part Two
The Rebirth of Radicalism, 1815–1824

1. *The Theological Inquirer*, 1815 175

Ode to Religion (1815)
F. [R. C. Fair] *175*

Scripture Soliloqu[i]es. Our blessed Saviour on Mount Calvary (1815)
F. [R. C. Fair] *177*

On Sectarian Persecution (1815)
S. *179*

The Ruined City (1815)
F. [R. C. Fair] *179*

2. *The People*, 1817 185

Spontaneous Verse (1817)
P. F. P—— *185*

An Englishman's Domestic View of his Political Situation . . . (1817)
R. W[edderburn]. *190*

3. *The Forlorn Hope/Axe Laid to the Root*, 1817 194

The Desponding Negro (1817)
R. W[edderburn]. *195*

The Negro Boy sold for a Watch (1817)
R. W[edderburn]. *196*

The African[']s Complaint on board a Slave Ship! (1817)
R. W[edderburn]. *196*

[Britons!] (1817)
[R. Wedderburn] *198*

4. *Sherwin's Political Register*, 1817–1818 199

On the New and Unconstitutional Legislative Acts . . . (1817)
H. W. *200*

On seeing in a List of New Music *The Waterloo Waltz* (1817)
R. S[horter]. *201*

Monopoly (1817)
Alfred *203*

Appeal to Englishmen (1817)
S. R. *204*

The Topic (1817)
A. D[avenport]. *205*

Ode on the Anniversary of T. Paine's Birth-Day . . . (1818)
Clio Rickman *206*

Contents

To Englishmen (1818)
M. *209*

England, at the Commencement of the Reign of George III. 1760 (1818) *210*

Sonnet. Written with a Pencil . . . (1818)
Clio Rickman *212*

Distress of the Poor; A New Song (1818)
G. Taylor *212*

A Hint to Congress (1818)
A. D[avenport]. *213*

5. *The Mirror of Truth*, 1817 215

The Devil's Thoughts (1817)
Professor Porson [S. T. Coleridge] *215*

6. *The Theological and Political Comet; or, Free-Thinking Englishmen*, 1819 217

[Let preachers waste their breath . . .] (1819)
[R. Shorter?] *217*

[When Babylon's notorious wh——re . . .] (1819)
[R. Shorter?] *217*

The Bloody Field of Peterloo! A New Song (1819)
R[obert] S[horter]. *218*

A Psalm, to the Praise and Honor of Liberty (1819)
[R. Shorter?] *219*

The Wanton Wife of Bath (1819)
[R. Shorter?] *220*

[Blush, *Christian* . . .] (1819)
["country correspondent"] *222*

Saint Ethelstone's Day (1819)
A. D[avenport]. *224*

A New Song (1819) *225*

7. *The White Hat*, 1819 226

Sonnet (1819) *226*

It is Lovely to Die for our Country (1819)
T. A. T. *227*

8. *The Medusa*, 1819 227

Majesty in the Shades (1819)
[T. Davison?] *228*

The Wrongs of Man. Or, Things as they Are (1819)
Spencean Philanthropist *229*

The Rights of Man, Or, Things as they were Intended to be by Divine Providence (1819)
Spencean Philanthropist *231*

Nature's First, Last, and Only Will! Or a Hint to Mr. Bull (1819)
E. J. B[landford]. *234*

A Real Dream; Or, Another Hint for Mr. Bull! (1819)
E. J. B[landford]. *235*

More Hints for Mr. Bull; With the last Hint, which at last Bull must take! (1819)
E. J. B[landford]. *238*

Invocation to Britain (1819)
C. P. *239*

An Ode, to Major Cartwright (1819)
A. D[avenport]. *240*

Man in Prospective, Or Things As They Are To Be! (1819) *240*

A Terrible Omen to Guilty Tyrants; or The Spirit of Liberty! (1819)
E. J. B[landford]. *243*

A Lord's Advice, and a Tradesman's Reply (1819)
S. D. *244*

On a Bloody Massacre (1819) *244*

Contents

An Address to "The Rabble" (1819) *245*

Paddy Bull's Epistle to His Brother John (1819) *246*

9. *The Black Dwarf,* 1817–1824 249

The Plot. A Letter to my Brother Robert in the Country (1817)
Dick (of Stepney) *250*

Answer to the Threats of Corruption (1817)
T[homas]. J. W[ooler]. *253*

A Tear (1818)
C. M. T. *253*

The Three Bulls and the Jackdaw. A Fable (1818)
Philo Taurus *254*

Insolence (1818)
F. [R. C. Fair?] *255*

Impromptu Reply to Impertinence (1818)
CLIO *256*

Ode to Major Cartwright (1818)
R. [C.] Fair *256*

To Belinda (1818)
Florio *257*

Ode to the Ladies on Their Alledged [*sic*] Rights (1818)
Roderick Random *258*

Rights of Women. Answer to Florio (1818) *261*

Napoleon in Exile (1818)
F. [R. C. Fair?] *262*

To Britons (1819)
Caledonius *263*

Stanzas Occasioned by the Manchester Massacre! (1819)
Hibernicus *265*

The Peterloo Man (1819) *266*

State Contrivances! (1820)
W. F. L. *267*

Sonnet to Reason (1820)
William Sturch *269*

The Queen's Triumph (1820)
J. W. Dalby *270*

Jeremy Bentham (1821)
B. *272*

The Banished Printer to his Trade (1821)
J. W. B. *272*

Tribute to the Memory of an Injured Queen (1821)
F. G. *273*

Ode to a Plotting Parson . . . (1821)
S. Bamford *274*

The Late Honourable Conduct of Radicals Justified (1822)
Radix *276*

A New Loyal Song, Meant to Please Mr. Murray (1824) *277*

An Ode . . . (1824)
G. Dyer *278*

Bibliography *283*
Author Index *289*
Subject Index *293*

Preface

I have tried to reproduce the poems as exactly as possible, without altering punctuation or spelling. Any additions to the text of the poems have been signalled by brackets, and sometimes I added a bracketed *sic* to signify an unusual spelling or misspelling. It may seem silly to preserve ancient typos but even typos can be meaningful: a large number of them might indicate hurried printing during a politically tense period. At any rate, since I did not want to judge what was a meaningless typo and what was a significant variant, I have preserved the original texts entirely. Entirely, that is, except for the titles and sometimes the first letter of the first word and sometimes the entire first word. Some titles were in huge upper case letters, and the first letter of the first word was oversized, or the first word itself of each poem was in large upper-case letters. As there was no easy way to reproduce this effect consistently, and since the conventions of titles seemed determined more by the typography of each periodical rather than by each poet, I decided to regularize the capitalization of the titles except when it appeared to be the product of the poet. Footnotes within poems are original, and not editorial.

When I have been unable to determine the identity of the poet, I have written within brackets "n. a."—no author identified. My identification of some of the initials and pseudonyms has been conservative. When I have had the slightest doubt I have added a question mark.

In the annotations I have tried to accommodate the needs of both the scholarly expert and the student who might not have the same literary and historical information at her fingertips. Obscure and fairly well-known historical figures, events, authors, and literary allusions have been identified. When I cite an author or historical figure, I provide when possible the birth and death dates; when the person has an entry in the *Dictionary of National Biography*, I add *DNB* after the dates (with royalty and major Romantic poets I omit the *DNB*, assuming anyone would know they are described in there). Some people in the reform movement who have no entry in the *DNB* are, however, written about in a very useful book, which I have

Preface

abbreviated B&G to signify the *Biographical Dictionary of Modern British Radicals, vol. I, 1770–1830* (1978), edited by Joseph O. Baylen and Norbert J. Gossman. In the notes to each periodical and in the annotations to the poems I have included bibliographical information that I hope will be useful. Quotations from the Bible are from the King James Version.

I wish to thank Professor Mary Thale of the University of Illinois at Chicago for her assistance, and I also wish to thank the Graduate School and the English Department of Wayne State University for a travel grant, and Wayne State University for two summer grants and a sabbatical leave which allowed me to work on the project. I wish to thank the following libraries: British Library, Carl H. Pforzheimer Library, Detroit Public Library, University of London Library, University of Michigan Library, Midrasha-College of Jewish Studies Library (Southfield, Michigan), State University of New York at Buffalo Library, Wayne State University Library, and Yale University Library. To the director, Arthur Evans, the professional staff of the Wayne State University Press, including Kathryn Wildfong, and the copyeditor, Cindy Bily, I wish to express my gratitude for their making the book better than it would have been otherwise. I cannot thank enough Donald H. Reiman and Betty T. Bennett, who read the book in manuscript and offered me many useful criticisms. To my wife, Mary Ann Simmons, my thanks for her valuable suggestions.

ABBREVIATIONS

Altick	Altick, Richard. *The English Common Reader. A Social History of the Mass Reading Public 1800–1900*. Chicago & London: U of Chicago P, 1957.
B&G	Baylen, John O., and Norbert J. Gossman, ed. *Biographical Dictionary of Modern British Radicals, vol. I: 1770–1830*. Sussex & New Jersey: Harvester P & Humanities P, 1979.
Bennett	Bennett, Betty T., ed. *British War Poetry in the Age of Romanticism: 1793–1815*. NY & London: Garland, 1976.
Butler 1984	Butler, Marilyn, ed. *Burke, Paine, Godwin, and the Revolution Controversy*. Cambridge: UP, 1984.
Chase	Chase, Malcolm. *"The People's Farm." English Radical Agrarianism 1775–1840*. Oxford: Clarendon P, 1988.
DNB	*Dictionary of National Biography* (1885–)
E. H. Coleridge	Coleridge, E. H., ed. *Coleridge. Poetical Works*. vol. 1. Oxford: UP, 1912.
Erdman 1969	Erdman, David V. *Blake: Prophet Against Empire*. rev. ed.. Garden City: Anchor Books, 1969.
Erdman 1986	Erdman, David V. *Commerce Des Lumieres. John Oswald and the British in Paris, 1790–1793*. Columbia: U of Missouri P, 1986.
Goodwin	Goodwin, Albert. *The Friends of Liberty. The English Democratic Movement in the Age of the French Revolution*. Cambridge: Harvard UP, 1979.
Hone	Hone, J. Ann. *For the Cause of Truth. Radicalism in London 1796–1821*. Oxford: Clarendon P, 1982.
Howell's State Trials	Howell, T. B., ed. *A Complete Collection of State Trials*, vol. 22. London: Hansard, 1817.

ABBREVIATIONS

Klancher	Klancher, Jon. *The Making of the English Reading Audiences, 1790–1832*. Madison & London: U of Wisconsin P, 1987.
Marlow	Marlow, Joyce. *The Peterloo Massacre*. London: Rapp and Whiting, 1969.
Oxford Shelley	Hutchinson, Thomas, and G. M. Matthews, ed. *Shelley. Poetical Works*. Oxford: UP, 1969.
Porter	Porter, Dale H. *The Abolition of the Slave Trade in England, 1784–1807*. New York: Archon Books, 1970.
Reiman 1979	Reiman, Donald H. Introduction. *George Dyer's Odes and The Poet's Fate*. New York & London: Garland, 1979.
Scrivener	Scrivener, Michael. *Radical Shelley*. Princeton: UP, 1982.
Smith	Smith, Olivia. *The Politics of Language 1791–1819*. Oxford: Clarendon P, 1984.
STC Letters	Griggs, Earl Leslie, ed. *Collected Letters of Samuel Taylor Coleridge*, 4 vols. Oxford: Clarendon P, 1956–72.
Sullivan	Sullivan, Alvin, ed. *British Literary Magazines. The Romantic Age, 1789–1836*. Westport & London: Greenwood P, 1983.
Thompson 1963	Thompson, E. P. *The Making of the English Working Class*. NY: Vintage P, 1963.
Thompson 1969	Thompson, E. P. "Disenchantment or Default? A Lay Sermon." In Conor Cruise O'Brien & William Dean Vanech, ed. *Power and Consciousness*. London & NY: U of London P & New York UP, 1969.
Walvin	Walvin, James. *Black and White. The Negro and English Society, 1555–1945*. London: Allen Lane, 1973.
Wickwar	Wickwar, William S. *The Struggle for the Freedom of the Press 1819–1832*. London: George Allen & Unwin, 1928.
Wiener	Wiener, Joel. *Radicalism and Freethought in Nineteenth-Century Britain. The Life of Richard Carlile*. Westport & London: Greenwood P, 1983.
WW Letters	Selincourt, Ernest de, & Chester L. Shaver, ed. *Letters of William and Dorothy Wordsworth. The Early Years 1787–1805*. 2nd edition. Oxford: Clarendon P, 1967.

INTRODUCTION

Until very recently there were only two anthologies that contained much nineteenth-century English reformist verse,[1] Betty T. Bennett's anthology of war poetry (1793–1815) and Y. V. Kovalev's anthology of Chartist poetry. Now there are Brian Maidment's anthology of Victorian laboring-class poetry and Peter Scheckner's anthology of Chartist poetry. Though not explicitly political or laboring-class, Roger Lonsdale's anthology of eighteenth-century women's poetry is another indication that our "canon" of poetry is indeed expanding.[2] *Poetry and Reform* is closest to Bennett's, whose collection extracts war poetry from the reformist and anti-reformist press. I have departed from Bennett's example by including only ostensibly pro-reform periodicals and structuring the selections around not the English-French war but the English reform movement from 1792 to 1824, roughly the period coinciding with the literary period of English Romanticism.

The periodicals represented—newspapers, weeklies, fortnightlies, monthlies—had a wide range of implied readers, from plebeian to genteel. The political spectrum encompassed by this anthology goes from insurrectionary laboring-class socialism to moderate liberalism. The different kinds of poems reflect the generic diversity at the time; except for epic, almost every poetic genre is represented here. Constituting some coherence within the diversity is that all the poems are from periodicals, and all the periodicals are informed by a political commitment to reform, whether radical or moderate, exclusively political or social and economic also. The poets and their periodicals ranged themselves against established political power—"Old Corruption"—and practiced some form of opposition politics. In other literary periods this focus would not necessarily yield much illuminating material, but the Romantic period was notably contentious politically, and all the major Romantic poets were, at one time at least, somewhere well left of center.

As literary background and context, Part 1 of the anthology is relevant to Blake, Wordsworth, and Coleridge as they wrote in the 1790s and shortly thereafter; Part 2 is most relevant to Shelley and Byron, less so to Keats who, though of the left, did not write much obviously political poetry. Accordingly, the literary commentary and notes after the poems reflect a concern with the major Romantic poets. Confining the Romantic period to only the "big six" poets has come under justifiable criticism as many now feel the canon needs to be broadened. There is a major feminist rethinking of Romantic poetry within the framework of women poets.[3] John Clare's poetry has been gaining so much attention that it seems his work will cease to be considered "minor." Clare is only one of a large number of laboring-class poets who have not received enough attention. Radical political motives animate some of the canon-expanders, but even if one does not share the same ideological commitment, one can applaud for literary reasons the broadening of the literature we can now read and study. To some extent, then, *Poetry and Reform* is more than background for the major Romantic poets; it also foregrounds some excellent poetry and poets that require understanding on their own terms.

The anthology also reveals some features of the reform movement's literary assumptions. It is historically meaningful how the movement responded in verse to important events such as the French Revolution, the political repression, the Peterloo Massacre, the Queen Caroline Affair, the Cato Street Conspiracy, and Napoleon. Accordingly, the poems have historical as well as aesthetic value in that they disclose things about the reform movement that are not presented in any other way. The poetry gives additional information for the historian of the reform movement to integrate.

The Reform Movement

When, in April, 1792, the London Corresponding Society (hereafter, LCS) issued its first public statement, there was a new moment in reform politics because a group of artisans and tradesmen was organizing for its own political enfranchisement, as had some similar groups in Sheffield, Derby, and Manchester that had been formed around the same time (Thompson 1963, 17–20).[4] That same month the Friends of the People was formed by liberal Whigs in favor of reform. The veteran reform organization, founded in 1780, was the Society for Constitutional Information (hereafter, SCI), which was dominated by middle-class Dissenters.[5] The reform movement was this unlikely set of groups, each with a different social composition, each with a different agenda. The plebeian LCS wanted universal manhood suffrage—"radical reform." The SCI's focus was repeal of the Test and Corporation Acts (1828), abolition of the Slave Trade (1807), and parliamentary reform (some in the SCI favored only a "moderate" reform, the kind that was enacted in 1832). The aristocratic and high

Introduction

bourgeois Whigs were the opposition to William Pitt (1759–1806; *DNB*) and wanted, if possible, to form a government; they generally supported the SCI program but were not limited to it; and rarely did they countenance universal manhood suffrage.[6] All three were sympathetic to the French Revolution and opposed the war with France, which began in January, 1793. In 1794 the leaders of the LCS and SCI were imprisoned and put on trial for treason. According to one historian, had Pitt been content with a sedition indictment the defendants would have been convicted, but instead all the treason trial reformers were acquitted (Goodwin 28). This reform victory was partial at best as public opinion had turned against the radicals. All three components of the reform movement were forced to retreat from political activism at least by July, 1797, when Earl Grey's (1764–1845; *DNB*) motion for parliamentary reform lost and the liberal Whigs withdrew from parliament. Prior to that, the repressive Two Acts of 1795 had crippled the plebeian movement. It was not until after Waterloo (1815) that the three elements of the reform movement came together again to push for political change, and this brief alliance did not endure after the Queen Caroline Affair (1820–21); the reform movement's three elements came together once again in 1830 when the political agitation culminated in the 1832 Reform Bill. Ordinarily the reform movement's groups acted separately, pursued separate interests, and distrusted one another.

The liberal Whigs, led until his death in 1806 by Fox (1749–1806; *DNB*), were the Opposition that could claim few victories in 1790s. Edmund Burke (1729–97; *DNB*) and the followers of Lord Grenville (1759–1834; *DNB*) left the Foxite Whigs over the French Revolution, thus crippling the parliamentary opposition to Pitt. Although the liberal Whigs succeeded with the new libel law (1792), authored by Fox, which gave juries discretion to decide what was libelous, they lost on parliamentary reform, slave trade abolition, civil liberties for Dissenters, and of course peace with France. Nevertheless, a month after the formation of the Friends of the People in 1792, the government issued the repressive Royal Proclamation Against Seditious Writing, which was aimed more at the liberal Whigs than the plebeian radicals (Goodwin 207). Pitt and his followers were more worried about the Foxites than the extraparliamentary reformers, even though, ironically, the Foxites repudiated the SCI and rejected the democratic ideas of Thomas Paine (1737–1809; *DNB*). The nightmare scenario was that the Foxites would come to power on the strength of a popular uprising. The Pitt government and Whig alarmists like Burke made sure that this nightmare never materialized by repressing the popular movement and discrediting the Foxites. In fact, the middle-class liberals had always distrusted the liberal Whigs, even as they acted as a pressure group on the party. The plebeian reformers liked Lord Stanhope

INTRODUCTION

(1753–1816; *DNB*) but had little faith in the Foxite Whigs. One of the few times all elements of the reform movement cooperated in the 1790s was during the unsuccessful attempt to stave off the repressive Two Acts of 1795.

The Foxites' calls for peace with France were quite popular after the initial pro-war feelings of 1793, and Pitt was forced to make some peace overtures to France, which were rebuffed. The Peace of Amiens (1802–03) was the consequence in part of strong English anti-war sentiment that could not be ignored. The Foxites, however, could not translate this anti-war feeling into parliamentary success. Indicative of their frustration and sense of futility, they boycotted parliament entirely from 1797 to 1800. Fox did enter the Ministry of All the Talents in 1806, but his death in the same year extinguished the hopes of the liberal Whigs. After Fox's death, the Whigs remained the Opposition until Grey's ministry in 1830. The Whig factions consisted of the conservative Grenvillites, the liberal Foxites led by Grey, and the "Mountain" radicals like Samuel Whitbread (1758–1815; *DNB*). The Whigs could muster 115 votes for moderate parliamentary reform in 1810 and 105 votes against suspending Habeas Corpus in 1817, but they were an ineffective opposition, outflanked on their left by the radical MP Francis Burdett (1770–1844; *DNB*) and the extraparliamentary reform movement. Moreover, its overall agenda—anti-war, Catholic Emancipation (1828), parliamentary reform, opposition to free trade—and its factions tended to immobilize it and yield the initiative to others.[7]

The reform group with the best organization, success record, and ability to pursue its goals was the middle-class reformers. The SCI was its most radical institutional form but by no means its only one: there was Christopher Wyvill's (1740–1822; *DNB*) association of moderate reformers; the Dissenting chapels and their schools, even institutions of higher learning; scientific societies, like Birmingham's Lunar Society. Most notably, perhaps, middle-class liberals dominated the book trade and exerted a disproportionate influence on the periodical press as well (Cookson 23; ch. 4). They could also point to real victories even before their greatest triumph in 1832: slave trade abolition in 1806, abolition of the Orders in Council (which restricted trade) in 1812, and the Unitarian toleration act in 1813. The reformist intelligentsia was not exclusively middle-class and Dissenting, but nearly so. Dissenters included Major John Cartwright (1740–1824; *DNB*), who helped found the SCI, and who propagandized for universal manhood suffrage and annual parliaments for decades; Joseph Priestley (1733–1804; *DNB*), theologian, philosopher, scientist, and reformer whose Birmingham house was attacked by a Church and King mob in 1791; Richard Price (1723–91; *DNB*), philosopher and reformer whose speech in favor of the French Revolution provoked Burke to write his

Introduction

Reflections on the Revolution in France (1790); Thomas Paine, who composed the most famous reply to Burke, *The Rights of Man* (1791–92), the popularity of which altered decisively the conditions of English literacy; Joseph Johnson (1738–1809; *DNB*), one of London's largest publishers, imprisoned and financially ruined in 1799 for publishing a "seditious" work; John Aikin (1747–1822; *DNB*), first and most successful editor of the *Monthly Magazine*, a periodical dominated by Dissenters; William Godwin (1756–1836; *DNB*), whose timely pamphlet on the 1794 treason trials influenced the acquittal of the defendants, and whose *Inquiry into Political Justice* (1793) was the most important political work among the avant-garde intellectuals; Mary Wollstonecraft (1759–97; *DNB*), the age's most prominent feminist, who studied under and wrote for Dissenting intellectuals. The middle class was hardly homogenous, and the notables in the above list are far more radical than were most liberals; nevertheless, this insurgent, self-confident, and successful minority presented the most serious challenge to aristocratic dominance. It is no accident that Burke pays special attention to Dissenters in his *Reflections*, and that when Coleridge becomes a conservative he centers so much attention on the dangers of Dissent.

Although there were many middle-class reformers sympathetic to poor people, favoring radical reform and even some form of socialism or what we now would call social-democratic institutions, most middle-class proponents of reform were either indifferent to or fearful of poor people, according to Cookson (28). For middle-class liberals, "Old Corruption" meant religious discrimination, aristocratic domination of parliament, disabling restrictions on trade and business, and overall a government that did not adequately represent the society. Sometimes they would look to the Whigs for help, and sometimes they would work with the plebeian reformers, but except for some individual reformers like Cartwright and Paine, whose involvement with plebeian radicalism was sustained, the middle-class reformers pursued their own interests.

For the plebeian radicals who founded the LCS the experience of reform politics was quite different. First, as the social world of the LCS is so remote and as we might tend to read back onto it a "working-class" quality, one has to see who exactly joined the LCS and constituted the plebeian part of the reform movement. According to one historian, at this time there was "no great gap between journeyman and small master or shopkeeper, tradesman, self-employed engraver, printer, apothecary, teacher, journalist, surgeon or Dissenting Clergyman."[8] Until the 1830s factory workers were not a great force, and unskilled laborers who lived in poverty, while numerous, were not active in reform politics. In the LCS, for example, most were artisans—shoemakers, weavers, and tailors predominating—while the

INTRODUCTION

leadership, mostly artisan, was also comprised of "a clerk ([John] Richter [d. 1830; B&G]), a lecturer ([John] Thelwall [1764–1834; *DNB*]), a mechanic ([Alexander] Galloway), a merchant ([Maurice] Margarot [1745–1815; B&G]) and a surgeon ([John Gale] Jones [1769–1838; *DNB*])" (Thale xix). Artisans, shopkeepers, and members of the "middling classes" defined plebeian reformism at the time. Artisans had their trade unions and friendly societies, but a literate education could be obtained only with difficulty, during scarce leisure hours. In the memoirs of radical artisans one finds an heroic and idealistic devotion to learning that is reflected in the plebeian periodicals and that seems to have been a feature of laboring-class society in general.⁹

Plebeian reformism could point to few political victories and instead found its own particular interests being eroded rather than otherwise. With successive waves of taxes and repressive legislation, periodical literature by 1824, the end point of this anthology, was less accessible than it was in the early 1790s. There were no significant moves toward free, compulsory elementary education. Trade unions, which had been banned by the Combination Acts (1799–1800), benefitted finally from their repeal in 1824, but the unions' campaign in favor of government enforcement of apprenticeship rules and state wage-regulation ended disastrously in the abolition of protective legislation (1813). The Luddite riots of 1812 were an attempt to "regulate" the textile industry according to the customary rules, but these were being ignored in favor of unfettered market forces, eventually resulting in the supplanting entirely of the artisanal mode of production. When the SCI was formed in 1780 there was considerable middle-class support for universal manhood suffrage, but by 1824 there was very little such support; indeed, some version of radical parliamentary reform did not succeed until 1867.

Running counter to these failures and defeats, however, are a few political victories—like repeal of the Combination Acts (1824)—and even more important, a decisive cultural movement away from traditionally deferential patterns and toward independence and self-assertion. Despite the repression, which was at times savage, plebeian literacy seems to have increased. It is difficult to gauge exactly the sales of Paine's *The Rights of Man*, but by the end of 1793, according to one estimate, 150,000 copies of part 2 had been sold (Goodwin 199 n.138). Even if this estimate is only close, it reveals an astounding level of political literacy in a country whose overall population then was less than ten million. To counter this spread of republican ideas Hannah More (1745–1833; *DNB*) produced her *Cheap Repository Tracts* (1795–98), which actually outsold Paine considerably. This anti-Jacobin propaganda was in some ways democratic despite itself as More imitated and lent legitimacy to plebeian language and concerns; moreover,

Introduction

the availability of inexpensive reading material would assist literacy.[10] Betty Bennett has noted the irony of the war poetry of 1793–1815: despite the predominance of pro-war, anti-Jacobin verse, the opponents of democracy were forced to use popular forms like songs and ballads, focus on popular concerns, and praise the dignity of common people, so that, like Hannah More, the anti-democratic propagandists despite themselves assisted in the democratization process.[11] If one looks at only the obvious effects of political repression—the closing down of the plebeian press, for example, by 1797—one might ignore the persistence and growth of laboring-class literacy which was to become dramatically evident from 1816 to 1819. Determined artisans somehow found ways to work around serious obstacles. For example, although the price, intellectual style, and reputation of Godwin's *Political Justice* would discourage laboring-class readers, there was in fact a significant set of such readers (Goodwin 475). Literature deemed important would be purchased collectively, or read out loud, or passed around, or circulated at a meeting place such as a tavern.

What made the "two-penny trash" of William Cobbett (1762–1835; *DNB*) so alarming to the government in 1816 when the first cheap editions of his *Political Register* were published was that the fifty thousand or so papers sold would circulate many more times by being borrowed, read out loud, or left in public places.[12] The number and variety of plebeian periodicals during the 1816–19 period indicated a sizeable growth in readers since the 1790s. The government could throw up obstacles, put people in jail, add more taxes to make periodicals prohibitively expensive, but it was fighting a losing battle: laboring-class literacy and cultural self-confidence were progressing inexorably. In the near future, opponents of democracy would be forced to use more sophisticated weapons than the crude ones of repression.

The plebeian reform movement from the 1790s to the Chartist period concentrated upon "radical reform": manhood suffrage and annual parliaments. The former was far more important than the latter, but together they stressed the concept of more direct representation and government responsiveness to popular needs; and they also repudiated the notion of "virtual representation," the idea that the already constituted franchise was adequate because parliamentary representatives owed their loyalty to the common good and not the small group of voters who put them in office. Defenders of restricting the franchise to those meeting property qualifications insisted that only those with a certain degree of economic independence could make rational decisions on state policy. Prior to 1789 proposals for manhood suffrage, such as the Duke of Richmond's (1735–1806; *DNB*) in 1780, and the SCI's, while never popular, were made occasionally and were not associated with threats to social order; however, from the 1790s to the middle of the nineteenth century, radical reform was associated with revolution, violent attacks on property, and class warfare.

Arguments for manhood suffrage were usually of two types, one based on constitutional precedent and one based on natural rights. The myth of the Norman yoke was appealing because it discovered in Saxon history precedent for democratic innovation, so that reform would not be innovation at all but restoration. Moreover, the monarchic and aristocratic domination of government could be ascribed to a foreign usurpation, un-English; additionally, as defenders of the status quo used the rhetoric of constitutionalism—asserting that democratic reforms violated the Constitution—the reformists could fight their opponents in the same language and frame of reference. Natural rights theory, which led to the concept of a social contract, never had the popular appeal of Saxon liberty. Paine was an overpowering presence in the 1790s, but his social contract ideas were not decisively influential; similarly, Godwin's even more abstract ideas on rational institutions had difficulty competing with the legend of Saxon liberty and an unbroken line of democratic heroes stretching from King Alfred (841–901) to the seventeenth-century republicans and contemporary revolutionaries and reformers. One finds, for example, in the reformist poetry of both the 1790s and the later period numerous tributes to the democratic heroes of the past, especially Alfred the Great, Algernon Sidney (1622–83; *DNB*), and John Hampden (1594–1643; *DNB*). In short, the plebeian movement preferred an image of conservative restoration of ancient rights violently usurped by foreign invaders. One can see why the reformers utilized the myth of native English liberty after looking at how their detractors characterized them: Edmund Burke, for example, portrayed the reformers as detached entirely from the tradition, merely projecting their own immediate wishes, selfishly, mechanically, and violently innovating and modernizing institutions that took centuries to evolve organically.

Parliamentary reform was not the only focus of the plebeian movement. Thomas Spence (1750–1814; *DNB*), adopting some of the ideas of James Harrington (1611–77; *DNB*), formulated an agrarian socialist plan for restructuring England, redistributing landed property, decentralizing power, and insuring access to wealth and education.[13] Although Spence's appeal was limited, he had a real following among some artisans who, after his death, formed the Society of Spencean Philanthropists, which was the most radical group in the reform movement. A split among the Spenceans emerged between the moderates, who wished to stress Spence's "plan" by educating the public, and the insurrectionists, who wanted to lead a violent revolution. With assistance from a paid government agent, the insurrectionists did indeed make an attempt to overthrow the government in 1820: the

Introduction

Cato Street Conspiracy.[14] Spencean socialism survived the execution and imprisonment of the conspirators, as Spenceans were active in Chartism. For reasons that deserve more study, some of the very best plebeian poets were Spenceans. Of course, Thomas Spence himself was a capable poet and effectively spread his message using songs and poetry. The later Spencean poets—Robert C. Fair, Robert Wedderburn, Allen Davenport (1775–1846; B&G), and Edward J. Blandford—had a much broader literary range than Spence himself and displayed genuine promise as poets. The artisan poets, one of whom, Wedderburn, was the son of a slave, are a testament to the high intellectual level of the Spencean movement.

The plebeian reformers—and the reform movement as a whole—were also internationalists and took a passionate interest in the fate of "liberty" in other countries. During the 1790s they followed closely the battles between the various counterrevolutionary coalitions and revolutionary France, and between the French loyalists and French revolutionaries. After Waterloo, they identified with the various freedom movements to challenge the Holy Alliance's settlement of Europe. Lord Castlereagh (1769–1822; *DNB*) was hated by the reform movement in part because of his role in suppressing the Irish rebellion of 1798 but more because of his role as Foreign Secretary.

The reform movement was hardly a single-issue phenomenon. Middle-class and plebeian reformers alike in their respective periodicals debated economic issues, feminism, birth control, religion, and philosophy. Moreover, while acknowledging the class divisions among the reformers, one cannot ignore what the reformers had in common: a common enemy, a common rhetorical and conceptual "grammar" by which they articulated their concerns and projected their visions, and many common issues. One can see this commonality in the poetry. The poetry of John T. Rutt (1760–1841; *DNB*), for example, appeared in Foxite Whig, middle-class Dissenting, and plebeian periodicals. At a literary level, reformist poetry itself, regardless of class, displays certain common features generically, symbolically, and thematically. One could ascribe this uniformity in literary and political discourse to the "hegemony" or the ideological power of the dominant class, but I find more useful a focus on reform hermeneutics: reformist writers engaged a variety of traditions to produce various revisions of those traditions in order to suit their particular needs. In political discourse, the notable instance is the myth of Saxon liberty and the ancient constitution, and in literary discourse a notable instance is the revision of Burke's "swinish multitude" phrase.

The relevant passage in *Reflections on the Revolution in France* is as follows:

> Happy if learning, not debauched by ambition, had been satisfied to continue the instructor, and not aspired to be the master! Along with its natural protec-

tors and guardians, learning will be cast into the mire, and trodden down under the hoofs of a swinish multitude.[15]

The reform movement took the phrase and turned it on its head, generating one satirical allusion after another, poking fun at Burke's elitist assumptions and defiantly asserting that the multitude was anything but swinish. This endless play with the swinish trope might strike some modern readers as tedious, but it was a way for a formerly subservient and deferential group to assert itself, make fun of its former deference, and stomp gloriously on the grave of its cultural inferiority. This necessary and purgative process helped create the cultural atmosphere within which further departures from and revisions of tradition could be made. Two of the best 1790s plebeian periodicals were "swinish": Daniel I. Eaton's *Politics for the People* (1793–95) was originally named *Hog's Wash* and Thomas Spence's journal was entitled *Pig's Meat* (1793–95). The swinish trope, although most intensely played with in the 1790s, continued to have some currency into the 1820s.

Burlesque and parody of anti-reform slanders were not the only revisionary tactics the reformist writers employed. Among many I will mention one: revision of established biblical interpretation. In the 1790s religion was politicized, contested territory, with the British government sponsoring "fasts" and prayers for victory over the French, and Church of England bishops aligning Christian morality with the suppression of democratic reforms. Reformist writers, however, refused to let the state church and the Tories claim for themselves ownership of the Bible and divine sanction. Some poems were anti-clerical, attacking church policy like the fasts (Dyer's "Hymn on the Fast" 1793), while others expressed their vision of a better society using biblical references (Spence's "Jubilee Hymn" 1793), and others were deistic critiques of institutional religion altogether (Fair's "Ode to Religion" 1815). There were, in the plebeian *Theological and Political Comet* (1819), numerous biblical allusions in the poems attacking and satirizing various social evils. The Bishop of Llandaff (1737–1816; *DNB*), and William Paley (1743–1805; *DNB*) all exerted considerable religious authority at the time but many reformist writers would not concede the authority of the Bible to those defenders of the status quo.

The Reform Press

Periodicals at the time included daily and weekly newspapers, political journals, magazines, and reviews. Even before the French Revolution reformers and Dissenters were a powerful force in periodical literature so that once the political struggle intensified in the 1790s, the reform movement was in a good position to take advantage of the opportunity. The press,

Introduction

however, was hardly "free." Although there was no pre-publication censorship, published material could be prosecuted by government officials for seditious, blasphemous, or personal libel; not until Fox's 1792 Libel Act were juries given some discretion to interpret what was libelous. Prosecutions could be brought against author, publisher, printer, and bookseller. Because of the libel laws, there was self-censorship in order to stay out of court. In addition, a series of taxes on paper, newspaper advertisements, and newspapers themselves elevated their price to prohibitive levels, so that only the wealthiest people could afford a daily newspaper; weekly newspapers were beyond the range of most people. The government was most concerned about newspapers because they communicated "news": contemporary events involving the government, including parliamentary activities—which could not be transcribed verbatim. To control information the government not only made newspapers expensive but by bribery and secret subsidies purchased propaganda vehicles.[16]

William Wickwar's *The Struggle for the Freedom of the Press, 1819–1832* tells an exciting story of repression and resistance and offers some revealing statistics: in the thirty years between 1760 and 1790 there were seventy libel prosecutions, but in the eight years between 1817 and 1824 there were 167 libel prosecutions, with the peak years being 1819, 1820, 1817, and 1821. During one of the reform movement's especially quiescent periods, 1825–28, there was only one prosecution.[17] Clearly, the government repression increased as the reform movement grew, and decreased as the movement subsided.

In the 1790s there were indeed opposition newspapers, and the three represented in this anthology are not untypical. The *Morning Chronicle* (1769–1862), a Whig paper, was with the Foxites during the 1790s and was well enough established to survive the tax increases and repression. The *Manchester Herald* (1792–93) was an early victim of repression as the editors, under indictment, fled to America not long after a violent Church and King riot in Manchester. The *Cambridge Intelligencer* lasted much longer, from 1793 to 1803, but the editor, Benjamin Flower (1755–1829; *DNB*), was fined and imprisoned in 1799 for libelling the Bishop of Llandaff. Flower noted in the January 6, 1798 issue, that after the 1797 tax increase on newspapers the *Cambridge Intelligencer*'s price rose to six pence and circulation dropped from 2,700 to 1,800. There were not many reform newspapers in the 1790s, and even fewer provincial papers that were reformist. The situation changed in the Regency period when more reform newspapers, even provincial ones, emerged along with an independent press not tied to the government or the reform movement; the *Times* developed in this direction. Circulation for newspapers at the time rarely exceeded the 5,730 that the *Times* could claim in 1822 (Altick 392).

INTRODUCTION

Another kind of periodical was the political journal that did not contain "news" so that, at least before the Six Acts of 1819, it avoided being categorized as a newspaper with its attendant heavy taxes. The political journal, usually published weekly, was the most appropriate vehicle for the plebeian writers. Costing one or two pence, offering political analysis, poetry, extracts from democratic texts—indeed, *Pig's Meat* (1793–95) was a *Reader's Digest* of reformist literature—the reformist journals were designed for a popular readership. Among the London political journals I have included four associated in some way with the LCS. Daniel I. Eaton (editor and publisher of *Politics for the People* and the *Philanthropist*), Thomas Spence (editor and publisher of *Pig's Meat*), and John Thelwall (editor and virtually the only writer of *The Tribune*) were members of the LCS, with Eaton being an important LCS printer and Thelwall being the LCS's most notable lecturer; all had been arrested and imprisoned at various times in the decade, Eaton and Spence many times. These periodicals plus the two official LCS publications, the *Politician* (1794–95)—not included here—and the *Moral and Political Magazine* (1796–97), constituted the periodical literature of the LCS. Estimating the circulation of the LCS periodicals is difficult. Dues-paying membership in the LCS was never large—peaking at 3,000 in 1795 (Thale xxiv)—but it could also orchestrate demonstrations in London of over 100,000 protesters.

During the period 1815–24 there was a burgeoning of very radical reformist journals. The reform movement of the period, torn between the moderates and the radicals, was far larger than it had been in the 1790s. Between Waterloo, ending the Napoleonic wars, and Peterloo, the massacre of unarmed demonstrators at St. Peter's Field in Manchester (August 16, 1819), an unusual conjunction of circumstances heightened political tensions to such a degree that some thought England was on the verge of a civil war. Precisely during this period plebeian journals flourished as they never had before, but after the Six Acts almost all of them were shut down. A similar growth of the plebeian press would not occur again until the 1830s.

All plebeian periodicals by virtue of price, format, ideology, and rhetoric generated a plebeian implied reader, and most were actually written and edited by plebeians. There were some exceptions: the *Theological Inquirer*'s George Cannon was a lawyer, and the most successful plebeian periodical's editor, William Cobbett, was the son of a farmer. The large number and high quality of the plebeian periodicals were remarkable, considering the physical, financial, and other difficulties involved with publishing a journal. David Vincent has pointed out that the first half of the nineteenth century was something of a golden age for literary self-expression: before publishing became too capital-intensive and professionally specialized, but after an artisan culture had matured to a rather high level of literacy.[18] Circulation

Introduction

figures for the plebeian journals are difficult to ascertain, but the *Black Dwarf* sold 12,000 copies—more than twice the number of the very successful *Times* newspaper. The two-penny version of Cobbett's *Political Register* was a national phenomenon, a spectacular 40,000 or so purchased. Of course many more people actually read the periodicals—or heard them read—than there were copies sold (Altick 392). The circulation for the less successful plebeian journals would have been much lower than the *Black Dwarf*'s 12,000—how many fewer is difficult to say.

There were few plebeian monthlies. The LCS's *Moral and Political Magazine* (1796–97) is an exception. More representative is the middle-class and largely Dissenting *Monthly Magazine* (1796–1843). At its peak—its first ten years—in terms of circulation (5,000) and quality, the *Monthly Magazine* was the periodical in which the most intellectually innovative writers in the middle class explored their ideas on topics as diverse as politics, religion, astronomy, classical and biblical scholarship, land drainage, population statistics, linguistics, metaphysics, and foreign and English literatures. The magazine had some regular writers, including John Aikin the editor, but the journal's vitality derived from the letters and articles submitted by its readers regarding various controversies. Radicalized by the French Revolution but disappointed by its development and ultimate outcome, the middle class in the 1790s had one of its heroic moments as some of its prominent intellectuals and publishers—Gilbert Wakefield (1756–1801; *DNB*), Joseph Johnson, and Benjamin Flower—were victimized by the Pitt repression late in the decade. Coleridge and Southey wrote for the magazine, which also introduced to English readers Kant and German Idealism. By price, format, ideology, and rhetoric, the magazine's implied reader was middle-class, but in its own ways it was as reformist and anti-aristocratic as anything created by the plebeian press.

Periodical Verse

In the *Monthly Magazine*'s first issue the preface included the following: "The term *Magazine poetry*, has usually been considered as synonymous with the most trivial and imperfect attempts at writing verse" (iv), and the editor was determined to include only good poetry. The *Monthly Magazine* in fact published not just good poetry but good innovative poetry, and the other reformist periodicals maintained high literary standards as well. Verse columns in newspapers and magazines were commonplace by 1789, so that when the reformist press also published poetry it was hardly deviating from custom.[19] Cheap ballads and chapbooks also precede the 1790s.[20] In short, the reformist periodicals were part of an already fairly sophisticated culture that was undergoing a complex process of democratization even before the

INTRODUCTION

1790s. Expanding literacy, greater educational opportunities for both children and adults, reading societies and libraries, inexpensive literature, and the increasing importance of "public opinion" even before the franchise enlarged in 1832, all constituted democratizing factors that the reformist periodicals could exploit.[21] Although the radicalism of the 1790s might have retarded the progress of political democratization, as liberal reforms became associated with Jacobin extremism, the overall effect of the political conflict during this turbulent period promoted democratization. The most dramatic example, as I have already noted, was the conservative effort to counteract the cheap democratic pamphlets like Paine's with Hannah More's *Cheap Repository Tracts*, which, despite the political message, helped spread literacy and legitimated plebeian readers. One can notice also the dramatic increase in plebeian literacy in the post-Waterloo period that can be inferred from the number and kind of reformist periodicals. The popularity of Robert Bloomfield's (1766–1823; *DNB*) poetry, especially in the first decade of the nineteenth century, illustrates the degree to which plebeian writers had some legitimacy, even if not full equality.[22]

The anthology illustrates that the category "political poetry" entails considerable diversity. Many of the poems are thoroughly political in focus, theme, content, and effect, but there are numerous poems whose political edge is somewhat concealed or even not apparent. Lucy Aikin's "On Miss Linwood's Pictures" (1798) does not address any political issue as such, but its focus is as implicitly feminist as the anonymous "Female Education at Two Periods" (1799): both poems put women's perceptions at the center of attention in a culture that does not. The long elegy by P. F. P____ in the *People* (1817) is an emotional and somewhat rambling lament by a father over his dead son; it does have a politically oppositional section, but the poem's overall affirmation of the poet's subjective being, mediated through the culture's significant conventions, is an act of empowerment with political implications.

Most of the poems are unapologetically political, however. There is no one poetic form through which the political message must come. There are sonnets, odes, couplet satires (tetrameter and pentameter), songs, ballads, animal fables, burlesques, blank verse meditations, tributes, narratives, ruins poems, dramatic monologues, poems about poetry and poets, epigrams, dream allegories, elegies, pastoral poems, and comic poems. The political focus can be as detailed as describing the specific features of repressive legislation ("Sedition Act" 1795) or as abstract as praising "Liberty." Agrarian socialists and republican democrats portray their visions of a better society and subject their own society to a variety of criticisms.

Introduction

Repression is a major theme. At various times it was so severe that it affected the periodicals and writing in general, dramatically and subtly. Habeas Corpus was suspended from 1794 to 1801 and again in 1817; the Two Acts of 1795 and the Six Acts of 1819 were designed specifically to silence the reform movement. Three of the Six Acts, for example, focused on periodical literature and seditious libel. In part, the excitement and energy of the reformist press and its poetry came from its being threatened by the political repression that was at times a source of inspiration as well as an occasion for fear. I have included twenty-five poems that deal explicitly with the issue, but there are few poems that do not bear the marks of having been affected in some way by the intense atmosphere of political repression.[23]

Repression provoked a wide range of poetic responses, from Aesopian allegory—the animal fables in *Politics for the People*—to revolutionary defiance in some of the post-Peterloo poems. Although one usually sees repression as the enemy of literature, it can be and has been a productive muse. In such times the written and spoken word are taken so seriously that literature itself is viewed as an action, ideas have consequences, and writing itself—as well as the writer—is elevated in importance. One can note, for example, the excellent literature produced by the Eastern Europeans who lived under Communist dictatorships, or by the Latin Americans who lived under rightist dictatorships. Some of the poems I selected for the anthology thematize the role of the poet in ways we have come to call "Romantic" as the reformist poets articulate versions of the bardic myth of the prophet, speaking truth to power. Indeed, a number of poems display a degree of literary self-awareness that will surprise those who fear dreary political verse.

I have already alluded to the ways in which the reformist poets played gleefully with the swinish multitude trope from Burke. Parody, burlesque, and other satirically humorous forms are perhaps the most successful genres of reformist poetry. The implied reader of this comic verse is an already committed reformist, so that the object of such poetry is not to persuade but to delight, and to triumph symbolically over the absurdities performed by their adversaries. Such poetry can be playful, exploiting puns, literary parallels, and analogies, and employing outrageous conceits. John Thelwall's "Sheepsheering Song" (1795) and Coleridge's "The Devil's Thoughts" (1817) are two examples of skillfully rendered poetic excess made possible by the reform movement's cultural defiance. The Cato Street Conspiracy (1820), part Spencean terrorism, part government provocation and set-up, received a humorous treatment in the *Black Dwarf*'s "State Contrivances!" that deliberately echoed *Macbeth* in order to ridicule the government. In

Introduction

1819–20 there were no pieces of literature as popular as the pro-reform satires of William Hone (1780–1842; *DNB*) with engravings by George Cruikshank (1792–1878; *DNB*).[24] Satire was an especially fruitful genre for the reformist poets. With satire so prominent in reformist poetry, one is reminded that satire was a major genre of the Romantic period: think of Byron's numerous satires, Shelley's *Peter Bell the Third* (1819) and *Oedipus Tyrannus* (1820), Blake's antinomian satires, Austen's satirical novels, Peacock's and Lamb's comic prose. By identifying "Romantic" exclusively with the Greater Romantic Lyric or some other notably "subjectivist" mode we might not realize how typical and representative the satires are in the reformist periodicals.[25]

Perhaps the most popular literary form, at least among the plebeian writers, was the song or ballad. Songs played an actual role in reform politics, as they were sung at political gatherings in taverns and at demonstrations, and as they were distributed as propaganda.[26] London balladmongers were bribed and otherwise coerced into promoting anti-reform songs, and arrested if they sang "Jacobin" songs.[27] It might be useful to look closely at one such "Jacobin" song in order to see how it worked as a piece of literature. Indeed, there is a connection between the songs in the plebeian periodicals and the experiments in verse undertaken by the major Romantic poets. Many of the political songs do the following: revise an already established tradition in a transgressive way; recreate symbolically a community by redefining fundamental values, thus discrediting the basis of the older, repressive social formation; transfer the guilt of the transgression onto the established authorities, therefore justifying the plebeian rebellion as a conservative gesture against the innovating forces from above. I will illustrate this pattern by examining a typical political song, "A New Song," from the *Philanthropist* in 1795 (94).

A New Song,   [N.A.]

(To the old Tune of "God save the King.["])

To be sung by the Corresponding Society, and the Friends of Liberty, at their Grand Meeting.

GOD send each Nation Peace,
May they victorious cease,
   Who in defence
Of Liberty has fought,
And has triumphant brought
Into tyrannic Courts,
   Freedom once more.

Introduction

> Let each example lead
> Britons to valiant deeds,
> 10   Worthy our praise;
> Rear up the glorious cause,
> Down with despotic laws,
> Let us no longer pause,
>   God will preserve.
>
> No longer inactive sleep,
> Tyrants already weep,
>   Freedom's our Right.
> Down with Corruption's sway,
> Freedom points out the way,
> 20   Virtue dictates my lay,
>   God save the Cause.
>
> The Banners of Reason spread,
> And by Liberty led,
>   Let us advance.
> Asserting our glorious claims,
> Free from all Courtly Chains,
> Jove will direct our aims,
>   MAN SHALL BE FREE.

First there is the framing of the song: it is to be sung to the tune "God Save the King," and it is to be sung by the LCS and "the Friends of Liberty at their Grand Meeting" protesting the imminent passage of the repressive Two Acts. By appropriating the almost sacred national anthem, the song boldly rewrites the meaning of nation, and what the sacred entails in relation to the state. The established anthem, which Church and King bullies would sometimes force suspected democrats to sing,[28] signifies a rigidly drawn "Constitution" that rules out both republican and democratic aspirations: the House of Commons, as already constituted, represents the interests of the common people, and whatever grievances the people have must be channeled through already existing routes. The social hierarchy, which the royal dominance symbolizes, is immutable and just. The democratic song, however, subverts the assumptions of established Church and King ideology at numerous points and on several different levels.

The song replaces the monarchy as central authority with God and a set of abstract values governed by God: Peace, Liberty, Freedom, Virtue, Reason. This is the principal transgressive action of the poem, a symbolic regicide. Moreover, the transgressive guilt is repressed by means of the

INTRODUCTION

concept of tyranny: the divine abstractions negate and are negated by "tyrannic Courts," "despotic laws," "Tyrants," "Corruption's sway," "Courtly Chains." That is, the agency that transgresses is monarchy and its aristocratic allies. Whatever authority this social group claimed for its own is discredited. Legitimate authority is assumed by those loyal to the true king, God, and the various divine qualities, namely the democratic forces of "the Cause." Indeed, there is a radical substitution of common people for monarchy in line 21: "God save" not the king but "the Cause." There is a similar reversal in the last stanza, where the abolition of the monarchy is rewritten thus: "our glorious claims" supersede "Courtly Chains," which will be negated under the guidance of "Jove," who will lend authority to "our aims" until there is universal liberation, humanity being free. There is yet another reversal in the song, replacing nationalism with internationalism, particular with universal claims. The first stanza establishes this: each nation deserves a libertarian peace—not peace at any price, not England alone. In the national anthem, God saves the king, but here, beginning in the first stanza, God sets different priorities by defining peace as the absence of tyranny.

The social group whose values are superseding the discredited ones is obviously alluded to by the inscription concerning the LCS and Friends of the People. The song then becomes the vehicle by which the democratic forces define themselves, almost as a revolutionary "convention," similar to the French. Accordingly, the song speaks to its implied audience: transgression is urged, but the guilt is negotiated in ways that repress guilt, and any doubts concerning the legitimacy of the cause are counteracted by strategies that foster democratic authority. First, there is the "we" against "them" structure in the song, repeated each stanza at least once, thus generating a redundant sense of difference. God and moral right are on the democratic, not aristocratic, side. Courage will be needed to fight against the established order, but divine assistance is invoked, and moreover, the established order lacks any moral legitimacy. The song suggests that only a coward could refuse to combat the aristocratic order because that order has no moral authority.

This is in fact a very militant song for a protest meeting of the sort that actually took place. But the song also has an Aesopian ambiguity, thanks to its reliance on abstractions. Only the last stanza is unambiguously radical; the other stanzas can be construed—and if necessary, construed in a courtroom, as Thelwall's "Chaunticlere" allegory was construed[29]—in harmlessly nationalistic ways, even though such interpretation runs counter to the spirit of the song. The peculiar use of "Jove" in the last stanza might have been used as a possible disclaimer. The poet could tell a judge the song was entirely in jest anyway, a mere literary exercise, since the deity was from

Introduction

Roman antiquity. Similarly, as a song for a meeting of aristocratic Whigs—Friends of the People—and plebeian democrats, it is sufficiently ambiguous to satisfy both sides.

The pattern of the song, then, is as follows: transgression is disguised and guilt repressed by turning the formerly legitimate authority into the agency for rebellion; a formerly recognized tradition is revised in a transgressive way to foster authority for the new ideology; at a symbolic level, there is both a redefinition of values and the replacement of one social group, once dominant, with another, now insurgent. One can see this pattern in Romantic poetry as well. Blake's *Songs of Innocence and of Experience* (1789–94) is an elaborate and involved enactment of transgression, appropriation, and revision of tradition, repression of guilt, and the symbolic destruction of one order and the celebration of another, emergent order. The *Songs* possesses as well an ambiguity so stubborn that there is still fundamental controversy about the meaning of its poems. Similarly, the *Lyrical Ballads* (1798; 1800) has a transgressive pattern in that—especially as the poems are framed by the provocative Preface—a poetic revolution is announced as a conservative movement, true to nature and the eternal rhythms of the countryside, in opposition to the innovating forces of the city. The seemingly innocent ballad stanzas quietly undermine the literary foundations of an aristocratic culture. The major Romantic poets, like the authors of the political songs in the reformist periodicals, typically rework established genres, revising and redefining conventions rather than breaking entirely with them.

Transgression and revision define the reformist poetry with some accuracy. Not only do the political songs revise transgressively established conventions, but other kinds of poems do so as well. The Whig "liberty" poem, praising progress and Whig heroes, acquires a dangerous Jacobin quality in the 1790s versions. Robert C. Fair's "ruins" poem, in heroic couplets, is fiercely anti-religious and politically far to the left, quite unlike the typical eighteenth-century "ruins" poem. Agrarian socialist poets like Thomas Spence and Edward J. Blandford draw upon the Bible and pastoral tradition as authority for their visions of a new society. The reformist poets do not reject traditional authority and precedent, as some writers, especially William Godwin and Thomas Paine, urged at the time; rather, they establish alternative authorities and precedents, ones more congenial to democratic reforms. Indeed, there seems to be no poetic genre the reformist poets will not use because of its being associated with monarchy, aristocracy, or the anti-reform forces. Moreover, the reformists are as nostalgic as Edmund Burke; the difference is the point in the past where the nostalgia waxes lyrical—for Burke, it is the age of chivalry, and for the reformists, it is the age of Alfred and Saxon liberty, or the Puritan Revolution.

Introduction

The relevance of the reformist periodical verse to the major Romantic poets is both direct and contextual. Southey, Wordsworth, and Coleridge actually wrote for the reformist periodicals; Shelley collaborated with the editor of the *Theological Inquirer*; Leigh Hunt's *Examiner*, John Hunt's *Yellow Dwarf*, and Thelwall's *Champion*—all middle-class liberal periodicals— involved major Romantic writers, including Hazlitt and Keats. Contextually, the very fact of so much reformist and democratic writing, plebeian and otherwise, provided a lively atmosphere for literary experimentation. I think that the great Romantic innovations in poetry between 1789 and 1824—innovations that set the agenda for English poetry for decades to come—are unthinkable outside the context of this remarkable democratic insurgence that increased literacy and established a defiant literary spirit.

Structuring the Anthology

I have weighted the anthology more heavily toward the 1790s than the later period because the revolutionary decade was indeed formative; accordingly, I have presented a representative sample of the different types of reformist periodicals. The reformist press in the post-Waterloo period was much more developed and had a much larger readership, and I have had to structure the post-Waterloo section quite differently from the first section. The periodicals of the revolutionary decade and its repressive aftermath are arranged according to type, from newspapers to monthlies, in order to illustrate the breadth and diversity of the democratic press. Although in the later period there is a similar breadth and diversity, I have concentrated in the anthology's second part mostly on the plebeian periodicals, almost all of them cheap weeklies or fortnightlies, in part because scholars are more acquainted with the more accessible middle-class periodicals like the *Examiner*. By so doing I am able to make available a significant body of work by laboring-class poets, something that could not have been achieved had I tried to present a balanced selection that was representative of the entire reformist press in the post-Waterloo period. There are no selections from Cobbett's *Political Register* because this most popular of the plebeian periodicals had virtually no poetry in it. Similarly, the *Republican* of the heroic Richard Carlile (1790–1843; *DNB*) published little verse, so it too has been excluded.

I have not duplicated any of the poems Betty Bennett included in her anthology of war poetry, and I have—with one exception—avoided reprinting periodical poems by the major Romantics, as such poems are already accessible. There were many considerations determining what to include: generic and ideological variety, quality of the verse, relevance for Romantic poetry and the reform movement, and so on. I am not pretending

Introduction

to be definitive here. Nevertheless, my selection does provide a fairly representative sampling of the reformist periodical verse in the first section and a representative selection of plebeian periodical verse in the second section.

In the 1790s the most important plebeian journals were the ones associated with the LCS, and the best middle-class periodical was the *Monthly Magazine*. The LCS's most ambitious poet was John Thelwall, whose work receives much attention in the anthology. I included a few special emphases such as maintaining a string of continuity with the Gilbert Wakefield episode as it was reflected in the verse columns of the *Monthly Magazine*, from his poetry in jail to the tributes to him after he died shortly after leaving jail. It was a poignant and historically important episode. Although there were not many women poets in the 1790s periodicals, some were notable, like Lucy Aikin (1781–1864; *DNB*) and Fanny Holcroft (d. 1844); the ultra-radical "F. A. C.," whose identity and further work need to be investigated, also wrote good poetry. George Dyer (1755–1841; *DNB*), J. T. Rutt, W. H. Green, and Clio Rickman (1761–1834; *DNB*) are also poets whose work deserves more attention. Dyer, the most well known, has poems in parts 1 and 2, and his ode to Major Cartwright, the veteran reformer who founded the SCI and worked for radical reform until his death in 1824, appropriately concludes the anthology. In the section on the *Monthly Magazine* I stopped rather arbitrarily at 1809 because that was the year in which Sir Francis Burdett revived a dormant reform movement by challenging the staid House of Commons and provoking it to imprison him. I could have continued providing selections from the *Monthly Magazine*, even until 1825 when Thelwall was editor for a year, but it seemed to me that the innovative nature of the periodical was not maintained much after the revolutionary decade, and that the Regency period needed to be represented by other periodicals.

In the second section I included a considerable selection of verse by Robert C. Fair, Spencean shoemaker, whose poetry is excellent and whose connection with Shelley remains mysterious. Fair and the other Spencean poets deserve much more research than they have received so far, and accordingly I have chosen quite a few of their poems. There needs to be bibliographical work on all of them. Perhaps Robert Fair's 1815 collection of poetry and Edward J. Blandford's *The Powers of Fancy* will be found someday.

The end-point of the anthology was fixed at 1824 in part because the *Black Dwarf* closed down that year, but it is also the year in which Byron died, thus signaling the end of one moment in English Romanticism. Of course both reformist politics and Romanticism continued beyond 1824, but by 1824 most of the decisive experiments in Romantic poetry had been written, and few plebeian journals were still publishing.

INTRODUCTION

Notes

1. I use "reformer" and "reformist" as the words were used at this historical period. Extreme radicals and even revolutionaries were called "reformers" at that time. During the controversies within the socialist movement at the time of the Second International, "reformist" acquired its moderate connotation in contrast to "revolutionary." I have also used throughout the book "laboring class" and "plebeian" instead of "working class" because the latter term evokes industrial factory workers rather than the artisanal and mixed character of the actual social group. For "reform" and "class" as words, see Raymond Williams, *Keywords. A Vocabulary of Culture and Society* (NY: Oxford UP, 1976).
2. Betty T. Bennett, *British War Poetry in the Age of Romanticism: 1793–1815* (NY & London: Garland, 1976); Y. V. Kovalev, *An Anthology of Chartist Writing* (Moscow: International, 1956); Brian Maidment, *The Poorhouse Fugitives. Self-Taught Poets and Poetry in Victorian Britain* (NY: Carcanet, 1987); Peter Scheckner, *An Anthology of Chartist Poetry. Poetry of the British Working Class. 1830s-1850s* (Rutherford et al.: Fairleigh Dickinson UP & Associated UP, 1989); Roger Lonsdale, *Eighteenth-Century Women Poets. An Oxford Anthology* (NY & London: Oxford UP, 1989). Many of the democratic and radical periodicals of the Romantic period are now on microfilm: Greenwood, Harvester, Research Publications, and University Microfilms.
3. Lonsdale's anthology includes many poets active during the Romantic period; Donna Landry's *The Muses of Resistance: Laboring-Class Women's Poetry in Britain, 1739–1796* (Cambridge: UP, 1990) has parts that are relevant to Romanticism; Stuart Curran's "The I Altered," in Anne K. Mellor, ed., *Romanticism and Feminism* (Bloomington & Indianapolis: Indiana UP, 1988), 185–207, discusses the numerous women poets active and popular during the Romantic age who now need serious attention, which has been supplied recently by Marlon Ross, in his pathbreaking *The Contours of Masculine Desire. Romanticism and the Rise of Women's Poetry* (NY & Oxford: Oxford UP, 1989). A feminist rethinking of mostly male Romanticism has been under way for some time; see Anne K. Mellor, "On Romanticism and Feminism," in Mellor, ed., *Romanticism and Feminism*, 3–9.
4. Thompson's *The Making of the English Working Class* is an indispensable study of plebeian radicalism from the 1790s to the 1820s; Thompson's narrative is also engaged, passionate, and readable. Complementing and at times correcting Thompson are Mary Thale, ed., *Selections from the Papers of the London Corresponding Society. 1792–1799* (Cambridge: UP, 1983); and Albert Goodwin, *The Friends of Liberty. The English Democratic Movement in the Age of the French Revolution* (Cambridge: Harvard UP, 1979).
5. For the middle-class liberals, see Carl Cone, *The English Jacobins. Reformers in Late Eighteenth-Century England* (NY: Charles Scribner's Sons, 1968); J. E. Cookson, *The Friends of Peace. Anti-War Liberalism in England* (Cambridge: UP, 1982); and Goodwin.
6. For the Whigs, see Goodwin; Arthur Aspinall, *Lord Brougham and the Whig Party* (Manchester: UP, 1927); and Michael Roberts, *The Whig Party 1807–1812* (1939; London: Frank Cass, 1965).
7. Aspinall 38–41.
8. Iorwerth Prothero, *Artisans and Politics in Early Nineteenth-Century London. John Gast and His Times* (Folkestone: William Dawson & Son, 1979), 20.

Introduction

9. For artisan memoirs, see *The Life and Literary Pursuits of Allen Davenport* (1845; NY & London: Garland, 1986), and *The Autobiography of Francis Place*, ed. Mary Thale (Cambridge: UP, 1972). For laboring-class views on education, see Thomas W. Laqueur, *Religion and Respectability. Sunday Schools and Working-Class Culture, 1780–1850* (New Haven & London: Yale UP, 1976).
10. For Paine and More, see Altick ch. 3 and Butler 1984.
11. Bennett 1; 47–51.
12. Thompson 1963, 744–63; Altick 324, 381, 392.
13. For Spence, see Chase, and the note to *Pig's Meat* (1793–95).
14. For the Spenceans, see Chase, McCalman, Hone, and Thompson 1963; for the Cato Street Conspiracy, see also David Johnson, *Regency Revolution. The Case of Arthur Thistlewood* (London: Compton Russell, 1974).
15. Edmund Burke, *Reflections on the Revolution in France*, ed. Conor Cruise O'Brien (1790; Harmondsworth, et al.: Penquin, 1969), 173. For commentary on the swinish trope, see Roland Bartel, "Shelley and Burke's Swinish Multitude," *Keats-Shelley Journal* 18 (1969): 4–9; Smith ch. 3.
16. On newspapers, see H. R. Fox Bourne, *English Newspapers*, vol. 1 (1887; NY: Russell & Russell, 1966); Arthur Aspinall, *Politics and the Press. c. 1780–1850* (London: Home & Van Thal, 1949); Altick; Lucyle Werkmeister, *A Newspaper History of England 1792–1793* (Lincoln: U of Nebraska P, 1967).
17. *The Struggle for the Freedom of the Press. 1819–1832* (London: George Allen & Unwin, 1928), 167, 315.
18. *Bread. Knowledge and Freedom. A Study of Nineteenth-Century Working Class Autobiography* (London & NY: Methuen, 1981), 10. Francis Hearn has argued that the English laboring class was the most critically thoughtful and independent in the earlier decades of the nineteenth century, and as workers gained political and economic rights they lost some of their cultural vitality. *Domination, Legitimation, and Resistance. The Incorporation of the Nineteenth-Century English Working Class* (Westport: Greenwood P, 1978).
19. Robert Mayo, "The Contemporaneity of the *Lyrical Ballads*," *PMLA* 69 (1954): 486–522.
20. Altick, 27–29; Albert B. Friedman, *The Ballad Revival. Studies in the Influence of Popular on Sophisticated Poetry* (Chicago: U of Chicago P, 1961).
21. For the process of democratization, see Raymond Williams, *The Long Revolution* (London: Chatto & Windus, 1961).
22. For Bloomfield, see *Collected Poems (1800–1822)*, ed. Jonathan N. Lawson (Gainesville: Scholars' Facsimiles & Reprints, 1971); *Selections from the Correspondence of Robert Bloomfield*, ed. W. H. Hart (1870; Walton-on-Thames: Robert F. Ashby, 1968); *The Remains of Robert Bloomfield*, 2 vols., ed. Joseph Weston (London: Baldwin, Cradock, & Joy, 1824).
23. On repression's effects on Romantic poetry, see David Erdman, *Blake: Prophet Against Empire. A Poet's Interpretation of the History of His Own Times*, rev. ed. (Garden City: Anchor Books, 1969), and *Commerce des Lumières. John Oswald and the British in Paris. 1790–1793* (Columbia: U of Missouri P, 1986).
24. Facsimiles of the Hone-Cruikshank satires are in Edgell Rickword, ed., *Radical Squibs and Loyal Ripostes* (NY: Barnes & Noble, 1971). See my discussion of these satires in Scrivener 200–06.
25. M. H. Abrams coined that eminently useful phrase for categorizing some common features in a number of different Romantic poems. "Structure and Style in the

Introduction

Greater Romantic Lyric," in Frederick W. Hilles & Harold Bloom, ed., *From Sensibility to Romanticism* (Oxford: UP, 1965), 527–60.

26. The LCS activist, John Binns (1772–1860; *DNB*), commented on the tavern life within which political songs played an important role. *Recollections of the Life of John Binns* (Philadelphia: Parry & M'Millan, 1854.
27. Mrs. Cecil Thelwall, *The Life of John Thelwall* (London: John Macrone, 1837), 208–9.
28. See, for example, the account of such an incident in *Politics for the People*, I, 377–79.
29. For John Thelwall's "Chaunticlere" allegory and Eaton's trial for publishing it in *Politics for the People*, see Butler 1984, 185–88.

PART ONE

The Revolutionary Decade and Its Repressive Aftermath, 1792–1809

NEWSPAPERS

1. *Morning Chronicle* (1792–1796)

This daily newspaper, a vehicle for the Foxite Whigs, was probably the most important periodical for the liberal Whigs during the 1790s. Owned by James Perry (1756–1821; *DNB*) and James Gray (d. 1796), the *Chronicle* was able to survive several prosecutions for libel when other periodicals could not. Circulation in the 1790s was in the several thousands; in 1803, the estimated circulation was 3,000 (Altick 392). At four pence an issue, the paper was expensive, as government stamp taxes of 1757, 1776, and 1789 had forced up the price. Of course many more than 3,000 would read it in coffee houses, taverns, and other public meeting places.

See Lucyle Werkmeister, *A Newspaper History of England 1792–1793* (Lincoln: U of Nebraska P, 1967), 34–35; Neil Robert Reinitz, "The French Revolution in London Newspaper Verse of the Seventeen-Nineties," diss., U of California, 1958. For a generous sampling of verse from this and other newspapers during this period on the theme of the war with France, see Bennett.

SENSIBILITY [N.A.]

    Soon as the smiles of Youth disclose
The radiance of the budding rose,
O fount of Beauty! fount of Joy!
Enchanting Sensibility!*
Tis thine, with every mental charm
The Virgin's breathing mien to warm:
Thine, o'er her native bloom to throw

---

*Sensibility is here intended to represent that exquisite moral sense which is the Soul of female Beauty.

Of sentiment the living glow;
Or make that radiant bloom appear
10 Lovelier, when moisten'd with a tear.
The charming air of Modesty,
Love's sweetest smile and melting eye
Are thine; and thine the livelier glance
That darts divine intelligence;
The blushes thine, that tinge the cheek,
And o'er the trembling bosom break;
Thine is each sweetly-pensive grace,
And thine the passion-breathing face,
O fount of Beauty! fount of Joy!
20 Enchanting Sensibility!
   Tho' lovelier than the dewy rose
That on the robe of Summer blows;
The Nymph, who dares thy graces scorn,
Shall sigh in solitude forlorn;
Her smile no living radiance show,
Her heart in throb of rapture know:
No flower shall deck her early bier;
Her grave shall drink no gen'rous tear;
No Daughter for a Guardian mourn,
30 No weeping Lover clasp her urn.

Morning Chronicle (Jan. 6, 1792). This particular poem, apolitical at a highly politicized time, is the exception to the rule of politically edged poetry. Here is an instance of the sentimental tradition becoming politicized in that the apolitical sensibility has become associated with "Jacobin" liberty. For an illuminating study of the politics of sensibility, see Marilyn Butler, *Jane Austen and the War of Ideas* (Oxford: Clarendon P, 1975).

ODE ON LIBERTY [N.A.]

Recited at the Meeting, in honour of the Anniversary of the French Revolution, held at the Mitre Tavern, Aldgate, on Saturday, July 14, 1792.

Hail! more refulgent than the morning star,
Fair QUEEN of BLISS—fair daughter of the sky,
We woo thee, LIBERTY, and hope from far
To catch the brightness of thy raptur'd eye!
While not unseemly streams thy zoneless vest,
Thy wild locks dancing to the frolic wind,
And born on flying feet thou scorn'st to rest,
Save where meek TRUTH her modest seat may find;

Morning Chronicle

    Hail! radiant form divine, blest LIBERTY!
10 Where'er thou deign'st to rove, oh! we will rove with THEE.

    Choosest thou, Nymph, to tread the mountain's brow,
    Or haunt meand[']ring stream, or wanton plain,
    Up the steep mountain's height, with thee we'll go,
    Or wake by rivers' brink the merry strain;
    Or, o'er the wanton plain we'll trip along,
    Like simple swains, 'midst hinds, and virgins gay,
    And still we'll chaunt to thee the evening song,
    Unwearied with the raptures of the day:
    And even when lock'd in sleep's soft arms we lie,
20 Still flatt'ring dreams shall wake the midnight EXTACY.

    Or art thou wont to couch, with lion pride,
    Near BRITAIN'S GENIUS, slumb[']ring as in ire,
    Waiting what time thy children shall abide
    Thy noblest form, and wake to purest fire;
    Sweet slumb'rer, rest! Yet shall the times be found
    When BRITAIN'S BARD shall wake no venal strain,
    Her prophets give no more a double sound,
    No more her PATRIOTS thirst for sordid gain;
    And lawless zeal shall sink to endless shame,
30 Nor longer keep thy seat, nor bear thine injur'd name.

    But should e'en Britons scorn thy generous sway,
    On Gallia's plains still linger with delight;
    Still to their sons thy sacred love convey,
    Direct their councils and their battles fight:
    May tyrants ne'er, those murd'rers of the world,
    Austria's proud Lord, and Prussia's faithless King!
    Their blood-stain'd banners to the air unfurl'd,
    O'er FREEDOM'S sons the note of triumph sing;
    Still with the GREAT RESOLVE the POLES inspire,
40 To live in thine embrace, or in thine arms expire!

Morning Chronicle (July 17, 1792). The third section (ll. 21–30) emphasizes the crisis in poetry that has arisen because of the French Revolution. The Romantic concern for a poet and a poetry fully adequate to the moment in the nation's existence is evident here, in a popular tavern ode, which indicates that the Romantic concerns in this area were hardly idiosyncratic. The poem, along with a description of the reform meeting, was also published in the *Manchester Herald* (July 21, 1792).

    (l. 1): The morning star as a libertarian symbol was developed with much complexity in P. B. Shelley's (1792–1822) poetry.

The Revolutionary Decade

(l. 36): Austria's Lord Leopold II (1747–92) and Prussia's King Frederick William II (1744–97) led the first coalition against revolutionary France.

(l. 39): In 1792 Poland was still a constitutional monarchy which had been instituted in 1791 and which was to be destroyed by the 1793 partition of Poland by Russia and Prussia; there was a revolution against foreign domination that started in March, 1794, and led to a third partition of Poland in 1795.

To Liberty   J. A.

O LIBERTY! thou brightest fair,
That gilds this scene of toil and care,
Who wont with kind benignant mien
To tread the plains, a Goddess-queen;
What alter'd features mark thee now;
What ireful frowns involve thy brow;
How fiercely glare thy blood-shot eyes;
How starts each limb with wild surprise!
Mercy! what hideous shrieks I hear!
10   What blood-stain'd forms of hell appear!
Why streams aloft the gory head,
And whence those ghastly piles of dead?

Say, hast thou drain'd the maddening bowl,
That turns to phrenzy all the soul?
Have furies roused the vengeful smart,
And fixed their vipers on thy heart?
Or view'st thou threat'ning from afar
The horrid face of impious War?

'Tis He—'tis He—the fiend accurs'd,
20   On spoil, and blood, and carnage nurs'd!
He comes, with Tyranny in hand,
And Kings and Princes fill the band;
In hellish league they sweep the ground,
Their slaves in countless thousands round;
On thee their hateful looks they bend,
To Thee the threat'ning arm extend,
Resolve to hunt thee o'er the plain,
And 'whelm in ruin all thy train.

What wonder, then, O pow'r sublime!
30   Thou tak'st a colour from the time,
And wear'st a brow o'ercharg'd with fate,
While all thy terrors round thee wait,

To dash the proud presumptuous foe,
And lay the guilty traitor low?
But, O! while Justice points the sword,
Far, far, be Massacre abhor'd,
Nor Cruelty her victims tear,
Nor Rapine, Riot, and Despair
Their deeds emblazon with thy name,
40   And brand thy sacred cause with shame.

March forth with all thy generous band,
And meet th' Invader of thy land;
There strike with giant arm the blow,
There bid the purple torrent flow,
Till in one mingled heap of slain
Tyrants and slaves bestrew the plain.
Then rise serene, thy ensigns furl'd,
And take the homage of the world.

Morning Chronicle (Sept. 14, 1792). The poet, J. A., could be John Aikin, prominent liberal man of letters, editor of the *Monthly Magazine* and *Athenaeum*. The poem tries to justify the troubling if also defensive violence of the French Revolution. The feminine Liberty contrasts starkly with the violently masculine tyrants of the third section, suggesting a rape.

STANZAS TO THOMAS PAINE   J. T. R[UTT].

Go, PAINE—'tis Freedom calls from Gallia's shore,
    Nor wilt thou linger in the glorious cause,
Chaunt to the rescued land her sweetest lore,
    And midst a patriot Senate teach her laws;
With Common Sense the social fabric plan,
And fix on Truth's firm base the equal Rights of Man.

For see mock-glory's robe of gaudy hue,
    By Reason torn, flutters with every wind,
Heroes, as savage plunderers we view,
10   And Princes but the dwarfs of human kind;
E'en courtly champions of the right divine,
Despise the grov'ling idol, while they deck the shrine.

What, tho' Corruption wreak her frantic rage,
    Till scap'd thy vessel, from our venal coast,
Yet my rous'd country in some happier age,
    With martyr'd ALGERNON'S thy name shall boast,

And now full many a Briton lauds thy zeal,
While the fond pray'r ascends for threaten'd Gallia's weal.

And sure, when blood-stain'd glory charms no more,
20 But war's dread clarion tunes the song of peace,
When friendly commerce joins each distant shore,
  And Victor Reason bids contention cease,
Wither'd the laurels reap'd on CRESSI's plain,
This godlike love of Man a nobler wreath shall gain.

Morning Chronicle (Sept. 28, 1792). Dated September 17, 1792, this poem by John Towill Rutt on Thomas Paine commemorates Paine's leaving England for France (in September, 1792) at a time when the second part of *The Rights of Man* had been the occasion for Paine's being brought to trial in absentia and outlawed (in December, 1792—see *Howell's State Trials*, 22: 357–472). Rutt wrote a number of poems for the *Morning Chronicle* and Daniel Isaac Eaton (d. 1814; *DNB*) published several of his works in *Politics for the People*. At this particular historical moment the various ideological and social differences among the partisans of the French Revolution are not nearly as important as the similarities, as Rutt appears in both a plebeian and genteel periodical.

 (l. 5): In *Common Sense* (1776) Paine argued for American independence.

 (l. 16): Algernon Sidney was a victim of Restoration repression and one of the most often cited martyr-heroes in democratic writing. His republican writings were reprinted in the nineteenth century.

 (l. 23): Cressi's plain is at Valmy, where the French Republicans beat the Prussians and French Royalists.

THE MAID'S ENIGMA   [N.A.]

Some merry girls one night, 'tis said,
When the old folks were gone to bed,
  Assembl'd round the fire:
They wish'd to laugh an hour away;
Their chat was harmless as 'twas gay;
  What more can you desire?

Enigmas, riddles, tales went round;
The knotty point, or guess profound,
  By turns their minds possess'd;
10 When Sue defies them to unfold
A *riddle*, which she had been told
  No *Maid* had ever guess'd.

"What's that which tickles us and men,
"And oft, when done, begins again?—

"A drug, they say, befriends it:
"But soon, says SUE, the pleasure's past,
"And, tickling more and more, at last
    "A slight convulsion ends it."

Some bit their lip, some wink'd their eye—
20 All giggled—and they knew not why—
    The joke somehow had pleas'd;
When KATE, less wicked than the rest,
Thinking to hit upon the jest,
    Discover'd it—and *sneez'd*.

Morning Chronicle (Oct. 13, 1792). That sexual jokes would be appropriate in a periodical as prestigious as the *Chronicle* tells us something about the social mores of the time and how different they would become in several decades. There is a slight revolutionary flavor to the poem in the allusion to repressive "old folks" whose presence inhibits the sexuality of the "merry girls." (Cf. the riddles in volume 1 of Jane Austen's *Emma* [1816]).

THE GENIUS OF FRANCE [N.A.]

While France, full of sense and of spirit, pursues
The cause of the world, with the noblest of views;
Where tyranny held her unbounded controul,
Made nature factitious, and fetter'd the soul.
Let us fill the gay glass, and with rapture advance,
The soul and the song, to the Genius of France.

See her swains render'd happy—her cities all shine,
Her hills "laugh and sing" with the gen'rous vine;
Fit emblem of ev'ry true patriot that lives,
10 He draws his support, from the embrace that he gives.
Then hail th' occasion, and boldly advance,
The glass and the song, to the Genius of France.

See Commerce delighted, extending her arm,
With virtues, all active, to bless and to charm;
Where monkery indolent, vicious and blind,
Laid man all in ruins, and rusted the mind.
Then lift up the song, and with spirit advance,
The full-glowing glass to the Genius of France.

See Sages all ardent—see Patriots burn,
20 The faith and the moral of nature return;
While grim superstition retires to her caves,

And beckons those rebels of nature—the slaves—
Then Britons join chorus, and nobly advance
The glass and the song, to the Genius of France.

Morning Chronicle (Nov. 30, 1792). Described as the "best" song sung at the Southwark Friends of the People meeting and public dinner, this song, with its four-stress meter, focuses on religious and intellectual enslavement. Commercial and intellectual freedom, the song asserts, go hand in hand. The song is historically interesting too as an example of the songs sung at prominent political meetings that someone like Horne Tooke (1736–1812; *DNB*) would be attending. Tooke, a linguist and an SCI leader, was acquitted for treason in the 1794 trial. The September Massacres of several months previous obviously had little effect in dampening their enthusiasm for the revolution.

Hymn on the Fast   George Dyer

Great Framer of unnumber'd worlds,
    And whom unnumber'd worlds adore!
Whose goodness all thy creatures share,
    While nature trembles at thy power;

Thine is the hand, that moves the spheres,
    That wakes the winds, and lifts the sea;
And man, who moves the lord of earth,
    Acts but the part assign'd by Thee.

Kings, at whose will a nation bends,
10   Bow at thy throne, and own thy sway;
And, though like Gods, they tread on earth,
    To thee shall duteous homage pay.

Chiefs, though with numerous hosts combin'd,
    They fellow-blood like torrents spill;
Eager for conquest and for fame,
    Do but thy great designs fulfil.

While suppliant crowds implore thine aid,
    To Thee we raise the humble cry;
Thine altar is the contrite heart,
20   Thine incense a repentant sigh.

But if injustice grind the poor,
    Or av'rice stain the sordid hand;
Or stern ambition thirst for blood,
    Or rude oppression waste the land;

The GOD, who hears the orphan's cry,
  The martyr's prayer, and prisoner's groan,
Still list'ning to the poor opprest,
  Would spurn the oppressor from his throne.

Nor would he heed the streaming eye,
  Th' uplifted hand, or bended knee;
Or altars grac'd with splendid rites,
  Or forms of solemn mockery.

Yet though unnumber'd sins abound,
  Should but a generous sorrow rise;
And as new troubles threaten round
  'Midst wasting wars, and angry skies;

Should Britain, in her sober hour,
  Confess Thy hand, and bless the rod;
Thou still would'st love to be her Friends,
  Who lov'd to own Thee as her GOD.

Morning Chronicle (April 18, 1793). Dyer, prominent liberal and man of letters, was a friend or acquaintance of most of the well-known poets and their circle: Charles Lamb (1775–1834), Coleridge (1772–1834), William Godwin, Wordsworth (1770–1850), and William Hazlitt (1778–1830). For Dyer, see Reiman 1979.

After the war between France and England started in January, 1793, the king periodically called for a public fast and prayers for military victory. The English Jacobins, of course, took a dim view of this militarization of religion. In comparison with other, more satirical responses to the fast, Dyer's is very moderate. There are numerous "fast" poems in Bennett.

SEDITION ACT   A LADY

One Justice of Peace alone is sufficient,
However in talents and virtue deficient,
To disperse any Meeting he chanceth to spy;
And, if one individual his power defy,
And this Meeting do not, at his order, divide,
As Felons they every one shall be tried;
And DEATH is the penalty for such decreed!—
No Benefit of Clergy such Felons shall plead.

And in case at these Meetings some persons stand prating,
And delay to disperse while the Law is debating,
  Reluctant to go, and most willing to stay—

And curious to hear what his Worship will say;
Should the Law's Proclamation be issued in vain,
And, for more than one hour, twelve persons remain,
When the rest are dispersed—such persons shall find
The penalty DEATH to that Crime is assign'd!

Moreover arm'd Soldiers shall be within call,
To spur lagging Obedience—with Powder and Ball;
And, in case any person or persons be kill'd,
20 As, *confus'dly* dispersing, some Blood *may be* spill'd,
If, with *impotent* rage, they, with *power* contending,
Should dare to oppose, and persist in Defending—
Then their Necks *may be* broke, and their Limbs *may be* maim'd
But no Justice for this shall, in future, be blam'd;
Indemnified, free, and discharg'd he shall stand
Of Maiming or Killing each man in the land!

This Magistrate also may persons arrest,
For using such words, whether earnest or jest,
As *he thinks* may destroy the people's content,
30 And stir up their Hate to the *good* Government—
Then a Prison awaits; and a Fine such must pay,
Or, perchance, take a voyage—to Botany Bay!

Moreover, this Act, in its wisdom, doth say—
Domiciliary visits this Justice may pay;
And when, without doors, he has done with the Riot,
He may come to our houses—to *see* that we're quiet;
For, mark how the words in this clause are express'd,
As thus, in the language of law, it is dress'd—
If a justice on oath should receive information
40 Against any man, or men, in the Nation,
Or, have cause to *suspect* any room, house, or place,
Where he a Political junto may trace;
Where is held any Lecture, Discourse, or Debate,
Which leads to discussion of Matters of State—
Such Justice may go, with the Law in his hand,
To this house, room, or place, and admittance demand;
And, in case any persons aversion betray
To these visits familiar this Justice may pay;
Should they *fancy* their House an asylum secure,
50 And bid him, in wrath, to begone from their door—
The same a *disorderly* house shall be deem'd,

However, before, it had *orderly* seem'd;
And, if firm in resistance such persons be found,
The Forfeiture penal is ONE HUNDRED POUND
To person or persons who sue for the same,
And take it they may—without fear or blame.

And this is the *Law* that so troubles the Land,
Which now has the sanction of Royal comand!

Morning Chronicle (Jan. 5, 1796). The poem had the following prefatory note: "It is of the utmost importance that a Law of this serious magnitude should not only be clearly understood, but correctly remembered. There is nothing fixed so surely on the Memory as *Verse*; and therefore, as a Caution to the Unwary, a FAIR CORRESPONDENT has kindly favoured us with the New Act in Metre."

The Two or "Gagging" Acts became effective Dec. 18, 1795. The identity of the poet is unknown. This witty description of the new law shows the specific aspects the reformers would have to know in order to be well prepared for the legal repression.

(l. 32): Botany Bay, Australia, was the destination for transported criminals.

2. *Manchester Herald* (1792)

In its brief existence (1792–93) the *Manchester Herald* represented provincial radicalism at its best. Printed and presumably edited by Matthew Falkner and Samuel Birch, both members of the Manchester Constitutional Society, the paper—at three and a half pence an issue—published articles by Thomas Cooper (1759–1840; *DNB*) and was finally victimized first by a Church and King riot (Dec., 1792) and then legal repression. While under indictment, Falkner and Birch fled to America in early 1793 and the paper was silenced (see Goodwin 147, 228–30, 235, 265, 271–72).

ON SUGAR   A CITIZEN OF THE WORLD

   Go, guilty, sweet seducing food,
Tainted by streams of human blood!
Emblem of woe, and fruitless moans,
Of mangled limbs, and dying groans!
To me, thy tempting white appears
Steeped in a thousand Negroes' tears!
I see the lash uplifted high;
I see the vainly-streaming eye;
The shrunk clasp'd hands that but provoke
10 Their tyrants to a harder stroke.
The varied punishments I view—
Invention[']s blackest pencil drew,

And did to cruel man impart,
To pierce and rend a Brother[']s heart.
Oh! Can I then a sweet enjoy,
That tempts me only to destroy?
No!—I abhor the luscious food
Purchas'd by many a *Brother[']s* blood!
I'll wage with habit, virtuous strife,
20   To save a fellow-creature's life;
And bless the day I scorn'd the food
Produc'd by *torments, groans*, and *blood*!

Manchester Herald (April 7, 1792). Agitation against the slave trade was a fairly broad based movement—supported by William Wilberforce (1759–1833; *DNB*), William Pitt, and Charles James Fox, for example—not exclusively attached to reformist radicals, but it was an important aspect of the reform movement nevertheless. The poem personalizes the issue of slavery by promoting the sugar boycott. For the anti-slave trade movement, see Porter.

THE REFORM.
BY THE RIGHT HON.
WILLIAM PITT.   [N.A.]

The Gentlemen say,
   They remember the day,
When I was an advocate warm;
   For equalization,
   Of representation,
And cry'd out aloud for REFORM.

   But indeed 'twould be strange,
   If my mind did not change,
As circumstance alters the case;
10   These short sighted men,
   May remember 'twas when,
Another man was in my place.

   Majorities did,
   What the Minister bid,
And he was the Nation's undoing;
   I was thin as a stag,
   And my empty green bag,
Presented no picture but ruin.

No Borough then rotten,
By me was forgotten,
I brought them all into disgrace;
But their timbers were found,
To be perfectly sound,
The moment I got into place.

I admit there are blots,
And a few little spots,
Which stain the white robe of the Nation;
But that is no cause,
For amending bad laws,
And changing the representation.

At some other season,
It might be a reason,
Though at present it is not the case;
I am Minister Prime,
And 'twill never be time,
So long as I keep in my place.

Manchester Herald (May 19, 1792). William Pitt last promoted parliamentary reform in 1785. Reformers liked to remind their opponents that Pitt once advocated reform, a fact that made the political repression of the reform movement seem that much more arbitrary and unjust.

TO THE ENGLISH FRIENDS OF FRENCH FREEDOM [N.A.]

Again, O ye spirits that feel for mankind,
  And who scorn what ye feel to deny,
Who would waft to all climes on the wings of the wind
  Those blessings which all should enjoy;
Again, tho' the tempest of bigotry howls,
  And menaces tyranny's foes;
Again let us meet to applaud the great souls
  At whose voice prostrate Gallia arose!

If resistance be wrong, O ye Britons! 'tis clear,
  By wrongs your own rights were regain'd—
And the fame of your Sires, whom the world will revere,
  Is stabb'd when the French are arraign'd:—
Each crown-pated miscreant they dar'd to annoy;
  Great Nature applauded each deed—

The Revolutionary Decade

Then, why should their cold-blooded offspring decry
    That stroke by which Frenchmen were free'd?

Shall warriors who drench the broad earth in man's gore,
    The applause of all ages obtain?
And shall men who that rights of our nature restore,
20   Be number'd in infamy's train?
Is this the result of those wonderful powers
    Which nature to man has assign'd?
Away with such weakness—and, O be it ours
    To extol but the Friends of Mankind!

Too long has the childhood of reason endur'd,
    In swaddles too long has she pin'd;
And tho' earth's haughty lords would still have her immur'd,
    Still cramp'd, still to crawling confin'd;
Yet with sinewy arm now she bursts their vile bands,
30   Superstition and prejudice fly,
And soon unrestrain'd may she sweep o'er the lands,
    And each tyran[n]ous system destroy.

With aspects all bluster and hearts all dismay,
    Lo! the scourges of Europe combine—
They see Reason's progress, they dread her blest sway,
    And to crush her is now their design.—
    At this striking period, tho' Kings may proclaim,
    Let us hear their invectives unaw'd:—
In Freedom's great cause let us scorn to be tame—
40   We feel—let us dare to applaud.

Manchester Herald (July 7, 1792). As the revolution became more radical and as England and France neared a state of war, the English sympathizers with the French Revolution became increasingly fewer, especially among the upper classes. This poem is at once a morale-boosting redaction of the revolution's justification and an aggressive figuration of the revolutionary process as adolescence. In fact, the fourth stanza (ll. 25–32) is almost Blakean—specifically reminiscent of the 1793 prophecy *America*—in its imagery.

A Song, Composed for the Anniversary of the French Revolution. July 14—1792.

Mr. Scott (of Dromore)

While tyranny marshals his minions around,
    And bids his fierce legions advance,

Manchester Herald

Fair Freedom! the hopes of thy sons to confound
    To restore his old Empire in France.

What friend among men to the rights of mankind,
    But is fir'd with resentment to see
The Satraps of pride and oppression combin'd
    To prevent a great land's being free?

Europe's fate on the contest's decision depend[s].—
10   Most important its issue will be—
For should France *be subdued—Europe's liberty ends.—*
If she *triumphs*—THE WORLD WILL BE FREE!

Then let every true patriot unite in her cause,
    A cause of such moment to man—
Let all whose souls spurn at tyrannical laws,
    Lend her all the assistance they can.

May the spirit of Sparta her armies inspire,
    And the star of America guide!
May a WASHINGTON's wisdom—a MIRABEAU's fire—
20   Iu[In] her camps and her counsels preside!

May her sons['] fatal discord no longer divide,
    'Mong her chiefs no dark traitors be found—
But may they *united* resist the rough tide,
    Till their toils be with victory crown'd!

And at length when sweet Peace from her sphere shall descend
    When the fiends of oppression have fled—
Immortal renown shall those heroes attend
    Who for freedom fought—conquered and bled.

Blazon'd high, then their deeds shall swell history's page,
30   And adorn lofty poetry's lays;
While the mem'ry of tyrants—the curse of their age,
    In oblivion's dark bastil[l]e decays.

Manchester Herald (July 21, 1792). This song was sung at a reform meeting and represents the intense idealism attached to the revolution at this time, when the best of the past and present were to have been embodied in a future victory of the revolution over its enemies.

    (l. 19): George Washington (1732–99) was then President of the United States; Mirabeau (1749–91) had been one of the leaders of the French Revolution until his death.

The Revolutionary Decade

Epigram   Sam Sly

Torn in a water closet lay
The long Addresses of the day;
When a proud fragment raised its head,
And thus in measured accents said:—
"Ah! happy sheets, 'twas yours to feel
"The glory of a ruby seal;
"'Twas yours in loyal love to bear
"The burthens of a people's care,
"New symptoms of esteem produce,
"And still though torn of ample use;
"'Tis yours, ah! service sweet indeed,
"To serve in time of ROYAL NEED!"

Manchester Herald (July 28, 1792). Using royal addresses for toilet tissue was one way to express irreverence towards the crown and this amusing poem is confidently defiant in its excremental puns.

Song. The Fire of Liberty.   [N.A.]

When o'er this sea encircled ground
   The Norman Conqu'ror grimly frown'd
   And quench'd the Nation's fires,
Th' oppressor could not all destroy
For thine, O heaven-born Liberty,
   Then glimmer'd 'mong our Sires.—

From reign to reign it moulder'd on
Scar[c]e warming—till dark-visag'd John
   Beheld the bursting flame—
10 He saw—and, by it, sign'd that deed
Which makes thy sword, O! Runnimede,
   For ever dear to Fame.

This sacred fire, through many an age
Of mental gloom and civil rage,
   A varied heat bestow'd—
But when at length 'twas sprinkl'd o'er
With some few drops of regal gore
   An awful flame it shew'd.

'Twas this which lighted William o'er[,]
20 This scar'd a bigot from our shore[,]
   And shew'd an abject world

With how much ease those dreaded things,
Those scourges, call'd despotic Kings,
    May from their thrones be hurl'd.

Chear'd by the soul enlivening blaze,
Our Sires did much to merit praise,
    Tho' much was left undone—
Then be it ours to feel the flame
And nobly act, till but the name
30   Of tyrant laws be known.

With awful charge from Sire to Son
O! may this fire be handed down,
    And watch'd with holy zeal.
O! may its heat expand the soul,
And teach us, while we spurn controul,
    For others['] wrongs to feel.

Whate'er their tongue, their hue, their state,
Whate'er the God they supplicate,
    Or clime which gave them birth,
40 O! Liberty, may'st thou be given,
All bounteous as the light of heaven,
    To all the Sons of Earth.

Manchester Herald (Dec. 8, 1792). In brief, the poem recapitulates the libertarian myth of the Norman yoke which was to have such powerful currency in the radical movement for many generations—far more influential than the more abstract libertarian theories of Thomas Paine and William Godwin. Liberty as a specifically paternal legacy is also standard, as the figure of a female Liberty fought over by jealous males was to persist also for many generations. The poem appropriates the Whig myth of the Glorious Revolution (stanza 4) by attaching the myth to something more radical than the usual Whig ideology.

   (l. 2): William of Normandy (1027–87) conquered England in 1066.

   (l. 8): King John (1167?–1216) granted the Magna Carta at Runnymede in 1215.

   (l. 17): Charles I (1600–1649) was beheaded during the Puritan Revolution.

   (l. 19): William of Orange (1650–1702) became king in 1689.

   (l. 20): James II (1633–1701), a Catholic partisan, was forced from the throne in 1688.

3. *Cambridge Intelligencer* (1793–1799)

Edited by the Dissenter Benjamin Flower, this radical provincial weekly newspaper at three and a half pence an issue—rising to six pence in 1797 after the new tax—had a national reputation as it promoted anti-war opinions from July 20, 1793, to

1803, when it ceased publication. The circulation of the newspaper was between two and three thousand. Flower was sentenced to six months in Newgate Prison and fined one hundred pounds in 1799 for "libelling" a member of the House of Lords, Richard Watson, Bishop of Llandaff. He later edited *Flower's Political Review* (see p. 165).

See also B&G, and Michael J. Murphy, *Cambridge Newspapers and Opinion, 1780–1850* (Cambridge: Oleander P, 1977), 25–42. Flower knew Coleridge (1772–1834), some of whose poems he published, including two from *Lyrical Ballads*; there are extant letters between Coleridge and Flower (see *STC Letters*, I: 196–97, 247–48, 266–69). There are a number of *Cambridge Intelligencer* poems reprinted in Bennett.

THE WRONGS OF POVERTY   J. T. R[UTT].

Occasioned by reading the Strictures on the practice of impressing, in Mr. Cooper's *Reply to Mr. Burke's Invective.*
"Come, by whatever sacred name disguis'd,
"Oppression come, and in thy works rejoice."
Thomson

Ah! could Ambition's harden'd bosom feel,
She'd tear the blood-stain'd laurel from her brow;
Drop from her nervous hand the murd'rous steel,
And trembling at the throne of Justice bow.

There—in repentant sighs would she confess
Her crimes, increas'd with time's advancing years;
But, ah! she triumphs o'er the human race,
Still drinks the widow's, and the orphan's tears.

See, at her call, the friends of lawless pow'r,
10   Approach the peasant's *unprotected* shed;
Intrude on weary Labour's resting hour,
And seek in night to hide the ruthless deed.

But keen-ey'd Justice marks the guilty scene,
And Pity hears the friendless suff'rer's cry;
While taught by Cooper's philanthropic pen,
The Muse gives language to the victim's sigh.

'In vain I listen'd to the grateful theme,
'That 'tis a Briton's birthright to be free:
'In vain deluded by a flatt'ring dream,
20   'I hail'd the land of Law and Liberty.

"'Tis mine, alas! the dire reverse to prove,
'To share the captive's, or the felon's lot;
'Torn from the soothing smiles of virtuous love,
'And all the joys that cheer'd my humble cot.

'No more at eve my pratt'ling babes repair,
'To greet their Sire, his daily labour done;
'But now, defrauded of a father's care,
'Some niggard hand may deal the scanty boon.

'"Tis mine, alas! to wage the bloody fight
30 'Against a brother-man, no foe to me;
'For pow'r controuls the feeble voice of right,
'And "State necessity," the *tyrant's* plea.

'Yet to HIS throne shall all my sorrows rise,
'Who looks on mortals with an equal eye;
'Beholds oppression through each artful guise,
'And hears the captive's unregarded sigh.

'Yet may the angel Peace from heav'n descend,
'And save the victims of Ambition's rage;
'The cause of man in ev'ry clime befriend,
40 'And bring the blessings of the promis'd age."[*sic*]

Cambridge Intelligencer (Aug. 31, 1793).
  J. T. R.: John Towill Rutt wrote political verse in the 1790s (for example in *Politics for the People*, I:2:10; 15–16; numerous poems in the *Morning Chronicle*); he also was a close associate of Joseph Priestley, whose writings he edited: *Theological and Miscellaneous Works*, 25 vols.(1817–31). This particular poem protesting the unpopular impressment of sailors was reprinted by the *Monthly Magazine* (March, 1797): 219. This is the sort of anti-war protest poem that provides the context for the innovations Wordsworth makes in *The Ruined Cottage* (1797–98).
  Mr. Cooper's Reply to Burke: Thomas Cooper was a Unitarian from Bolton who wrote *Reply to Mr. Burke's Invective against Mr. Cooper and Mr. Watt* (Manchester: Falkner & Co.,1792). Edmund Burke had attacked James Watt (1769–1848; *DNB*) and Cooper in a parliamentary speech of April 30, 1792, for fraternizing with the French Jacobins in Paris (see Erdman 1986). Cooper's house was attacked by a Church and King mob on December 11, 1792; he eventually settled in the United States.
  Thomson quotation: from James Thomson (1700–48; *DNB*), "Liberty," part 1, ll.123–24. In context, these lines are sarcastic.
  (l. 8): Although the tears of widow and orphan are conventional sentimental references, they are also biblical. According to the Hebrew Bible, the treatment of the widow and orphan is an important index of social justice.

SONG.
INVOCATION TO LIBERTY. [N.A.]

Where—the poor *Negro* with desponding heart
   And busy thoughts still stretch'd across the main;
Plies with unceasing toil his destin'd part,
   While the fierce sun-beams scorch the naked plain,

CHORUS. Appear! appear! and set the captive free,
   O guardian Goddess, sainted LIBERTY!

Where—in some loathsome dungeon's solitude,
   All means denied to cheer the heavy day,
His noble soul by wrongs still unsubdued,
10   The patriot *Statesman* wastes his life away,

CHO. Appear! appear! and set the captive free,
   O guardian Goddess, sainted LIBERTY!

Where—the bold *Warrior*, first in freedom's cause,
   Friend, Soldier, Champion of the human race,
Feels the keen rigour of a Despot's Laws,
   And scorns to purchase mercy with disgrace,

CHO. Appear! appear! and set the captive free,
   O guardian Goddess, sainted LIBERTY!

Where—the sad *Victim* of fanatic zeal,
20   Lifts his imploring eye to Heav'n, and sighs,
And fearless of contempt, or fire or steel,
   A Tyrant's empire o'er the mind denies,

CHO. Appear! appear! and set the captive free,
   O guardian Goddess, sainted LIBERTY!

Cambridge Intelligencer (Oct. 19, 1793). For a somewhat similar series of images figuring libertarian defiance, see P. B. Shelley, *Prometheus Unbound* 1. 672–800 (1820).

   (*ll. 1–4*): Parliamentary debate over abolishing the slave trade (1789–93), and the slave revolt in French Santo Domingo (1791) and the subsequent granting of freedom to slaves by the French in 1793 all raised the issue of black slavery for radicals and reformers. See Walvin; Erdman 1969, 228–29; Porter.

   (*l. 10*): Imprisoned radicals at that time included Thomas Muir (1765–98; *DNB*) (sentenced to transportation for 14 years) and Rev. T. F. Palmer (1747–1802; *DNB*), Unitarian minister and Cambridge alumnus (sentenced to 7 years transportation); both were sentenced in Scotland in the fall of 1793. See Thompson 1963, 124–25.

   (*l. 13*): Perhaps the "bold Warrior" is Thomas Paine, convicted and outlawed on December 12, 1792.

Cambridge Intelligencer

SOLILOQUY   T. R.

Who lives, and is not weary of a life
Expos'd to manacles, deserves them well.—Cowper

Ah me! how many a soul on life's wide plain,
Unheard of and unknown, hourly bewails
The frowns of fortune and the world's neglect!
How many oft, when bitter storms disturb
The peaceful breast, to crowded scenes repair,
And in the busy world's tumultuous throng,
Strive to forget the griefs that haunt them still.
Far from the blaze of pleasure let me fly,
Remov'd from life's vain scenes, to some lone spot,
10   Where my sad soul may linger out the day,
And memory there to sooth its cheerless haunt;
Back to my mind recal[l] the hours of youth,
When oft I rioted in dreams of joy,
Exulting in the thoughts of future bliss,
Unknowing then of all the various scenes,
The storms and sunshine of this chequer'd life;
But most of all unknowing that o'er man
By nature free—free as the vital air,
Oppression frown'd and check'd each generous thought,
20   Or that regardless still of nature's rights,
A sceptered Infant, with a glittering Crown
Upon his baby brow, could violate
The sacred laws of liberty and life,
And madly triumphing o'er freedom's bust,
Prescribe the bounds of thinking to mankind!

Cambridge Intelligencer (April 5, 1794). These Cowperesque lines of blank verse are a somewhat oblique and sentimental protest against the political repression, especially as it affects literary culture—"the bounds of thinking."
    T. R.: perhaps John Towill Rutt.
    Cowper quotation: from William Cowper (1731–1800; *DNB*) *The Task*, 5: 365–66.

THE WISH   RENEGE *TRIN. COLL.*

My utmost wish would favouring fortune grant,
    And all the treasures of her wheel display,
Riches and useless honours would I scant,
    And cast ambition's longings far away.

57

From all her various lots some one I'd cull
  Where peace, content and quiet mildly shone,
Remote from nobles proud, and pedants dull,
  From church oppression, and tyrannic throne.

In some sweet village, friendly, small, and clean,
10   On Severn's banks, or Camus' sedgy side,
I'd rear a dwelling comely to be seen,
  Neat without splendour, handsome without pride.

There highly blest in all my soul holds dear,
  To virtue, beauty, sense and candour join'd,
How oft would start the sparkling grateful tear,
  How oft extatic joys transport my mind.

There—free from envy, discord, faction, strife,
  Sweetly each day, each month, each year would roll,
'Midst calm domestic pleasures glide my life,
  And on religious comforts rest my soul.

Cambridge Intelligencer (July 19, 1794). Pastoral retreat from urban strife is somewhat topically politicized in the second stanza, but otherwise this poem is in the sentimental tradition. Life will imitate art when later in the 1790s Coleridge, Robert Southey (1774–1843; *DNB*), Wordsworth, and even John Thelwall retreat in fact to the countryside.

Domestic Felicity   C. V. L.

Though grandeur flies my humble roof,
  Tho' wealth is not my share,
Tho' lowly is my little cot,
  Yet happ'ness is there.

A tender wife with mild controul,
  By sympathy refin'd,
When rage the tumults of the breast,
  Becalms my troubled mind.

Three pledges of our mutual love,
10   Kind Providence has given,
And competence to nurse their hopes,
  Is all we ask of Heaven.

Still from the little we enjoy,
  A little we dispense;

And watch the buddings of their mind
　　Just blossoming to sense.

With arm entwined in arm we sit,
　　And join their hands to pray;
And teach the accents of their tongue,
20　　To hail the rising day.

At eve again they kneel and bless
　　The hours, which now have past;
And hope their cherished virtues may
　　Prove happiness at last.

Accept, Great Father of us all,
　　Accept their little prayers,
And grant the nurslings of our youth,
　　May crown our silver hairs.

Let those whose weak and infant limbs
30　　With tenderness we guide,
Be props unto our age, when down
　　The steep of life we glide.

Cambridge Intelligencer (March 21, 1795). It is hardly a uniquely Wordsworthian-Coleridgean maneuver—the turn toward domesticity, family, and country living, and retreat from the city and contentious politics. At some point in the future this turn will be *instead of* reformist politics but at this historical point it coexists with such politics (see Thompson 1969).

SONNET [N.A.]

Ye woods that darken o'er the steep hillside,
Ye rocks that rise terrific o'er the tide,
　　Not with less transport do I wander o'er
Your mazy paths, or mount the rude ascent,
Fill'd with less joy than one who ne'er had bent
　　His way delightful thro' your scenes below.
Tho' many a year familiar to my sight,
These hanging woods, and yonder ivy'd height;
　　The glorious scenes yet satisfy and fill
10　My soul: I call to mind the day when first
On my young mind their mighty beauties burst
　　And time and memory make them dearer still;
With deeper joy your wilds I traverse o'er,
As thoughts arise of days that are no more.

Cambridge Intelligencer (March 30, 1799). The Wordsworthian qualities in this excellent sonnet are striking, particularly the way memory and landscape interact as in "Tintern Abbey" (1798).

SONNET [N.A.]

O! Thou sweet Lark, that in the Heav'n so high
Twinklest thy wings, and singest merrily;
   I watch thee soaring with no mean delight;
And when at last I turn my aching eye,
   That lays how far below thy lofty flight,
Still silently receive thy melody.
O! thou sweet Lark that I had wings like the[e]—
   Not for the joy it were in yon blue light
   Upward to plunge, and from that giddy height
Gaze on the creeping multitude below;
   But that I soon would wing my eager flight
To that lov'd spot, where Fancy, even now,
   Has fled, and Hope looks onward with a tear,
   Counting the hours that keep her prison'd here.

Cambridge Intelligencer (June 5, 1799).

LONDON POLITICAL JOURNALS

1. *The Patriot* (1793)

This short-lived periodical (1792–93) was published in London by the Robinson brothers (who published William Godwin, *Political Justice*—first edition, 1793), and produced by "A Society of Gentlemen." George Robinson (1737–1801; *DNB*), with his brother John (1753–1813), was one of London's largest publishers; for Paine's *The Rights of Man* (1791–92) they were fined on November 26, 1793. *The Patriot* was designed to spread knowledge "among all Ranks of People, at a small Expence." The identities of the editor and particular poet here remain unknown.

THE PRESENT WAR   TELL.

Manchester,
August 15, 1792.

Why sleeps the Muse, when half the world's in arms,
And rouses pity by it's stern alarms?
Why the dire discord? Why the battle's rage?
For what great purpose do the powers engage?
Alas! the truth must wound each pitying mind,
The war now raging is 'gainst human kind;
The war of DESPOTS 'gainst the "Rights of Man,"
Whilst Hell-kin'd Nobles the black horrors fan.—
Lately, when Liberty, fair Goddess came,
10   And gave to Gallia a more honour'd name,—
"*The land of freedom*"—then the powers of Hell,
Who burn in Chains, in envy, roar'd a yell;
Which made its entrance to their Kinsfolk's ears,
And gave a birth to ev'ry Despot's fears.

>   Each took th' alarm, and made the cause his own,
>   And each o'er Europe the death-blast hath blown.
>   Hell's minions hasted to the French domains,
>   Brandish'd death's weapons—and fell Slav'ry's Chains;
>   Anath'mas pour'd with horrid murd'rous breath,
> 20   Which threat'ned nought but massacres and death.
>   The knew[sic]-known Goddess, heard their threats and smil'd,
>   And closer press'd each new adopted child:
>   She smil'd on each, on each her influence shed,
>   And as she press'd them, all their terrors fled.
>   With voice in *Union* all the nation cries,
>   Freedom we'll have, though half our number dies!
>   The *God of Freedom*, never made a slave!
>   In vain may Austria and proud Brunswick rave!
>   The cry of *Frenchmen* with their latest breath
> 30   Shall be, like *Britons*, ["]LIBERTY OR DEATH!"

The Patriot (Feb., 1793), 360. The poem, written before England's declaration of war on France but published just after the declaration, represents the Austrian and Prussian war against France in strictly dualistic terms as one of liberty against tyranny, with "Britons" clearly on the side of liberty. There is, then, an irony with the poem as it is being published so soon after England and France go to war. The title, "The Present War," originally meant between the counterrevolutionary coalition and France, but it now means also between England and France. Especially in lines 11–20 there is an almost Blakean sense that war is a product of jealousy and repression of desire.

This poem, in a slightly different version, appeared earlier in the *Manchester Herald* (August 16, 1792).

(l. 7): Probably refers to France's "Declaration of the Rights of Man" (Aug. 4, 1789), not Thomas Paine's *The Rights of Man* (1791–92).

(l. 28): Austria's Leopold II (1747–92) and Prussia's Frederick William II (1744–97) were fighting against the French revolutionaries when the Duke of Brunswick (1735–1806), commander of the Austro-Prussian army from 1792 to 1794, issued his inflammatory "Manifesto" on July 25, 1792, which declared no compromise with French revolutionary ideas and practices.

2. *Pig's Meat* (1793–1795)

Pig's Meat was edited by Thomas Spence. For the first year Spence's title for the one-penny weekly was *One Penny's Worth of Pig's Meat*, which he changed in 1794 to *Pig's Meat, or Lessons for the Swinish Multitude*. Spence, an active member of the London Corresponding Society, designed his weekly journal to "promote among the Labouring Part of Mankind proper Ideas of their Situation, of their Importance, and of their Rights." He moreover declared his intention to teach them "that their forlorn Condition has not been entirely overlooked and forgotten, nor their just Cause unpleaded, neither by their Maker nor by the best and most enlightened of Men in all ages." Accordingly, most of the magazine consists of extracts from various texts. The first volume, for example, has the extracts and other contributions to the magazine distributed thus: about 46 percent from contemporary sources, mostly already published; about 29 percent from eighteenth-century sources; about 14 percent from classical and biblical sources; and the remaining 11 percent from seventeenth-century sources, almost entirely Commonwealthman material, especially Spence's favorite author, James Harrington, whose *The Commonwealth of Oceana* (1656) influenced Spence's own utopian ideas. The distinctive Spencean emphasis was the agrarian socialist "plan" that he articulated in many different literary forms and to which he was loyal up to his death, after which his vision of agrarian socialism was taken up by the ultra-radical Spencean Philanthropists (see the sections on the *Theological Inquirer*, the *Forlorn Hope* and *Axe Laid to the Root*, the *Theological and Political Comet* and the *Medusa*).

There is not a great deal of poetry in *Pig's Meat*, but most of it is authored by Spence himself, who was a proficient writer of songs that were often then sung at meetings of radicals held at taverns. Radical songs sung at taverns usually evaded the political repression that was used against pamphlet literature, so that political songs during especially repressive times served an important function in the radical culture: the songs articulated the radical ideology, maintained morale, and served as a symbolic defiance of the authorities.

Spence is finally getting the treatment he deserves by historians who no longer regard him as an eccentric crank but rather as an important figure in radical and labor history. See the following: B&G; Olive Rudkin, *Thomas Spence and His Connections* (London: George Allen & Unwin, 1927); Thompson 1963, 161–63; T. M. Parssinen, "Thomas Spence and the Origins of English Land Nationalization," *Journal of the History of Ideas* 34 (1973): 135–41; H. T. Dickinson, ed., *The Political Works of Thomas Spence* (Newcastle upon Tyne: Aero Publications Ltd., 1982)— includes reprints of Spence poetry; G. I. Gallop, *Pig's Meat: The Selected Writings of Thomas Spence, Radical and Pioneer Land Reformer* (Nottingham: U of Nottingham P, 1982); Smith ch. 3; Chase ch. 2 and 3.

[JUBILEE HYMN] FROM SPENCE'S RIGHTS OF MAN. A SONG, TO BE SUNG AT THE COMMENCEMENT OF THE MILLENNIUM, WHEN THERE SHALL BE NEITHER LORDS NOR LANDLORDS; BUT GOD AND MAN WILL BE ALL IN ALL. FIRST PRINTED IN THE YEAR 1782. TUNE— "GOD SAVE THE KING."

1.
Hark! how the trumpet's sound*
Proclaims the land around
   The Jubilee!

---

*See Leviticus, Chap. 25.

Tells all the poor oppress'd,
No more they shall be cess'd,
Nor landlords more molest
   Their property.

2.

Rents t'ourselves now we pay,
Dreading no quarter day,
   Fraught with distress.
Welcome that day draws near,
For then our rents we share†,
Earth's rightful lords we are
   Ordain'd for this.

3.

How hath the oppressor ceas'd,‡
And all the world releas'd
   From misery!
The fir-trees all rejoice,
And cedars lift their voice,
Ceas'd now the Feller's noise,
   Long rais'd by thee.

4.

The sceptre now is broke,
Which with continual stroke
   The nations smote!
Hell from beneath doth rise,
To meet thy lofty eyes,
From the most pompous size,
   How brought to nought!

---

†Though the inhabitants in every district or parish in the world have an undoubted right to divide the WHOLE of the rents equally among them, and suffer the state and all public affairs to be supported by taxes as usual; yet from the numerous evils and restraints attending revenue laws, and number of collectors, informers, &c. appendant on the same, it is supposed, they would prefer, that after the whole amount of the rents collected in a parish from every person, according to the full value of the premises which they occupy, so much per pound, according to act of parliament, should be set apart for support of the state instead of all taxes; that another sum should next be deducted for support of the parish establishment, instead of tolls, tythes, rates, cesses, &c. and that after these important matters were provided for, the remainder of the money should be equally divided among all the settled inhabitants, whether poor or rich.
‡Isaiah, Ch. 14.

5.

Since this Jubilee
30   Sets all at Liberty
Let us be glad.
Behold each man return
To his possession
No more like doves to mourn
By landlords sad!

Pig's Meat (1793), 1: 42–43. This often reprinted song became known as the Jubilee Hymn, of which there are different versions. The idea of the Jubilee comes from Leviticus 25 ("And ye shall hallow the fiftieth year, and proclaim liberty throughout *all* the land unto all the inhabitants thereof: it shall be a jubilee unto you; and ye shall return every man unto his possession, and ye shall return every man unto his family"[10]), and much of the song's imagery comes from Isaiah 14 ("The Lord hath broken the staff of the wicked, *and* the sceptre of the rulers" [5]; "Yea, the fir trees rejoice at these, *and* the cedars of Lebanon, saying , Since thou art laid down, no feller is come up against us" [8]; "Hell from beneath is moved for *thee* at thy coming" [9]).

(*l. 5*): "Cess'd" means taxed, assessed.

(*l. 9*): Quarter days were four annual days on which taxes and/or rents were due: Lady Day (March 25), Midsummer Day (June 24), Michaelmas Day (September 29), and Christmas Day (December 25).

BURKE'S ADDRESS TO THE "SWINISH MULTITUDE!"

[THOMAS SPENCE]

Tune, "Derry down, down," &c.

Ye vile Swinish Herd, in the Sty of Taxation,
What would you be after?—disturbing the Nation?
Give over your grunting—Be off—To your Sty!
Nor dare to look out, if a KING passes by:
Ge[t] ye down! down! down!—Keep ye down!
Do ye know what a KING is? By *Patrick* I'll tell you;
He has Power in his Pocket, to buy you and sell you:
To make you all Soldiers, or keep you at work?
To hang you, and cure you for Ham or Salt Pork!
10   Get ye down! &c.
Do you think that a KING is no more than a Man?
Ye Brutish, Ye Swinish, irrational Clan?
I swear by his Office, his Right is divine,
To flog you, and feed you, and treat you like Swine!
Get ye down! &c.

65

To be sure, I have said—but I spoke it abrupt—
That "the State is *defective* and also *corrupt*."
Yet remember I told you with Caution to peep,
For *Swine* at a Distance WE prudently keep—
20   Get ye down! &c.
Now the *Church* and the *State*, to keep each other warm,
Are *married* together. And where is the Harm?
How healthy and wealthy are Husband and Wife!
But *Swine* are excluded the conjugal Life—
    Get ye down! &c.
The *State*, it is true, has grown fat upon SWINE,
And *Church*'s weak stomach on TYTHE-PIG can dine;
But neither you know, as they *roast* at the Fire,
Have a Right to find fault with the *Cooks*, or enquire.
30   Get ye down! &c.
"What Use do we make of your Money?"—You say;
Why the first Law of Nature:—*We take our own Pay*—
And next on our Friends a few *Pensions* bestow—
And to you we apply when our *Treasure* runs low,
    Get ye down! &c.
Consider our *Boroughs*, Ye grumbling SWINE!
At Corruption and Taxes, they never repine:
If we only *Proclaim*, "YE ARE HAPPY!"—They say,
"WE ARE HAPPY!"—Believe and be *Happy* as they!
40   Get ye down! &c.
What know ye of Commons, of KINGS, or of LORDS,
But what the dim *Light* of TAXATION affords?
Be contented with that—and no more of your Rout:
Or a new *Proclamation* shall muzzle your Snout!
    Get ye down! &c.
And now for the SUN—or the LIGHT of the DAY!
"It doth not belong to a PITT?"—You will say.
I tell you be silent, and hush all your Jars:
Or he'll charge you a *Farthing* a piece for the Stars
50   Get ye down! &c.
Here's MYSELF, and *His Darkness*, and *Harry Dundas*:
Scotch, *English*, and *Irish*, with Fronts made of Brass—
A Cord plated three-fold will stand a good pull,
Against SAWNEY, and PATRICK, and old *Johnny Bull*!!!
    Get ye down! &c.
To conclude: Then no more about MAN and his RIGHTS,
TOM PAINE, and a Rabble of *Liberty Wights*:

That you are but our "SWINE," if ye ever forget,
We'll throw you alive to the HORRIBLE PIT!
60   Get ye down! down! down!—Keep ye down!

Pig's Meat (1793), 1: 250–51. A slightly different version appeared earlier in the *Manchester Herald* (Sept. 9, 1792).

(*l. 44*): Royal Proclamation against Seditious Writings, May 21, 1792; this inaugurated a severe repression of reformist publications.

(*l. 46*): Window glass was taxed so that the poor were discouraged from having adequate light in their dwellings.

(*l. 48*): "Jars" were contentious conflicts.

(*l. 51*): Henry Dundas, Viscount Melville (1742–1811; *DNB*), member of Pitt's government; June, 1791, he became Home Secretary.

l. 52: Dundas was Scots, Pitt English, and Burke Irish.

l. 54: nicknames for Scots, Irish, and English.

ALTERATION   [THOMAS SPENCE]

No longer lost in shades of night,
   Where late in chains we lay!
The sun arises, and his light
   Dispels our gloom away.

No longer blind, and prove to lye
   In slavery profound;
But for redress aloud we cry!
   And Tyrants hear the sound.

The pomp of Courts *no more* engage;
10   The *magic spell* is *broke*;
We hail the bright reforming age!
   And *cast away* the *yoke*.

Our *substance* and our *blood* no more
   So tamely shall we yield;
Nor quit like slaves our *native* shore
   To *deck* the MONSTER's field.

The *rotten lumber* of the land,
   The *courtly-pension'd train*;
Shall hear their sentence and disband,
20   As we our Rights regain.

The mitred villain as he rolls
   In luxury and lust,
He blinds and robs the silly souls
   Committed to his trust.

Amus'd no more with empty lies,
   Of bliss we *never* knew;
The traitors lose the state disguise,
   And closely we pursue.

Pig's Meat (1794), 2: 2.
  (l. 21): Anglican bishop.

EXAMPLES OF SAFE PRINTING   [THOMAS SPENCE]

To prevent misrepresentation in these prosecuting times, it seems necessary to publish every thing relating to Tyranny and Oppression, though only among brutes, in the most guarded manner.

The following are meant as Specimens:—

That tyger, or that other salvage wight
Is so exceeding furious and fell,
   As WRONG,
        [*Not meaning our most gracious sovereign Lord*
        the King, or the Government of this country]
   when it hath arm'd himself with might;
Not fit 'mong men that do with reason mell,
But 'mong wild beasts and salvage woods to dwell;
   Where still the stronger
        [*Not meaning the great men of this country*]
   doth the weak devour,
And they that most in boldness doe excell,
   And draded most, and feared by their powre.
                      E. Spencer

Pig's Meat (1794), 2: 14. Repression, the theme of the poem, was something Spence was well acquainted with. He was arrested—between 1792 and 1794—on December 6, 1792, December 10, 1792, January 1793, and December 1793, and was imprisoned from May 20, 1794, to December 22, 1794. The particular ploy here of inserting the bracketed material of denials, which act in an opposite direction, derives probably from the trial of Daniel Eaton for publishing John Thelwall's "Chaunticlere" allegory in *Politics for the People* (1793), 1: 102–7. During the trial (February 24, 1794), there were some hilarious exchanges, embarrassing to the government, as the prosecuting attorney was forced to keep saying that the gamecock whose head gets chopped off in Thelwall's allegory is "our lord the king." (See Butler 1984, 185–88). Radicals at this time gleefully exploited the ambiguities of animal allegory.

The Edmund Spenser (1552?–99; *DNB*) imitation was motivated by the obvious pun and the typical radical ploy of creating historical distance from the referents of the poem. The irony is that these various gestures that acknowledge the repression are in fact defying the repression and articulating an uncompromisingly radical criticism of the monarchy and aristocracy.

(l. 7): "Mell" means mix.

TRIBUTE TO LIBERTY   W. D. GRANT

Tune—Lullaby.

Generous PATRIOTS, nobly daring,
   Regal Ruffians rage defy;
Ev'ry toil and peril sharing,
   In pursuit of LIBERTY.
        Liberty! Liberty! Liberty! Liberty!
        In pursuit of Liberty!

In their train see TRUTH appearing,
   JUSTICE and EQUALITY: Reason's rays supremely cheering,
True-born *Sons of Liberty*!
        Liberty! Liberty! &c.

Nature Virtue bids us cherish,
   Those who wish ALL mankind free;
Then let ev'ry tyrant perish,
   Ev'ry foe to liberty.
        Liberty! Liberty! &c.

Pig's Meat (1794), 2: 43–44.

W. D. Grant: also published songs in Eaton's *Politics for the People*, 2: 72; 159–60; 207–8.

(st. 3): A real political group of English radicals in the 1790s used the name Sons of Liberty.

EDMUND BURKE'S ADDRESS TO THE SWINISH MULTITUDE.   [THOMAS SPENCE]

"Here is the constitution, which we have made for you and for your posterity for ever. We buckle it on your back, for you are beasts of burden, you must not dare to touch it," Burke.

Ye Swinish Multitude who prate,
   What know ye 'bout the matter?
Misterious [*sic*] are the ways of state,
   Of which you should not chatter.

Our church and state, like man and wife,
    Together kindly cuddle;
Together share the sweets of life,
    Together feast and fuddle.
        CHORUS.
Then hence ye Swine nor make a rout,
    Forbearance but relaxes;
We'll clap the muzzle on your snout,
    Go work, and pay your taxes.

Ye apron men to labour bred,
    How dare ye thus to quarrel;
We'll take your children's beer and bread,
    And you shan't smell the barrel.
'Tis ours to take your needful scot,
    When e'er we lack assistance;
Passive obedience is your lot,
    And humble non-resistance.

Then hence ye Swine, &c.

How dare you rail at noble lords,
    Remember Richmond's power:
To bind you[—]neck and head in cords,
    Bastile [*sic*] you in the Tower.
Stormount [*sic*] and we shall break your hearts
    With writs and declarations;
And Fox no longer takes your parts,
    Or vindicates the nations.

Then hence ye Swine, &c.

No reformation you shall have,
    We tell it to your faces;
Make every mother's son a slave,
    And yet we'll keep our places.
In vain you swear at Billy Pitt,
    At George in vain you grumble;
We'll take two thirds of all you get,
    To keep you poor and humble.

Then hence ye Swine, &c.

Equality, that crime abhor'd,
    Of this you dare to prattle:

Pig's Meat

Of different clay, is made my lord,
   He shepherd, you the cattle.
So hence ye herds, and graze below,
   Where'er he bids be jogging,
First lick the dust from off his toe,
   Or patient bear his flogging.

Then hence ye Swine, &c.

Now when we see you mend your lives,
   And live in humble quarters:
We'll let you kiss in peace your wives,
   Nor tax for new born daughters.
Let us at will reap all you've sown,
   Nor deal in turn vexation;
John Bull should bear, and never frown,
   Beneath immense taxation.

Then hence ye Swine, &c.

Remember all I say, for shame,
   I say ye Swine remember;
Or else we'll play you such a game,
   We did in last November.
Our proclamations sent about,
   'Tis Billy Pitt shall plan'em,
Of plots that never yet came out,
   Except of Richmond's cranium.

Then hence ye Swine, &c.

My mandate should you now neglect,
   Ye multitude of grunters;
We'll tax ye still, without respect,
   To feed us fortune hunters.
Chains, gibbets, axes, soon shall rise,
   And batter in terrorum
And you ye Swine, shall greet our eyes,
   By dangling high before them.

Then hence ye Swine, nor make a rout,
   Forbearance but relaxes.
We'll clap the muzzle on your snout,
   Go work and pay your taxes.

Pig's Meat (1794), 2: 39–41.
   (l. 8): "Fuddle" means to drink to intoxication.

(*l. 9*): "Rout" refers to a disorderly crowd.
(*l. 17*): "Scot" means tax payment.
(*ll. 19–20*): Passive obedience and nonresistance were old Tory doctrines.
(*l. 23*): The Duke of Richmond, Charles Lennox, proposed radical reform in 1780 (annual parliaments and universal manhood suffrage), but became an anti-radical apostate to the reform cause, most notoriously in the 1792 debate over the Proclamation concerning Seditious Writings when the still-liberal Lord Lauderdale (1759–1839; *DNB*) challenged Richmond to a duel. Richmond's proposal for reform was often reprinted by the reform movement.
(*l. 26*): Viscount Stormont, David Murray Mansfield (1727–96; *DNB*), Lord Justice General of Scotland.
(*l. 28*): Charles James Fox was the liberal Whig leader.
(*l. 31*): The most recent failure of parliamentary reform proposals was Charles Grey's in May 7, 1793.
(*l. 35*): William Pitt was the Prime Minister.
(*l. 36*): King George III (1738–1820).
(*l. 61*): The "proclamation" referred to here is perhaps the Royal Proclamation against Seditious Associations, November, 1792.

The two songs following were Written by T. Spence, when a Prisoner in Newgate, under a charge of High Treason, in the memorable Year 1794.

THE RIGHTS OF MAN FOR ME
A SONG—TUNE—*MAID OF THE MILL*

There are twenty fine schemes held up by the great,
    To deceive silly souls, d'ye see?
And render them passive for pure conscience sake,
    And mould them to fell tyranny;
Yet for all their fine arts with their priests in their aid,
    Their threats and their deep policy,
I'll laugh them to scorn, while loudly I sing,
    The Rights of Man boys for me.

This world for the poor they say never was made,
10   Their portion in the heav'ns be,
And say that they envy them their happy lot,
    So certain's their felicity;
But thank them for naught, if the heav'ns they could lett [*sic*],
    Few joys here the poor would e'er see,
For *rents* they must toil and for *taxes* to boot,
    The Rights of Man then for me.

Then cheer up all you who have long been oppressed,
    Aspire unto sweet liberty;

Pig's Meat

No fetters were form'd for a nation to bind,
20   That had the brave wish to be free:
To Gallia then look and blush at your chains,
     And shake off all vile slavery,
And let each man sing, till loud echoes ring,
     The Rights of Man boys for me.

As for me though in prison I oft' have been cast,
     Because I would dare to be free,
And though in black Newgate I now pen this song,
     My theme I've not alter'd you see;
In jail or abroad whatever betide,
30   My struggles for freedom shall be,
Whate'er fate bring, I will think, speak and sing,
     The Rights of Man* boys for me!

Pig's Meat (1795), 3: 249–51.
   The title: His Newgate term, May 17 to December 22, 1794.
   (l. 25): In addition to the 1794 term, Spence was imprisoned on December 10, 1792, January, 1793, and December, 1793. After his 1794 prison term, he was jailed in 1798 and 1801; in the lattermost year he began serving a twelve-month sentence.
   (note): One of Spence's propaganda techniques was to chalk political grafitti in London, echoed here in his "writing with chaulk."

The Downfall of Feudal Tyranny, Severely felt by the Moderns, under the System of Landlord and Tenant

That conquering blade, who did us invade,
     Ev'n William the Norman by name,

---

*The composer of the above song, was the first, who as far as he knows, made use of the phrase, "Rights of Man," which was on the following remarkable occasion: A man who had been a farmer, and also a miner, and who had been ill-used by his land-lords, dug a cave for himself by the sea side, at Marston Rocks, between Shields and Sunderland, about the year 1780, and the singularity of such a habitation, exciting the curiosity of many to pay him a visit; our author was one of that number. Exulting in the idea of a human being, who had bravely emancipated himself from the iron fangs of aristocracy, to live free from impost, he wrote extempore with chaulk, above the fireplace of the freedman, the following lines:
   "Ye landlords vile, who man's peace mar,
   Come levy rents here if you can;
   Your stewards and lawyers I defy,
   And live with all the Rights of Man."

Among his proud band he divided our land,
    Nought leaving but slav'ry and shame,
        My poor boys.
    Nought leaving but slav'ry's shame.

These plundering bands, thus strengthen'd by lands,
    For ages have rul'd us with awe,
Whilst we once so free, now without property,
10   From conqu'rors received the law,
        My poor boys.

The priests them to aid, they lib'rally paid,
    And gave them good share of the spoil,
The poor to persuade, that if nothing they said,
    In heav'n they should end all their toil,
        My poor boys.

Thus lords and priests leagu'd together intrigu'd,
    Completely poor man to enthrall,
And when thus befool'd, their vassals they rul'd
20   And kept them in chains one and all,
        My poor boys.

But now reason's ray, begins to display,
    To man his dear rights once again,
While all wond'ring how they've been duped till now,
    Make haste to declare they are men,
        My brave boys.

The sons and the heirs* of those old murderers,
    Observe how they fly now to arms,
For mankind they see, are resolv'd to be free,
30   Which ev'ry proud tyrant alarms,
        My brave boys.

Sad ruin's their fate, though they associate,
    No rents now the poor will soon pay,
For when in a mass, like a flood o'er they pass,
    They'll sweep all their greatness away;
        My brave boys.

For whom do we toil and feed with our spoil?
    Is now through the nations the cry,

---

*The associators.

Infuriate men sing, till heav'ns concave ring,
40 O, give me death or liberty!
My brave boys,
O give me death or liberty!

Pig's Meat (1795), 3: 249–51. Spence draws upon the myth of Saxon liberty and the Norman yoke here. This was an influential political myth for nineteenth-century radicalism. See Thompson 1963, 86–89. The poem targets, in typically Spencean fashion, the three key oppressors, the monarchy, the aristocracy, and the church.

(l. 2): William of Normandy (1027–87).

(l. 27): "Heirs" is a reference to the Association for the Defence of Liberty and Property against Republicans and Levellers, formed—with government help—by John Reeves (c. 1752–1829) in 1792. The Association actively promoted the repression of reformers, including Spence, by bringing prosecutions for seditious and blasphemous libel.

3. *Politics for the People* (1793–1794)

The editor of this journal was Daniel Isaac Eaton, member of the London Corresponding Society, bookseller and publisher. Like Spence's *Pig's Meat*, Eaton's *Politics for the People; or, A Salmagundy for Swine* (1793–95) was inexpensive (two pence), designed for a plebeian audience that it tried to educate with a variety of extracts. Eaton's journal includes far more poetry and original material than Spence's. Almost all the verse is politically oriented, but there is quite a diversity among the poems: songs and ballads (43 percent); satires in couplets (31 percent); epigrams (15 percent); fables (8.5 percent); blank verse (2.5 percent). For the prose selections, the predominant source is the eighteenth century, both English and continental writers, older and contemporary; the prose extracts are rather similar to those in Spence's *Pig's Meat*. One striking difference between the two periodicals is that Eaton's clearly invited reader participation, and Spence's did not. Consequently, *Politics for the People* has a definitely collective tone as a "movement" periodical, whereas *Pig's Meat* is stamped throughout as the production of one individual.

It is not possible to determine circulation numbers for Eaton's or Spence's journal, but if one factors in the low price, the political repression, the London Corresponding Society's activist membership, and the several editions of both journals in bound volumes—five editions of *Politics for the People* by 1795—then one can infer a figure much higher than that for newspapers (about 3,000) but considerably lower than the circulation of William Cobbett's *Political Register* in the Waterloo to Peterloo period (about 50,000). LCS dues-paying membership peaked at 3,000 in 1795, but the LCS could lead protest demonstrations of around 100,000 (see Thale xxiv).

For Eaton and his periodical, see Daniel L. McCue, Jr., "Daniel I. Eaton and *Politics for the People*," diss., Columbia U, 1974; McCue, Jr., "The Pamphleteer Pitt's Government Couldn't Silence," *Eighteenth-Century Life* 5 (1978): 38–49; Smith ch. 3. There is a facsimile reprint of the periodical published by Greenwood Press (1968).

What Makes A Libel?
A Fable [N.A.]

In *Aesop's* new made World of Wit,
   Where Beasts could talk, and read, and write,
And say and do as he thought fit;
   A certain Fellow thought himself abus'd,
And represented by an *Ass*,
   And *Aesop* to the Judge accus'd
That he defamed was.
Friend, quoth the Judge, How do you know,
   Whether you are defam'd or no?
10 How can you prove that he must mean
   You, rather than another Man?
Sir quoth the Man, it needs must be,
   All Circumstances so agree,
     And all the Neighbours say 'tis Me.
That's somewhat, quoth the Judge, indeed;
   But let this matter pass,
Since 'twas not *Aesop*, 'tis agreed,
   But *Application* made the *Ass*.

Politics for the People (1793), 1: 53. This particular poet exploits the animal fable tradition, as do many of the journal's writers. Although not present here, the "swinish multitude" phrase and its various permutations mark not just the journal's title but so much of the original material sent to the magazine. The animal fable crossed with the swinish trope produced a large quantity of satirical verse. The fable itself, with its Aesopian ambiguity and ability to withstand politically repressive situations, was especially popular in the journal in the first volume, before and shortly after Eaton's acquittal for the Thelwall "Chaunticlere" allegory (see Butler 1984, 185–88).

Two ways pointed out by which any poor Manufacturer deprived of work by this blessed War, may be enabled to obtain a morsel of bread.   No Work

Being thrown by this ruinous War, out of Work,
Dick blest, in *his* way, DUNDAS, PITT, and BURKE:
Then his wits he employed to find out the way,
To prevent being forced to keep fast on chopt hay;
After puzzling awhile, he cried out in a rage,
That times are so bad that one cannot engage,

Politics for the People

One's belly to fill without selling one's Soul,
To Slaughter our Brethren, or Wolves like to prowl,
For no way I see there's to weather the Storm,
But to *'list* for a *Soldier,* or—*rogue* like *inform.*

Politics for the People (1793–94), 1: 53.

 (l. 2): Henry Dundas, Viscount Melville, was a member of Pitt's government who in June, 1791, became Home Secretary; Burke was author of *Reflections on the Revolution in France* (1790).

1694   [N.A.]

The false rapacious Wolf of France,
 The scourge of Europe, and its curse
Who at his subjects['] cry would dance,
 And study how to make them worse.
To say such Kings, Lord, rule by thee,
Were most prodigious blasphemy.

Such know no laws but their own lust;
 Their Subjects['] substance, and their blood,
They count it tribute due and just,
10 Still spent and spilt for Subjects['] good.
If such Kings are by God appointed,
The Devil may be the Lord[']s anointed.

Such Kings curst be their power and name,
 Let all the World henceforth abhor 'em,
Monsters which knaves sacred proclaim,
 And then like Slaves, fall down before 'em,
What can there be in Kings divine?
The most are Wolves, Goats, Sheep, or Swine.

Then farewell sacred Majesty.
20 Let's pull all Brutish Tyrants down,
Where Men are Born, and still live Free,
 There Every Head doth wear a Crown.
Mankind like miserable Frogs,
Prove wretched, King'd by Storks and Logs.

Politics for the People (1794), 1: 68. The last two lines of this poem, like the next poem, draw upon the Aesop fable of the frogs who ask Jove for a king: at first they get a log, which proves inadequate, then a stork, which starts eating the frogs. The "Wolf of France" (l. 1) is obviously Louis XVI, executed in January, 1793. The "1694" of the title is a transparent way to avoid the charge of seditious libel. In the last stanza the poem moves toward a republican position that seems to call for the overthrow of George III and the English monarchy, but the animal allegory provides the poet with a convenient ambiguity. In line 18 there is yet another turning upside-down of Burke's swinish trope.

Logs, Storks, and Asses [N.A.]

A generous race of croking frogs,
Which lay intrench'd between two bogs,
Who, as the morning sun did shine,
Daily increas'd their stock divine;
Just as the solar influence burn'd,
Prolific spawn to life as turn'd,
Until the young one's had at length
An equal vigour, equal strength.
So numerous at length they prove,
10 They supplicate to mighty Jove;
A king and governor they crave,
As other beasts and insects have;
But Jove allow'd all mortal elves,
To choose a monarch for themselves,
The croking elders now consult
About a king, and the result
Was, that a neighb'ring log should be
Executor of monarchy.
About the log their heads they raise,
20 In sounds uncouth they croke his praise;
At length some crawl upon his top,
And frisk about, and croke and hop:
Says one frog, here's fine business done,
Was e'er a king thus trampl'd on?
Troth, says another antient frog,
We'll ne'er be govern'd by a log.
The heat at length so far arose,
They did the Loggerhead depose.
   To new election they proceed,
30 And to their hearts['] content succeed:
A neighbouring stork at length they chose,
Which should their heats and feuds compose;
He took upon him the command
Of all the people in Frogland;
But he, as t'other 'fore had done,

Made it an arbitrary throne;
Up from the mud the frogs would pick,
And squeeze their corps within his beak.
One frog, much wiser than the rest,
40 To those about him thus address'd:
Good friends this is confounded work,
Shall we be govern'd by a stork;
To have our bones in pieces torn,
Our young ones ate just as they're born?
As if kings only had a pow'r
To ruin subjects, and devour;
I think 'tis just to choose again:
The brood of frogs all crok'd, Amen.
    The next they chose was a dull ass,
50 Which prov'd as bad as t'other was;
For though he was not so malicious,
His folly made him as pernicious;
Stumbling on empire, oft he stood
Upon his subjects chok'd in mud:
Whole beds of spawn he did destroy,
At ev'ry flounce did frogs annoy,
The devil's in't, said one, for we
In choosing kings still wretched be.
THUS OFTEN WE HAVE CHOSE[N] A K——,
AND STILL HAVE FOUND IT THE SAME THING.

Written in the Year 1694.

Politics for the People (1794), 1: 69. These tetrameter couplets explore the Aesop fable from a republican perspective, developing what we might now call a critique of the authoritarian personality that creates and needs "monarchy." The recent French regicide, a dramatic illustration of republican theory in action, stimulated poems like this. Again, the bogus date for the poem is a transparent fiction, calling attention to the political repression rather than circumventing it.

(*l. 34*): There is a pun here, with *Frogland* referring to France.
(*l. 56*): "Flounce" is a sudden, violent movement.

The Goitre.*
A Fable. [N.A.]

Reader! you've seen perchance, (for every sight
    John Bull's devout attention draws)

---
*A wen, or swelling in the throat.

The Revolutionary Decade

You've seen, with equal wonder and delight,
   The Monstrous Craws—
Now if you feel your vigorous fancy able
   To give a mere unform'd excresence
   Existence personal and essence,
See how a *Wen* can figure in a fable.
A *Goitre* in an Alpine valley bred,
   In shape and size full rival to the head,
   Esteem'd among the belles of Syon
The prettiest lump of flesh was e'er set eye on,
Made vain, as we may well suppose,
   With admiration, like a noddy,
Puff'd with self-consequence and folly, chose
   To stand in competition with the body.

And thus he argued,—"In the general plan
That forms the commonwealth of man,
We may presume that every single part,
   In bulk, and growth, and distribution,
Was made, by never-erring art,
   Best suited to the human constitution.
'Twere then enough for me to sound pretensions
On my long standing, place and large dimensions;
   But be it known, that, if I please,
I can bring better claims than these.

And, first, my *privileges*. When the head,
   Fatigu'd with thinking, or with raking,
Lies on the pillow pale and dead,
   Ready to split with aching;
When the heart flutters, and with direful rumble
   The cholick'd bowels grumble;
   When limbs are on the rack,
And grinding pains run through the long long back;
   I loll upon the breast,
   In ease and rest,
With nought to do, but put my juices
   To all their proper uses:
And thus I fatten, grow, and thrive,
   While they, poor souls! scarce keep themselves alive.

Now for my *services*. I need not tell ye
How once the members quarrell'd with the belly;
   And still the resty rascals led

Politics for the People

    By the rebellious head,
    Are prone to riot.
'Tis then my task to keep them quiet,
By draining off superfluous humours,
Suppressing ferments and plethoric tumours,
And by the wholesome system of starvation,
50 Maintaining peace and due subordination.
    And thus I keep the balance even,
    And fit the body-politic for heaven.

These things consider'd, reason must agree
    That place and preference are due to me;
Yet, for the gen'ral welfare, I'm content
    To make a close and firm ALLIANCE,
That we may all live easy and content,
    And bid our foes defiance."

While thus, Sir Goitre, swaggering and vap'ring,
60 Led his poor passive partner such a life,
Comes a *French Surgeon* flourishing and capering,
Who whipping out his knife,
    Made an incision to the quick,
    Like boys about a stick,
And presently proceeded to dissever
The ill-match'd pair for ever and for ever.
Here Goitre lay, a wither'd lifeless lump,
While the disburthen'd body vigorous grew and plump.

Most states abound in hangers on and tumours,
70 From petty warts to wens of monstrous size,
That suck the blood and waste the precious humours,
Yet call themselves supporters and allies.
The *French practitioners* are bold and able,
    None better understand the art of lopping;
    When *English Surgeons* come to practise cropping,
I'll try to find the *Goitre* of the fable.

Politics for the People (1794), 2: 10–13. Published during the Reign of Terror, this bold poem exploits the figure of the body politic to allegorize a parasitic, cancerous aristocracy, although the monarchy is also suggested here, as is the church. The goitre in the poem seems to represent all three in a process of condensation. Violently anti-aristocratic, this poem deserves the label "Jacobin." This poem, minus the last four lines, was published earlier in the *Morning Chronicle* (Jan. 1, 1793).
    (l. 11): Sion is an Alpine city on the Rhone in the Vallais canton, Switzerland.
    (l. 14): A "noddy" is a simpleton.

(l. 43): "Resty" means restive.
(l. 75): "Cropping" here means cutting.

HYMN TO LIBERTY [N.A.]

    Hail! heaven born fair,
Who easest life from misery
    And makes it worth our care;
My constant vows are all addresst to thee,
Thou guardian goddess, Liberty[.]

    Let other swains
Carve plaintive sonnets on each tree
    Lamenting love[-]sick pains,
But let my noble verse be ever free
10 To sing the charms of Liberty.

    Should civil broil,
Of foreign force to slavery
    Subdue my native soil;
My native soil would have no charms for me,
Without thy presence, Liberty.

    Birth, titles, wealth,
The trappings of posterity;
    Soft peace, nor smiling health,
Nor love itself, can yield felicity,
20 Without the joys of Liberty.

    Should she remove
To Scythia, China, Tartary
    Or 'mongst rude Indians rove,
To frozen coasts, to burning sands I'd fly,
In search of lovely liberty.

    To sultry waste,
With far more temperate climes might vie
The sun in Scythia with a milder sky
30 Would smile on thee, sweet Liberty.

    Riches adieu!
Instructed by Philosophy
    I'll freely part with you;
Nor sigh for blessing which the gods deny,
Whilst they indulge me Liberty.

Politics for the People (1794), 1: 178–79.
   (*l. 22*): Scythia was an ancient nation north of the Black Sea in southeastern Europe and Asia; Tartary refers to the land stretching from Siberia down through Russia. These are archaic references.

INDEPENDENCE [N.A.]

Happy the Bard, [(]though few such Bards we find)
Who 'bove controlment, dares to speak his mind,
Dares, unabash'd, in ev'ry place appear,
And nothing fear, but what he ought to fear,
Him fashion cannot tempt, him abject need
Cannot compel, him pride cannot mislead
To be the slave of greatness, to strike sail,
When, sweeping onward with her peacock's tail,
Quality in plumage passes by;
10 He views her with a fix'd contemptuous eye,
And mocks the puppet, keeps his own due state,
And is above conversing with the great.
Perish those slaves, those minions of the quill,
Who have conspir'd to seize that sacred hill
Where the nine sisters pour a genuine strain
And sink the mountain level with the plain;
Who, with mean, private views, and servile art,
No spark of virtue living in their heart,
Have basely turn'd apostates, have debas'd
20 Their dignity office, have disgrac'd,
Like Eli's sons, the altars where they stand,
And caus'd their name to stink through all the land;
Have stoop'd to prostitute their pen
For the support of great, but guilty men,
Have made the Bard, of their own vile accord,
Inferior to that thing we call a *Lord*.

   O my poor conutry [*sic*] . . .
With unavailing grief thy wrongs I see,
And, for myself not feeling, feel for thee,
30 I grieve, but can't despair—for, lo, at hand
Freedom presents a choice, but faithful band
Of loyal patriots, men who greatly dare
In such a noble cause, men fit to bear
The weight of empires; fortune, rank, and sense,

The Revolutionary Decade

> Virtue and knowledge, leagued with eloquence,
> March in their ranks; Freedom from file to file
> Darts her delighted eye, and with a smile
> Approves her honest sons, whilst down her cheek,
> As 'twere by stealth—her heart too full to speak,
> 40 One tear in silence creeps,———

Politics for the People (1794), 1: 179. These forty lines of heroic couplets seem to be written by the poet of the previous poem. Especially in the second part of the poem, where the poet's identity becomes merged with the sons of freedom in military formation, what might have been vague is pointed and clear. The "independence" of the Tory satirists like Alexander Pope (1688–1744) and Jonathan Swift (1667–1745) has been appropriated to support a democratic revolution.

(l. 21): Reference to I Samuel: 4; Eli's sons were corrupt priests.

Effects of War   Philanthropos

> Come proud unfeeling Pomp—Come Luxury,
> And ye who thoughtless frolic in the round
> Of Mirth and Joy, or revel out the night
> Where Dissipation mads her festive sons!
> A scene I will disclose, a piteous scene,
> At sight of which proud Pomp shall shrink aghast;
> The tear shall start from the chang'd-eye of Mirth,
> And, from the unnerv'd bacchanalian hand,
> The cup shall fall, untasted, to the ground.
> 10 Behold yon wretched hovel, once the seat
> Of Industry and Health, Content and Love:
> There the poor labourer, from his daily toil
> Releas'd at eve, enjoy'd his little home.
> With every sweet endearment, his fond wife
> Welcom'd his glad return; rejoic'd to share
> A father's smile, the little prattlers strove
> To climb his knee, and play'd their gambols round,
> Thoughtless of future ills, each parent smil'd,
> Gaz'd on the pledges of their mutual love
> 20 With heart-felt joy, and thought them wealth enough!
> Blest was the cot with innocence and peace.
> Alas! how chang'd! each smiling joy is fled,
> Fled—to return no more!—while sickness, want,
> Famine, and all the complicated woes,
> That haunt the desolating steps of war,
> With dismal gloom, o'erspread the sadden'd scene.

See on yon wretched bed, which ill excludes
Rude winter's piercing blast, with sickness wan,
A wife, a mother, lies; oft had she spar'd
The hard-earn'd morsel from her famish'd lips,
To save her children from untimely death;
Long had she struggled with the cruel force
Of Sickness, preying on her tender frame,
Too carefully conceal'd, lest she should add
Another pang t'encrease her partner's woes;
She sinks at last, and feels the icy grasp
Of Desolation waste her feeble frame.
Resign'd, she welcomes death, nor heaves a sigh,
Save for her husband's and her children's fate.
In vain to shield her sinking in his arms,
And ward the dart, a wretched husband strives!—
She clasps his hand, and looks a last adieu!
In speechless agony he stands, while death,
Remorseless, mocks his prayer, and strikes the blow.
See o'er the clay-cold corpse he hangs,—despair
Rolls in his eye, and anguish fills his soul!
Have we no HOWARD left,—Heaven's messenger
To poverty distrest, to pour the balm
Of comfort on Affliction's wounded heart?
But here the stores of charity would fail,
Lo Commerce sickens, and the toiling hand
Of Industry droops lifeless, unemploy'd;
Dire is the curse, and wide the ruin spreads,
War sounds an echoing blast, and havoc stalks around!
Britannia, weeping, mourns her hapless sons,
But frowns indignant at a nation's wrongs.
Despots delight in war; to them 'tis sport,
A Royal Game—their subjects['] lives the stake:
But why will brother against brother lift
The murderous steel, to gratify the pride
Of one ambitious man, yclep'd a King?
If we must fight, let freemen fight with slaves;
Hurl'd from their thrones let despots feel the force
Of Britain's vengeful thunder, nor insult
The RIGHTS of NATIONS, and the RIGHTS of MAN.
Tremble, ye tyrants, for your doom is seal'd!
Tremble, ye slaves, for ye shall bite the dust;
Triumphant Freedom, in her blood-stain'd vest,

>   Despots combin'd, drags at her chariot-wheels,
> 70   And nobly manumits a world enslav'd!

Politics for the People (1794), 1 (part 2), no. 8: 10–12. These seventy lines of blank verse illustrate the generic range of even the most politically committed verse aimed at a plebeian audience. The vignette of the poor laborers being victimized by war is somewhat reminiscent of *The Ruined Cottage* (1797–98). The poem also fuses sentimental conventions—even the allusion to Howard is sentimental—and militantly reformist conventions, which predominate in the last fifteen lines or so.

(l. 47): John Howard (1726?–90; *DNB*) was one of the most famous philanthropists, most noted for his efforts exposing the atrocious conditions in English jails.

A Parallel between Riches and Poverty. From the Greek of Rhianus. [N.A.]

>   An ancient bard had reason to complain,
>   That all mankind are ignorant and vain;
>   Nor in prosperity their pride repress,
>   Nor with calm dignity support distress;
>   To those below them with contempt behave,
>   To those above them act the downright slave.
>
>   Thus, he who is in want of daily food,
>   Feels no bold courage animate his blood;
>   Nature to him no beauties can display,
> 10   He curses fate and shuns the light of day.
>   The rich, in public, tell aloud their mind,
>   The poor, in servile silence, slink behind.
>   "Chill Penury" each generous thought controls,
>   And freezes all the ardour of their souls.
>   Nor should we rail at the corrupted times,
>   'Tis Poverty which fills the world with crimes;
>   For very few begin to rob or steal,
>   Till once they've fear'd the want of many a meal.
>   If halters only for the rich were made,
> 20   Ketch soon might starve, or seek a better trade;
>   His office merely keeps poor rogues in awe,
>   For great men's crimes are sanctified by law.
>   To what I say, exceptions will be found;
>   But 'tis a common case the world around.
>
>   The great adopt a surer, safer course,
>   They neither break a shop nor steal a horse

They seldom pick a purse, or forge a note,
Or point a pistol at a coachman's throat.
Yet all to vice are equally inclin'd,
30 Their misdemeanours vary but in kind;
The poor dare only cheat, the rich oppress,
The first must hide, the last avow success;
The blushing footpad plunders in the night,
The *noble* felon dares the noon-day light.
And sure of mortals, the most foolish thing,
Is, for the most part, what we call a k—;
Vile sycophants, devoted to his will,
Define his right to conquer and to kill;
And some poltroon, who, bred among the poor,
40 Had scarce dar'd thrust a vixen from his door;
Commits whole empires to the sword and flame,
Dreaming destruction dignifies a name.
But instant vengeance treads upon his heel,
And all his pride inflicted makes him feel.
Survey that class with an impartial eye,
How few have died as wise men wish to die;
Though fools may deem the day of vengeance past,
Guilt in repentance always ends at last.

Politics for the People (1795), 2: 107–9. These heroic couplets show a familiarity with the form that provides for a relaxed, conversational meditation. Classical thought is made relevant to reformist literary concerns. This poem is reprinted without attribution in *Sherwin's Political Register* (1818), 3: 175–76, and the author is "S. A. B."

The Greek of Rhianus: Rhianus (275–195 BCE) was a Greek poet and grammarian from Crete, ten of whose epigrams are extant.

(*l. 13*): From Thomas Gray (1716–71; *DNB*), "Elegy Written in a Country Churchyard," l. 51. Gray's "Elegy" was in general very popular and was frequently cited in the reformist periodicals.

(*l. 19*): "Halters" refers to the hangman's noose.

(*l. 20*): Jack Ketch was the proverbial executioner, the hangman.

(*l. 33*): "Footpad" is a term for highwayman.

(*l. 39*): "Poltroon" means coward.

A TALE   TOMMY PINDAR

Two beggars seated in a sunny lane,
Each finding he'd too many to maintain,
Began to rid them of their retinue,
As some great folks are sometimes forc'd to do.

    The one, for very spite, his tatters tore,
    And, as his fell back-biters he attack'd,
    His sanguine nails were all distain'd with gore,
    And still he crack'd and swore, and swore and crack'd.

      The other, seiz'd with a religious fit,
10   No longer could endure the bloody sport,
        But, quite forgetting how he had been bit
          Stopp'd short.
    'Shall we,' says he, 'thus impiously employ
      'Our barb'rous hands in shedding insect blood!
    'Shall we th'Almighty's creatures thus destroy,
      'Created for his pleasure and our good?
    'Perhaps to bite us, they're by God appointed,
    'And ev'ry louse may be the Lord's anointed;
          _____'For, this we know,
    'That some three dozen centuries ago,
20   'Their ancestors were sent to plague th' Egyptians,
    'Like certain folks of certain high descriptions.'

    At this, the other of his wits had doubt,
      And at the speech his sides began to shake,
      And soon as e'er he could for laughing speak,
        He thus broke out,——
    'Surely, my friend, thy carcase is thine own,
    'Do as thou wilt with every louse of thine,
    'Let them so please thee bite thee to the bone;
30   'But, d____n their bodies, I'll kill mine.[']

    This, please your kingships, is a pretty fable,
    You'll understand it—that is, if you're able.

Politics for the People (1794), 1 (part 2), no. 11: 13–14. The author's pseudonym is derived from "Peter Pindar," that is John Wolcott (1738–1819; *DNB*), probably the most famous satirist at the time. This poem's humor, confident use of colloquial language, and skillful rendering of the republican allegory of regicide—and class war against the aristocracy—make this one of the better poems in the journal.

An Hymn for the Fast Day, To Be Sung by The Friends of Mankind [N.A.]

    Thy judgments, Lord, proclaim abroad
    The dreadful vengeance of a God,

Extending wide o'er Europe's land[;]
Destruction flies, at thy command.

Methinks we hear the cannons roar,
And see a sea of human gore,
We hear our brethren's dying cries,
We feel their pangs,—and sympathise.

We see the devastation made
10   By fire and the destructive blade;
Cities and towns in ruins lie,
And tens of thousands tortur'd die.

Monarchs and Princes wield the sword,
And mar the people's peace, O Lord!
How wide their desolations spread,
And fill the astonish'd world with dread.

Long as those murderers tread the ground,
Horror and misery will abound;
When shall the blood of ***** atone,
20   For all the crimes which they have done[?].

Does not their measure yet run o'er,
Or is there mischief still in store,
Which sceptr'd despots may devise
On men and brethren to practise?

O Lord of Hosts! in man's defence
Exert thine own omnipotence.
O save thine image, man—O! spare
From horrors of destructive war!

Let the dread tyrants of the world
30   Down from their lofty thrones be hurl'd;
O scatter those, almighty God,
Who gorge themselves with human blood.

All wars and tumults then shall cease,
And men enjoy perpetual peace,
As one large family of thine,
As brethren knit in bands divine.

Then shall th' fetter'd slave go free,
And man rejoice in liberty,
Enjoying all those rights divine,
40   Which nature did for man design.

With holy transports of the soul,
Shall worship thee without controul,
Own thee their King, and thee alone,
Detesting rivals of thy throne.

Th' industrious hand from cultur'd soil,
Shall reap the profits of his toil,
The beauteous verdure of the field,
Shall nature's gifts profusely yield.

Then shall no vultures take away
50 Our earned comforts as their prey;
No locust shall our land devour,
Nor Virtue feel Oppression's power.

Then none shall dare insult the poor,
Nor spurn the aged from his door,
Nor want, nor wretchedness despise,
But free relieve with tearful eyes.

For this we meet, for this we pray,
To this alone devote the day:
Let tyrants from their thrones be hurl'd;
60 With peace and freedom bless the world.

Politics for the People (1794), 1 (part 2), no. 4: 3–5. The king periodically proclaimed fast days for victory against the French; these fast days were well organized by the Church of England. Naturally, radicals did not share in the ideological support for the war, but this particular radical poet does not want to permit the Anglican Church to appropriate religion altogether, as the poem expresses an almost millennial perspective.

(l. 19): The missing word is "kings."

ON ABUSES [N.A.]

Though plenty yearly fills her horn
With milk and honey, wine and corn,
It nought avails the sons of need,
'Tis only that th' *Elect* may feed.
They, while it please them, may devour
The honey, wine, and oil, and flour,
The reprobated swinish clan
Were only made to chew the bran;
For fit it is such vulgar tusks

10   Should grub away among the husks.
Ye prodigals of wealth and power,
Who think far off th' evil hour,
When swarming locusts, fatal bands,
Have famine spread through all the lands,
You then in vain may think to dine
Among the grunting angry swine.
But think you they would so befriend you,
No, they'd surely turn and rend you.
Should *Old Nick* put it in their head
20   (As once he did, 'tis somewhere said,)
To take a gallop down the steep,
And headlong plunge into the deep;
What with their keepers would they do,
Why, tumble them down headlong too:
But if they would redress our wrongs,
Thousands and thousands porkers['] tongues
Would scream and grunt, and yell, and cry,
And raise their praises to the sky;
They still might *plenty* have and *ease*,
30   We want not PEARLS, we ask but PEASE.

Politics for the People (1794), 2: 272. Like so many poems in this journal and others like it, this draws much from the Bible in terms of imagery, symbolism, and frame of reference; here, the exodus from Egypt is invoked as contemporary allegory. The poem effectively communicates the class resentment by means of the food imagery, and it is rhetorically powerful by developing a politically moderate line in the poem's conclusion. Once again, the swinish trope is exploited, alluding not just to Burke's "swinish multitude" but also to the Gadarene swine in the New Testament.

   (*l. 19*): Old Nick is Satan.

   (*l. 20*): Allusion to the Gadarene swine story, in which demons possess a herd of swine that drowns in the sea (Mark 5).

4. *The Philanthropist* (1795–1796)

As Daniel Isaac Eaton's *Politics for the People* ceased in March, 1795, so a new periodical began in the same month, to run continuously until early 1796, when the newly passed repressive legislation—the Two or Gagging Acts—silenced magazines like this. In connection with other radical publishing ventures, Eaton was forced to emigrate to America to avoid prosecution in 1796.

    As one compares *Politics for the People* and the *Philanthropist*, there are the obvious differences: the latter cost one penny, the former two pennies; the former has more words per weekly issue. The similarities are so strong, however, that the latter is really a continuation of the former.

1795 was an eventful year for English radicalism because it was a deceptively good year: the treason trials were over, the defendants having been acquitted; the London Corresponding Society enjoyed its largest membership and could command large crowds for demonstrations (over 100,000); there was some cooperation among the genteel reformers, the Whig liberals, and the plebeian LCS; in France, the Reign of Terror was over. In reality, however, the reformist cause was very much in jeopardy, despite its temporary health in this year which was also a serious famine year with numerous food riots and great public concern about the scarcity and high prices of bread. Reading the *Philanthropist*—or John Thelwall's *Tribune*—for 1795 one would not realize that the end of at least one phase of radical history was imminent.

There has been some speculation that William Wordsworth might have worked with the *Philanthropist*, but there is no definitive evidence. See Kenneth R. Johnston, "The Politics of 'Tintern Abbey,'" *Wordsworth Circle* 14 (1983): 6–14; Nicholas Roe, *Wordsworth and Coleridge: The Radical Years* (Oxford: UP, 1988), 276–79.

ADDRESS TO POVERTY [N.A.]

'Tis not that look of anguish bath'd in tears,
O, Poverty! thy haggard image wears,
'Tis not those famish'd limbs, naked and bare
To the black tempest's rains, or the keen air
Of winter's piercing winds, nor that sad eye
Imploring the small boon of charity!—
'Tis not that voice, whose melancholy tale
Might turn the purple cheek of grandeur pale,
Nor all that host of woes thou bring'st with thee,
10   Insult, contempt, disdain, and contumely,
That bid me call the lost of those forlorn,
Who 'neath thy rude oppression, sigh, and mourn—
But chief, relentless Power! thy hard controul,
That to the earth bends low the aspiring soul,
Thine iron grasp, thy fetters drear, which bind
Each generous effort of the struggling mind!
Alas! that genius' melancholy flow'r,
Scarce opening yet to even's nurturing show'r,
Should, by thy pitiless and cruel doom,
20   Wither, ere nature marks her smiling bloom—
That innocence, touch'd by thy dead'ning wand,

Should pine, nor know one out-stretch'd guardian hand—
For this, O, Poverty! for them I sigh,
The hapless victims of thy tyranny!
For this, I call the lot of those severe,
Who wander 'mid thy haunts, and pine unheeded there!

The Philanthropist, no. 1 (1795), 8. This particular poem, which concludes the first issue, is typical of 1790s radicalism in its idealism: what is so unforgivable about poverty is that it inhibits and compromises the intellectual ambitions of those without wealth.

SONNET   SYLVANUS AMICUS

Who loves his Country, and with-holds a sigh,
    Its wasted Hamlets, ruined towns to see;
Who meets, which way soe'er he turns his eye,
    The various forms of Want and Misery?

Who but must feel his indignation strong?
    On Nature's honest, broad, and gen'ral plan,
Against that head, that heart, that hand, that tongue,
    Which makes mankind a foe to fellow-man?

I hate ALL Wars, because I love mankind,
    And execrate that Wretch's odious name,
However dignified, who first design'd,
    Or still protracts, the sanguinary game.

If man be form'd the image of his God,
Sure he who mars the stamp must feel Heav'n's vengeful rod!

The Philanthropist, no. 7 (1795), 8.

CATO'S SOLILOQUY PARODIED.   M.[W.] H. GREEN

Being a REFLECTION and ADDRESS to the PEOPLE, supposed to be Spoken while reading the PAMPHLET entitled

COOPER'S REPLY TO BURKE'S INVECTIVE.

It must be so—COOPER, thou reason'st well—else why this
Visible fear, this guilty dread of Political Investigation!
Why shrink our Governors back upon Themselves, and
Startle at the Truth!—because it wounds their Souls—It
Wounds their Pride; it wounds their Hypocrisy!—Hypocrisy,

Thou well-tim'd dismal thought—through what sad
Scenes of Blood and Ruin!—through what confusion and
Changes have we past—and all to support this state.
Hypocrisy—who's [sic] views have ever been to enslave us—
10 But here we rest; for Reason illumes the World. Behold
Her offspring LIBERTY now bursts to birth; she ever must
Delight in Virtue, and that which she delights in must
Be happy—then why and wherefore hang you thus between
As if you'd doubt her Blessings; soon she'll prove 'em.
Meanwhile her enemies must fall.—The Sons of
Liberty in Reason, clad smiles at the *Combination, and
Defies its Fury.—for STARS and GARTERS shall fade
Away; MONARCHY! himself, grow dim with age; and
Kingcraft! sink in year, but these shall flourish
20 In immortal fame, unhurt amidst the War of Nation's,
The wreck of DESPOTISM! and the crush of KINGS!

The Philanthropist, no. 11 (1795), 8. The poet is undoubtedly W. H. Green, not M. H. This poet's name is attached to more poems in the *Philanthropist* than any other author's. However, he wrote no poems for *Politics for the People*. The poet, who could be the "H. Green" appearing in documents as an LCS member (see Thale), experiments with imitating the voice in a dramatic situation. Moreover, the poem's meter is irregular, and the various enjambments generate some energy. The Cato referred to in the title is probably the play of that name by Joseph Addison (1672–1719; *DNB*).

(l. 1): Thomas Cooper; see the note on p. 55.

A New Song, [N.A.]

(To the old Tune of "God save the King.["])

To be sung by the Corresponding Society, and the Friends of Liberty, at their Grand Meeting.

God send each Nation Peace,
May they victorious cease,
   Who in defence
Of Liberty has fought,
And has triumphant brought
Into tyrannic Courts,
   Freedom once more.

Let each example lead
Britons to valiant deeds,

---

*The present Combination of Kings against Men.

10   Worthy our praise;
    Rear up the glorious cause,
    Down with despotic laws,
    Let us no longer pause,
        God will preserve.

    No longer inactive sleep,
    Tyrants already weep,
        Freedom's our Right.
    Down with Corruption's sway,
    Freedom points out the way,
20   Virtue dictates my lay,
        God save the Cause.

    The Banners of Reason spread,
    And by Liberty led,
        Let us advance.
    Asserting our glorious claims,
    Free from all Courtly Chains,
    Jove will direct our aims,
        MAN SHALL BE FREE.

The Philanthropist, no. 16 (1795), 8. The political occasion for the song was the joint meeting of the plebeian LCS and the Whiggish Friends of Liberty. Composing radical songs to the tune and model of "God Save the King" was not uncommon then or later. Indeed, Shelley composed a radical song along these lines in 1819–20 (see Oxford *Shelley* 574).

SONG   T. BEST

    On the white Cliffs of Albion Britannia reclin'd,
        Was seen with a face full of woe;
    Commotions much stronger affected her mind,
        Than the turbulent billows below:
    Tears flow'd down her cheeks like the source of a rill,
        Bereft was her bosom of rest;
    She pour'd forth a sigh—the waves became still,
        And gave ear to the words she express'd:

    "With England—Old England! I fear all is o'er,
10   Peace and plenty alas! now are fled;
    With broils and with civil dissentions is tore,
        And the poor are depriv'd of their bread:
    Yon vessel, which now I behold from afar,
        The wild waves may shortly o'erwhelm,

On quicksands may run and destroy ev'ry tar,
  If the pilot's untrue at the helm!

Poor country! dear country!—how alter'd and chang'd,
  How harrass'd [sic] and sorely distress'd!
From your ancestors['] glorious examples estrang'd,
20   Whom Providence shielded and bless'd:
But how shou'd we ever its favours expect,
  Or suppose we shall prosper or thrive,
When our great men of state, ev'ry duty neglect,
  And at Old England's ruin connive.

Horrid!—horrid the thought!—my poor bosom bleeds,
  Fresh torments arise in my breast;
Lo!—adown the gold sky, the sun slowly recedes,
  And the world will be shortly at rest:
But to me the dear blessing of life was not giv'n,
30   To live to see ENGLISHMEN slaves!"—
Then lifting her eyes and her hands up to Heav'n,
  She headlong plung'd into the waves.

The Philanthropist, no. 22 (1795), 7. Thomas Best wrote poems for the *Imperial and Biographical Magazine* (when John Thelwall was editor) and published a long poem, *Matilda* (London: C. Stalker, 1789). Best was most famous for his book on fishing, *A Concise Treatise on the Art of Angling* (London: C. Stalker, 1787); the British Library catalogue reports twelve editions in the early nineteenth century.

POLITICAL CONUNDRUMS   W. H. GREEN

Why is Billy Pitt like a great whore?	Because he debauches the State.
Why are the great people of England like lice?	Because they prey upon the poor.
Why is John Bull like an infant?	Because he is lulled asleep with delusive tales.
Why is war like a seven-headed monster?	Because it devours all ways at once.
Why is peace like an heavenly messenger?	Because it brings blessings to world.
Why are the revenues of England like the Spanish gold mines?	Because they support the great people in licentiousness, pride, luxury, and idleness.
Why were last year's taxes like the French arm?	Because they was too many for us.

Why are we taxed again?	Because we bore the last patiently.
Why do we bear these?	Because we are degenerate swine!
Why are we degenerate swine?	Because we have lost our liberties! and our oppressors call us so.

The Philanthropist, no. 23 (1795), 1. The question-answer form was popular in 1790s propaganda on both sides. Hannah More, for example, employed this form in her anti-democratic "tracts" in the 1790s.

THE CARMAGNOLE [N.A.]

This Song received its name from the Inhabitants of Carmagnan, in the Department D' Herault, formerly a Province in France, who composed and sung it on the occasion of their marching against the enemies of their country. It was then called the Carmagnanole *which name was contracted to the Carmognole; and hence it is that the slavish satellites of despotism have taken occasion to call the gallant men, who compose the French Army, Carmagnoles.*

Thy cannon, France, begins to sound,
Let all thy warriors march around;
   Citizens and Soldiers
   In flying to the Frontiers,
     Dance, dance the Carmagnole, &c.

In vain are millions of mankind
Against our liberties combin'd;
   Great dangers and deep treason,
   Fright not the sons of reason.
                      Dance, &c.

They said *great* General Brunswick
Of liberty would make us *sick*:
   We to his senses brought him;
   Our cannon manners taught him.
                      Dance, &c.

They said DUMOURIER also
Would lay our *laurel'd Freedom* low.
   But if Kings reckon'd thus—tis plain,
   We'll make them reckon o'er again.
                      Dance, &c.

The Philanthropist, no. 23 (1795), 8. The most radical aspects of the French Revolution appealed to some reformers on the other side of the English Channel, as this song makes clear. The dance represented here seems very innocent compared to the representations in Thomas Carlyle's *The French Revolution* (1837) and Charles Dickens' *A Tale of Two Cities* (1859).

(*st. 3*): Brunswick (1735–1806) was the commander of the Austro-Prussian army from 1792 to 1794; his "Manifesto" of July 25, 1792, was a notorious and inflammatory instance of counter-revolutionary rhetoric and bravado.

(*st. 4*): General Dumouriez (1739–1823) turned against the revolutionary Convention in March, 1793.

An Ode to Kentucky   An Emigrant

Hail modern Eden!—hail thy blooming sweets!
Thy promis'd favours, and thy fragrance, greets
My ardent wishes to salute thy plains,
And plant thy meadows with European grains.
Hail happy spot! that yields thy sweets profuse,
To waste in air, or rot in morning dews
Uncultivated—unenjoy'd by Man,
Reserv'd for latter ages in th' Almighty's plan.
No longer let thy fertile region waste
10   Its fruit (spontaneous fitted for the taste),
But let me now thy proffer'd sweets caress,
Thy rich profusion taste, thy meads possess.
May heav'n inspire a train of honest swains,
To emigrate, and cultivate thy plains,
And prove in earnest, what was said before,
That Eden now, is what in days of yore
It was to Adam, 'ere the Garden fence
Had felt a breach from Satan's impudence.
May many sons of Freedom catch the fire,
20   And from those *guilty madd'ning scenes* retire,
(Which now envelope Europe more and more,
And threaten judgments on Great Britain's shore)
To those sweet Arbours in KENTUCKY's grant,
Whose rich production will supply each want;
Whose ample resources, with little toil,
Will crown their labours, and their cares beguile.
No taxes there oppress the lab'ring kind,
No tyrant KINGS in chains their slaves to bind;
There are no game laws to prevent a man
30   From shooting hares, or pheasants if he can,
The Rivers there are free as we can wish,
And every man may catch a dish of fish.

The Philanthropist

No laws of primogeniture, to wrong
The most uncar'd for infant of the throng;
There are no lay Parsons, who demand
The tenth of all the produce of the land;
Nor Pope, nor Bishop, to enslave the mind,
But all may liberty of conscience find.
No Burke's, no Pitt's, no Windham's, nor Dundas's,
40   To stigmatize you all as *swine* or asses;
There is no tax for "apeing* your superiors,"
For all are equal there, and none inferiors.
There are no Nabobs, who from Indian plunder
Return, and fill their neighbours all with wonder;
No pamper'd hosts of pensioners you'll find,
To live upon th' industry of mankind.
No hireling spies, nor foul informers there,
To herd amongst you, merely to ensnare;
No harden'd crimps in government employ,
50   To steal your children, or your youths decoy.
No prostitution stains that happy clime,
Because no Prince to patronize the crime;
But every man may there in peace combine,
Those blessings which Heav'n did for all design:
And whensoever death shall call him hence,
He leaves his progeny a competence.
Then hasten to KENTUCKY's fruitful soil,
Nor longer in European fetters toil;
Possess this land of liberty and plenty,
60   And say "the *despots* of the earth have sent ye."

The Philanthropist, no. 24 (1795), 3–4. More than a few English radicals of the 1790s immigrated to the U.S. permanently or temporarily: John Binns (1772–1860; *DNB*), Thomas Cooper, Daniel Eaton, Joseph Priestley. The Coleridge-Southey pantisocratic scheme on the banks of the Susquehanna, however sneered at later, was in the mainstream of radical thought at the time. The poem here makes some fun of the recently passed tax on wig powder (March 10, 1795).

(*l. 27*): Taxes on consumer goods used by the middle classes and poor provided a high proportion of government revenues. Even after the 1799 income tax on the wealthy (a tax abolished shortly after the war's conclusion), indirect taxes that affected mostly the poor and middle classes accounted for a higher percentage of revenues.

(*l. 29*): The game laws were unevenly enforced but in many instances it was a

---

*Mr. Pitt[']s speech on the Hair-powder Tax.

capital crime to kill any of the animals on the landlord's estate without his permission.

(l. 39): William Windham (1750–1810; *DNB*) became Pitt's war secretary in 1794; Henry Dundas, Viscount Melville, member of Pitt's government, who became Home Secretary in June, 1791.

(l. 43): Nabobs—those who had become rich in India—were sometimes satirized as vulgar *nouveaux riches*.

(l. 49): Crimping was the process by which government agents would trick men into becoming sailors and soldiers (see Thompson 1963, 81).

(l. 52): The Prince Regent (1762–1830) had a reputation for frequenting prostitutes.

THE ATTRIBUTES OF LIBERTY — W. H. GREEN

Liberte sous la Loi.

Hail Beauteous maid of Heavenly light,
   Thy important truths pervade my soul;
And while I gaze with fond delight,
I see thee spread from pole to pole.

To thee my feeble lays I sound,
   Thou only joy I wish to have;
And if on earth thou can't be found,
   Why then I'll seek thee in the grave.

But yet not so while tyrant powers,
10   Usurp and chain thy generous will;
And while destruction o'er 'em low'rs,
   Unite thy votaries['] blood to spill.

But these whilst justice rules the ball,
   And sheds his influence round the world,
These! these! by heaven's behest shall fall!
   And down to endless ruin hurl'd.

For now thy torch PHILOSOPHY,
   Begins to light our darken'd minds,
And led by thee sweet Liberty,
20   Their rights the sons of Gallia finds.

No more beneath the tyrant's nod,
   His killing frown, his vile deceit,
They fall before him as a God!
   And kiss the dust from off his feet.

The Philanthropist

No more oppression's outstretch'd hand,
    Can awe the gallant Frenchman's soul;
No more can scourge! the happy land,
    Where liberty inspires the whole.

Yes—Gallia her tenfold chains has broke,
    And liberty thy blessings found,
And now reliev'd from every yoke,
    She shines a *star* to Nations round.

Let history boast of ancient wars,
    Of Cato's worth, of Caesar's name;
Be this the great, the glorious cause,
    Which truth enrolls in endless fame.

On REASON's pole behold on high,
    The flag of truth has France unfurl'd;
The glorious flag that sweeps the sky,
    And reaches round a slumbering world.

See *Poland adopts the Heaven-born plan,
    And Russia's Hydrae rage defies;
†Holland asserts the RIGHTS OF MAN!
    And *pierc'd by truth oppression* dies!

So now while France unveils the state,
    Which Kings and Priestly fraud uphold;
Let every tyrant view their fate!
    And liberty thy laws behold.

Come then Eternal fame advance,
    And to the list'ning world proclaim,
That Freedom shall preside in France,
    And as the world's example reign.

The Philanthropist, no. 24 (1795), 7–8. Most of the elements of a Shelleyan poem are here: the fire and light imagery; the uncompromising idealism (ll. 7–8); the personification of Liberty as a deity; the historical references. Green and P. B. Shelley were working in the same reformist tradition.

---

*Although since this was wrote, the gallant Poles have been forced to yield to their more powerful enemies,—let not the friends of universal LIBERTY despair, for notwithstanding the sparks of Freedom at present appear in some degree quenched in that Country, they do but lie smothered in each courageous breast to burst forth with double fury on the heads of its oppressors.
†It may now be said, Holland enjoys.

The Revolutionary Decade

(l. 41): The constitutional monarchy instituted in 1791 was destroyed by the 1793 partition of Poland by Russia and Prussia; the revolution against foreign domination started in March, 1794, and led to a third partition of Poland in 1795.

(l. 43): Becoming a republic in 1789, Holland was attacked by Austria in 1790 and from 1792 became under the influence of France.

For the Tenth of August, 1795 [N.A.]

Tho' the day on which Gallia first rais'd her strong arm,
    And laid the proud fabric of tyranny low;
Tho' the day which made privilege thrill with alarm,
    And sorrow's pale wretch with philanthropy glow;
        Tho' we praise that great day
        Which overturn'd lawless sway,
    Yet a King still remain'd Freedom's cause to betray;
But the day we have chosen saw Monarchy fall,
And man's dearest blessing extended to all.

10   What are Peers, Princes, Sov'reigns, with all their gay band,
    But reptiles maintain'd by the groans of the poor?
Like reptiles, 'midst darkness, they harrass a land,
    But if light beam around, the foul pests are no more.
        And as beasts that love night,
        When they ken glaring light,
    Tho' burning for blood, dart away in a fright;
So at this awful moment, from Liberty's fire,
Growling death and dismay, Man's oppressors retire.

As yon luminous orb, the vast emblem of God,
20   Gilds alike the low cot and the tall doom of pride,
So wherever pure Liberty makes her abode,
    Her soul-lifting smiles will by all be enjoy'd.
        Shall the poor man be told,
        That, because he lacks gold,
    His name among freemen shall ne'er be enroll'd?
No! perish such jargon, whate'er be man's store
He is MAN, and pure Freedom can never ask more.

Oh! be wise then ye French! be the world's mental sun,
    And pour your strong light o'er all prejudic'd nations,
30   'Tis for Man, and Man only, your work must be done;
    Then on Truth's lasting adamant lay your foundations,
        Let talents and worth
        From their haunts be call'd forth;

The Philanthropist

Let these, and not gold, be respected on earth;
Yes! shew that 'tis worth, and worth only, you prize,
And then Man, slighting wealth, may aspire to be wise.

On this glorious day, with sublimity crown'd,
    And with spirit all ire, the Republic arose;
And tho' perils and death have encompass'd her round,
40   Yet with arms strong as fate she has vanquish'd her foes:
        Then let Britain's proud race,
        To their lasting disgrace,
    Still back a curs'd court in a contest so base.
The day will arrive, and oh! speed it ye pow'rs,
When Freedom, *true* Freedom and Peace shall be ours.

The Philanthropist, no. 25 (1795), 6–7.

THE REPUBLICAN CROP.
A NEW SONG.   W. H. GREEN.

May the crops be triumphant all over the world,
And down from all power be their enemies hurl'd,
For nature ordains that we should be all shorn,
And thus are we crops from the time we are born.
Yes nature doth teach, even Paul doth declare,
'Tis a scandalous shame not to cut off your hair.
Then every brave freeman no more be a fop,
But shew to your foes a Republican crop.

In each gallant age men of greatest renown,
10 Disdain'd to appear with long hair on their crown,
At Athens each hero who scorn'd to wear chains,
And triumph'd for freedom on Maratha's plains,
At Rome every man who adored Liberty,
Who drove out the Tarquins, and resolv'd to be Free.
Each Brutus, each Cato, were none of them fops,
But all to a man wore Republican crops.

When Frenchmen appeared with long hair on each head,
Then tyranny triumph'd, and Liberty fled,
But cropt they have thrown off the despots['] controul,
20 And the love of fair freedom inspires every soul,
Behold with what spirit their Rights now they scan,
And gallantly fight to emancipate man.
Their foes with long hair to fly and won[']t stop.
For how can they face a Republican crop.

In England's proud days no long hair was seen,
Unless on the heads of base scoundrels I ween,
The Aristocrats then to freedom sworn foes,
To bind us in chains, with a tyrant arose.
To repel the vile slaves and our rights to maintain,
30   Up sprung the brave crops and subdued them amain.
The tyrant himself they caught tho' he fled;
And to end all his schemes they cropt off his head.

Britons off with your hair, and you are sure to prevail,
For a crop strikes with terror, a slave with a tail,
When your ancestors wore short hair on their head,
They valiantly fought, and they nobly bled.
For Equality's laws, and the freedom of man,
Can you ever submit to betraying their plan,
Then follow their steps, and no longer be fops,
40   Your Hampdens, your Miltons, your Sydneys were crops.

The Philanthropist, no. 42 (1796), 5–6. The frequently anapestic four-stress lines make for a rousing song that is comparable to Thelwall's "Sheepsheering" song. In these highly politicized times, even hair had rich political resonance, and Green also exploits the easily exploitable puns to endorse regicide and anti-aristocratic violence.

  (l. 5): The allusion is apparently to I Corinthians 11: 14, where Paul says it is a "shame" for a man to have long hair.
  (l. 12): The Athenians defeated the Persians at Marathon in 490 BCE.
  (l. 14): Tarquin, last king of Rome, died 495 BCE.
  (l. 15): Lucius Junius Brutus (fl. late 6th century BCE) was a famous figure in republican writing for deposing the last Tarquin, instituting the Roman republic, and showing his republican fervor by condemning to death his own sons who conspired to restore the Tarquins; Cato the Elder (234–149 BCE) was a republican figure famous for his stern civic virtue.
  (l. 32): Charles I (1600–49) was beheaded by the closely cropped "Roundheads."
  (l. 40): John Hampden, John Milton (1608–74), and Algernon Sidney were English republican heroes, Hampden and Sidney being martyrs.

EVERY INCH A PATRIOT, A NEW SONG   R. M.

The sun of liberty is nigh,
The flying night now quits the sky,
All means was tried to bind the tongue,
When firmly thus the patriot sung.

CHORUS.
A patriot[']s life's the life for me,
Who deems the world his country,

The Philanthropist

  If tyrants threaten still he'll be,
  Firm to the cause of Liberty,
  With manly voice I hear him cry,
10 I'll nobly live—or nobly die.

  Prolong the night the despots say,
  And tries to stem th' approaching day,
  But light oe'rpowers, 'tis all in vain,
  And patriot's [*sic*] sing in manly strain.
          A patriot's life, &c.

  A Bill, a bill, can Britons see,
  The downfall of their liberty,
  No—Albion's sons with heart and hand,
  Unites while echoes through the land,
20   A patriot's life, &c.

  Dark ignorance see none can save,
  Dispell'd it finds a truth-bound grave,
  The sun of reason darts her rays,
  On mortals—who chant forth her praise.
          A patriot's life, &c.

  And now from persecution free,
  To enjoy the fruits of Liberty,
  From exile to their friends and home,
  See faithful patriots singing come.
30   A patriot's life, &c.

  For tyranny see what disgrace,
  It dare no longer shew it's face,
  Mankind perceive, th' oppressive cheat,
  And hark I hear in ev'ry street.
          A patriot's life, &c.

The Philanthropist, no. 42 (1796), 6–7. The historical occasion for the poem is interesting because this song expresses a defiance in the face of political repression, namely the soon-to-be-passed Two Acts or Gagging Acts, which effectively ended the activist phase of the LCS.
 The poet R. M. could be Robert Merry (1755–98; *DNB*); see Erdman 1986.

ODE TO FREEDOM   [N.A.]

  Rouse, lyre, tune all thy warbling strings,
  Whilst I the praise of Freedom sing;
   Ye Muses lend your aid.

Ne'er did your powers of song supreme
Assist to sing a nobler theme
   In your Thessalian shades.

To Heaven alone her birth she ow'd,
Its loveliest boon on earth bestow'd,
   O man, to break thy chains.
Ah, hear ye not her cheering voice,
Which makes each glowing heart rejoice
   On Gallia's verdant plains?

Thou, Seine, didst hear the lofty strain,
When all the tyrant powers in vain
   Essay'd to stop her tongue,
And softly roll'd thy gentle tide,
While crowds along thy flow'ry side
   Delighted heard her song.

Methinks I hear th' enraptur'd song
In lofty numbers roll along,
   Which on thy banks was heard;
Methinks I hear that high decree
Which bid all human kind be free;
   No hostile power she fear'd:

When lo! so swiftly rushing forth
   To every region of the North
   The winds convey the sound;
Fame, with a thousand babbling tongues,
Did all her cheering notes prolong,
   And soon dispers'd them round.

They stole along the Baltic shore,
The Swede, the Dane, the Pole, no more
   Can bear the tyrant's chain;
The Russ, tho' savage as a bear,
Shall the glad voice with transports hear,
   Charm'd with the lofty strain.

Thro all Italia's winding shore
Her bigot sons have heard once more
   That song so much revered;
That strain of old ador'd by Rome,
Where lovely Freedom owned her home,
   When Rome her altars reared.

The Philanthropist

Old Father Tibur lifts his head
As one just rising from the dead,
   To hear the well known voice;
He to the goddess calls once more,
"Hail, welcome to my flow'ry shore,
   "Let all my sons rejoice."

He hopes to hear sweet Maro's lyre,
From ev'ry lofty warbling wire,
   Delight fair Mantua's plains;
He hopes his much loved Cicero's tongue,
With all its eloquence, ere long,
   Will bless his shores again[.],

Madrid hath heard the mighty sound,
Her sons, aroused, are gathering round,
   Emerging from the Night.
From Superstition's horrid shades
Oh call them forth, delightful maid,
   Oh let them claim their rights.

Indignant at thy voice they rise,
Their glowing breasts, their sparkling eyes,
   Alarm the guilty throne;
Her bloody Inquisition's walls
Already totter to their fall:
   Spain thy glad sway shall own.

Hark, by the Muse's springs and shades,
Her flow'ry vales and opening glades,
   By every wandering stream,
The voice of Freedom steals around,
And Graecia's sons, wak'd by the sound,
   Start from the midnight dream.

Once more thro' Tempe's flow'ry vale
Shall Perseus bear th' enchanting tale,
   Breath'd from the lyre's soft sound,
And fair Illissus, when he roves
By Academus['] shady groves,
   Shall hear the welcome sound.

And lo! o'er Afric's burning sands,
Her golden streams and fertile lands,
   The voice of Freedom flies;

Where Niger rolls her copious tide,
The sable nations on his side
  With souls expanded rise;

Her sooty sons, supinely laid
Beneath the umbrageous palm-tree's shade,
  Rouse at the welcome sound;
No more they'll bear the galling chain,
Nor, ravish'd from their native plains,
90   In servile fetters bound.

But chiefly thou, O Gallic fair,
To all thy sons be freedom dear;
  O guard her sacred shrine!
No more let Faction rear his crest,
With blood-stain'd hand to tear thy breast,
  Then Freedom's palm be thine.

The Philanthropist, no. 43 (1796), 4–6. The journal's final poem is appropriately elevated in tone, subject matter, and genre. Most notable in terms of the poem's ideology are the centrality of the classical republicanism as it is embodied in the French Revolution and the concomitant neglect of Anglo-American "liberty." The poem's internationalism, not unlike that of William Blake's in his mid-1790s prophecies, alludes to Greece, France, Sweden, Denmark, Poland, Russia, Rome, Spain, Greece (again), Africa, and France (again).

  (l. 6): Thessaly was in ancient Greece, in the northeast.

  (l. 49): Vergil (Publius Vergilius Maro, 70 BCE–19 CE) of Mantua (l. 51) wrote the *Aeneid*.

  (l. 52): Cicero (106–43 BCE) was a Roman statesman and Stoic philosopher.

  (l. 73): The vale of Tempe, in Thessaly, like the river Illisus (l. 76)—which ran through Athens—figured in Greek culture and mythology.

  (l. 74): Perseus slew the Gorgons for Athena in Greek legend.

  (l. 77): Academus was the Platonic school c. 387 BCE–529 CE.

5. *The Tribune* (1795)

John Thelwall, one of the leading members of the LCS, was the third prisoner brought to trial and acquitted during the famous Treason Trials of 1794. Upon release he resigned from the LCS to avoid legal entanglements that could ensue from his weekly lectures, which were transcribed and published in *The Tribune* (1795–96). Thelwall, a poet, inserted into his journal his own poetry but not much original, previously unpublished verse. There were two editions of the periodical, the cheap three-pence edition, and the "fine" six-pence version. Apparently he lost 400 pounds because of the *Tribune* (see Cestre 119). Exact circulation figures are impossible, but one can safely infer that Thelwall's *Tribune*, as lecture and published material, had a wide circulation among both LCS partisans and more genteel reformists like Coleridge. Between 400 and 500 would attend his lectures to hear the most popular radical orator.

For biographical and bibliographical information on Thelwall, see Mrs. Thelwall, *The Life of John Thelwall* (London: John Macrone, 1837); Charles Cestre, *John Thelwall, A Pioneer of Democracy in England* (London: Swann Sonnenschein; NY: Charles Scribner's Sons, 1906); Thompson, 1969; Vernon Owen Grumbling, "John Thelwall: Romantick and Revolutionist," diss., U of New Hampshire, 1977; Donald H. Reiman, Introduction, *Ode to Science by John Thelwall* (NY & London: Garland, 1978); and Michael Scrivener, "The Rhetoric and Context of John Thelwall's 'Memoir,'" in G. A. Rosso & Daniel Watkins, ed., *The Spirits of Fire* (Rutherford, et al.: Fairleigh Dickinson & Associated UP, 1990), 112–30.

ODE ON THE DESTRUCTION OF THE BASTILLE   JOHN THELWALL

    Now Science, by thy genial beam
    Awaken'd from the torpid dream
Of bigot Ignorance, and servile Fear,
Her awful brow, lo, Freedom rear!—
      See her hand, with generous rage,
      From sable limbs the shackles rends;
      Afric's wrongs her cares assuage,
And Hope, a long-lost guest, to Ethiop's race descends!
    Then, as indignant round she turns,
10   And snaps the Gallic yoke in twain,
    (While her patriot bosom burns
      With generous rage, and just disdain),
The flashing fires her eyes indignant shed
Shake the proud tyrants of the earth with dread!

    Shall then no Muse, with generous aim,
      Wide diffuse the sacred flame?
And shall not, chief, the patriot theme inspire
The raptures of the British lyre?
      Yes, Britons, yes—this artless hand,
20   While bright the inspiring ardour glows,
      The shell of Freedom shall command,
Indignant of Oppression's countless woes!—
    Yes, Britons,—Freedom's magic shell,
      Sacred of old in Britain's isle,
    This hand, with trembling touch, shall swell,
      Nor ask a laurel for my toil:—

The Revolutionary Decade

Blest, should my wild notes thro' one bosom roll
The genuine ardours of the free-born soul!

From Tyranny's insatiate sway
    What woes, what coward crimes prevail!
How generous Courage dies away,
    While Anguish sobs in every gale!

Cross but one narrow creek of raging waves,
    Set but thy foot on Gallia's bleeding shore,
Where bold Resistance proud Oppression braves,
    Who sinks, despairing, to revive no more!

There see (and seeing—smile with generous pride)
    Where, on the ruins of her noble rage,
Freedom, enthron'd by *Patriot Valour*'s side,
    Seeks a brave people's sorrows to assuage.

Say,—Rolls not then the agitated eye?—
    Does shuddering Nature no wild terrors feel,
When, with Reflection's retrospective sigh,
    Thou view'st what once was call'd the dread Bastille?

There sullen Tyranny, in murky cell,
    With spleen-born Cruelty, and ruthless Pride,
Hid from all human pity, loved to dwell,—
    To coin new torments, and new woes provide.

There loathsome Horror, from the dark, dank cave,
    Breath'd rank infection round the victim's head:—
————Perhaps, because his virtue, nobly brave!
    Awak'd the guilty tyrant's jealous dread:

Perhaps, because his manly tongue was warm
    To plead the cause of Innocence opprest;
Or from the rage of Power, with filial arm,
    He dar'd defend a Sire's devoted breast:

Perhaps, because the child his cares had nurst,
    Or the fond partner of his nuptial flame,
Had wak'd some pamper'd menial's sordid lust—
    And he refus'd the proffer'd bribe of shame.

Nay, not these vile pretexts does it require
    To urge the wrong, the cruel malice screen;

The Tribune

Enough if caprice, or suspicion fire
    The booby monarch, or his strumpet queen!

Think the vile tools of arbitrary sway,
    With all their tyrant's noxious power array'd,
Seizing the wretched victim ye survey—
    Of guilt unconscious—yet with fear dismay'd.

Hark! does not fancy hear the shrieking wife,
    The frantic parent, and the clinging child?
Each bosom torn with Passion's painful strife!—
    Must *guiltless sorrow* feel a pang so wild?

'Tis past—The prison opes its gloomy door;
    Deep—deep the ruffians plunge their victim down;
Heaven's common light—heaven's breath is now no more;
    Despair and darkness all the senses drown.

Chill Horror creeps thro' every vein,
And Frenzy racks the giddy brain,
While (ere it close, to ope, perhaps, no more)
    Sudden creeks the iron door;
See the loath'd abhorrent cave—
Helpless Virtue's living grave!

There sits Disease, 'midst filth-born vapours vile,—
Disease that knows no cheering smile;
While, trickling down the murky walls,
The aguish fiend Infection crawls.

"Den of horrors!—Cave of Woe!
"Emblem of the realms below!
"Why ope to me thy death-denouncing jaws?—
    "Why frown'st thou thus on Misery's guiltless son?
"I never broke my Country's sacred laws!—
    "I am no murderer!—Ruffians! I am none."

But, ah! the creeking doors remorseless close;
    Light, and the soul's best light, soft Hope, is fled.
Year after year he broods o'er lingering woes:
    To all but Horror and Reflection dead.

Yet walls, nor bars, nor deep descending cave,
    Shut a loved consort from his aching sight:
Her pictured sorrows find him in his grave,
    Haunt the long day, and scourge the restless night.

There, too, his babes in wakeful vision rise—
    Pale images of Want and friendless Woe!
To pierce his soul with unavailing cries;
    And bid afresh the floods of Anguish flow.

"Ah! save them—save!" he cries in wild despair—
    "My wife—my babes!—Ah! how could they offend?
"Me with your racks—your wildest tortures tear!
    "But, oh! to them your pitying succour lend!

    "'Tis phantom all.—Ah! restless train!
110   "Creations of the frantic brain,
    "Depart—depart!—
    "Oblivion come—and o'er my aching head
    "Thy opiate-dripping pinions spread—
    "Sole hope—sole soother of this bleeding heart."

While thus, perhaps, perturbed Fancy's sting
Aids the base fury of a tyrant King,
And the pale victim of each noxious cell
Hears, in each sullen breeze, the deathful yell—
Strange sounds of new-born ardour burst around,
120   And falling towers rush headlong to the ground;
France, from the slumber of a thousand years,
Starts forth to Freedom, and, vindictive, rears
Her giant arm; and while her conquering cries
Warm her brave sons, and bid new prospects rise,
The cheering sounds that change the captive's doom
Pierce the deep dungeon's solitary gloom.

    "Heav'ns!" he exclaims, "what sounds are these I hear?
        "Sure, from without, the pealing voice of Joy!
    "Again—again!—The gathering shout comes near!
130   "Liberty!—the rapt'rous cry!"

    "'Tis so!—The dungeon's bars are broke,
        "And cheerful light pervades the horrid gloom:
        "Awakening Gaul shakes off the yoke,
    "And, freed from slavish awe, her patriot honours bloom!"

The Tribune 1, no. 1 (1795): 21–24. The following introductory note precedes the poem: "The following Ode, occasioned by the first of those splendid events that have distinguished the French Revolution, was the earliest political production of the Lecturer." Also, "The poem was inserted in one of the periodical publications of the day, but he has never made its appearance in any collection of the author's works." The periodical referred to is the *Biographical and Imperial Magazine* 2 (1790): 312–15, which Thelwall edited (1789–92).

The revolution's initial appeal for Thelwall and many others was not that it heralded utopian change but that it enacted a Gothic melodrama in the sentimental tradition. It is typical of Thelwall as editor to use his own old poem in the poetry column. Like Blake (1757–1827) and Wordsworth, Thelwall connects the English anti-slave trade agitation with the triumph of liberty in France, and he indeed became active politically for the first time during the debates over the slave trade (see Porter).

NEWS FROM TOULON; OR, THE MEN OF GOTHAM'S EXPEDITION. SUNG AT THE GLOBE TAVERN, AT THE GENERAL MEETING OF THE LONDON CORRESPONDING SOCIETY. JOHN THELWALL

Silence, men of Gotham, all, in country, court and city,
With drooping hearts and downcast eyes, attend unto my ditty,
A ditty all so sad and strange, from Toulon late I brought it,
And sure you ought to love it dear, fordearly you have bought it.
                        Hum! hum! hum!

The burthen of my song is a wondrous *transformation*,
That late (by *hocus pocus* sure) befel a neighbouring nation,
For while *Bastilles* were tumbling down, and palaces of *Neroes*,
Lo! a *Swinish Multitude* were chang'd to *men* and *heroes*.
10   Hum! hum! hum!

There SOLDIERS, *hir'd to cut the throats of those whom they protected*,
Transform'd to zealous Citizens, the Court's commands rejected;
While LAWYERS (wondrous strange to tell!) to honest men converted,
Plac'd *Reason on the seats of Law*, and quirks and fees deserted.
                        Hum! hum! hum!

There cloister'd MONKS, who dream'd and pray'd, with shaven skulls so bare, sirs,
Transform'd to useful lab'rers, itch no more in shirts of hair, Sirs,
E'en PRIESTS their *holy frauds* forsake, the public weal to plan, Sirs,
And chaste and pious NUNS demand to learn the *rights of man*, Sirs.
20   Hum! hum! hum!

There *Superstition's temples* too—(but hush! I fear 'tis treason![)]
Are chang'd to temples (strange indeed!) of liberty and reason!

The Revolutionary Decade

While *crucifixes, relics, shrines, apostles, saint, and martyr*,
These *sans culottes* (oh! impious dogs!) for beef and brandy barter.
                        Hum! hum! hum!

Oh! WOEFUL TIMES! when schemes like these can madden every brain, Sirs,
When *priests, saints, lords and ministers* come tumbling down amain, Sirs;
Then those who've plunder'd long the land, alas! refused their riches,
That every villain *Sans-culotte* may get a pair of breeches—
                        Hum! hum! hum!

But woe, alas! not here can stop the renovating fury,
But *Kings* and *Princes*, *Queens* and *Lords* must bow to judge and jury;
Nay, *little* CAPET, so 'twas said, since changes went so fast, Sirs,
Must *cobble* up his *royal thoughts*, and labour at his last, Sirs,
                        Hum! hum! hum!

This news to GOTHAM late arrived, when her wise men assembled,
While *pensioners* were struck aghast, and every *placeman* trembled;
"To arms!" cries each *Aristocrate*, "for if the tempest gathers,
"They'll slay us all, and tan our hides, to furnish upper leathers."
                        Hum! hum! hum!

A mighty man, and mighty mighty fleet, then sought a mighty harbour;
He *came, saw, conquer'd*—GOTHAM'S CHIEFS declar'd it *quite the barber*.
Then thus says he "To France at large I bring most glorious news, Sirs;
"For *Louis*, by my NOSE I swear! shall never cobble shoes, Sirs."
                        Hum! hum! hum!

But, ah! those base-born *sans culottes* kick'd up a mighty riot,
Nor man of *Gotham, Naples, Spain*, could sleep a night in quiet:
The panic seiz'd on man and beast, of terror all were full, Sirs;
And e'en his POPESHIP'S *cows* and *calves* were silent as his BULL, Sirs.
                        Hum! hum! hum!

Thus while the rout and ruin reign, which nothing could controul, Sirs,
Each would himself a *Cobbler* be, might he but save his *soul*, Sirs;
Nay, *Gotham's Captain*, while the balls were whizzing in his ears, Sirs,

Began to think he was not like to live a *thousand* years, Sirs.
      Hum! hum! hum!

Thus ends, the woeful tale, good friends, of *Gotham's* expedition;
A tale must fill each loyal breast with sorrow's sharp attrition,
And so God save kings, priests, and lords, and princes altogether,
And shield them, in these changeful times, from lapstones, lasts, and leather.
60   Hum! hum! hum!

The Tribune 1, no. 1 (1795): 166–68. This and the subsequent song were used against Thelwall at his treason trial and his publishing both of them in full was part of his overall attempt to clear his name and fight against the "misrepresentations" of the prosecuting government.

The song's strongly anti-clerical thrust can be understood in part as showing how far the revolutionary French had departed from their Catholic heritage and had become more like the Protestant English, exchanging their superstititious relics for beef and brandy (ll. 23–24). The image of the cobbling Capet and the play on tailoring are both aptly designed for an artisan and tradesmen audience; one finds this image of manic cobbling in Dickens's Dr. Manette (*A Tale of Two Cities* [1859]); in fact, cobbling was one of the common occupations at the time for those imprisoned in solitary confinement.

The poem alludes to the ill-fated expedition at Toulon led by Admiral Samuel Hood (1724–1814; *DNB*). On August 29, 1793, the very important Mediterranean naval port of Toulon was offered to Hood by the French royalists. Quarrels among the coalition allies, poor communications with London, and inadequate reinforcements led to the English losing Toulon. The young artillery captain Napoleon Bonaparte (1769–1821) led the republican forces in its capture of Toulon on December 19, 1793; hundreds of royalists were executed afterwards. In short, Britain and the allies missed an opportunity to cripple France's navy, link up with the insurgent royalists during the revolt of the Vendée, and establish a southern front.

(l. 8): Nero (37–68), proverbially evil and tyrannical Roman emperor.

(l. 33): The son of Louis XVI (1754–93), Louis XVII (1785–95?).

(l. 42): The allusion to Julius Caesar's "*Veni, vidi, vici.*"

(l. 59): The allusions are to shoemaker tools, the lapstone by which leather is beaten and the lasts, or molds, around which the cobbler forms the leather.

A SHEEPSHEERING SONG   JOHN THELWALL

Come to a song of rustic growth
    List all my jolly hearers,
Whose moral plainly tends to prove
    That all the world are sheerers,
How *shepherds* sheer their silly sheep,
    How *statesmen* sheer the state,

And all when they can sheer no more
   Are sheer'd themselves by fate.
        Then a sheering we will go, &c.

10 The *farmer* sends his clippers forth,
   And deems it not a sin
To sheer the *lambhog* of his fleece,
   And sometimes snip his skin[;],
Then if his *landlord* rack-rents him,
   Can he deem it unfair
That he thus, in his turn, again,
   Is nipp'd and fleec'd as bare[?].
        Then a fleecing, &c.

Nor is the wealthy *landlord's* self
20   Of fleecing free from fears;
How oft his rent-roll shrinks beneath
   His *steward's* clipping shears;
And if he chances, for redress,
   The *lawyer* in to call,
Why he takes out his legal sheers,
   And fleeces worse than all.
With his capias, alias, and plurias, declaration, plea, replication, rejoinder, surrejoinder, rebutter, surrebutter, writ of enquiry, writ of error, habeas corpus—flaws; fees; three and fourpence, six and eightpence, thirteen and fourpence, one pound one, &c. &c. &c. &c. &c. ad infinitum.
        Thus a fleecing he does go.

But when the hour of sickness comes,
   And fevers mar his sleep,
30 This legal fleecer proves, alas!
Himself a *silly sheep*;
Grave *doctor's* call'd, whose potions, pills,
   The speed of death encrease,
While his prescription sheers the while
   Strip off the golden fleece;
        When a fleecing he, &c.

At length the patient trembling feels
   His latter end is nigh—
And conscience brings his crimes to view
40   And makes him fear to die,

The Tribune

That holy fleecer, call'd a *priest*,
   Is then call'd quickly in,
Who, finding all the wool is gone,
   E'en strips him of his skin.
        Thus a fleecing, &c.

But hold, cries *Mrs. Piety*,
   And lifts her goggling eyes,
O wicked lout, these holy men,
   Thus for to scandalize!
To steal the fleece, or strip the skin
   Not wicked robbers they,
But watchful dogs, whose pious care
   Keeps fox and wolf away.
        Lest a fleecing they should go, &c.

Yet tell me, honest neighbors all,
   When oft with fresh demands,
For rates, for fees, for Easter dues
   They tax your rack-rent lands,
While for their tythings often they
   Perpetual warfare keep,
Do they look more like *dogs* who *guard*,
   Or *wolves* who *tear* your sheep?
        When a fleecing they, &c.

Nor think that they in country shades,
   Can all the fleecing own,
Full many a sheepish flat, each day,
   Is fleec'd in London town:
There *tradesmen* fleece their customers,
   Them *sharpers* fleece, and then
Your thieftakers, for hanging fees,
   The sharpers fleece again.
        When a fleecing, &c.

There *misses* too, patch'd painted pink'd,
   With fashion's gaudy arts,
With mincing wiles, and fraudful guile
   Would fleece us of our hearts.
Yet while you're roving thus at large,
   You bachelors may find,
Miss will not only fleece your backs,

80   But leave her mark behind.
          When a fleecing she, &c.

But these are petty sheerers all,
    And fleece a little flock;
Behold where *haughty ministers*
    Fleece the whole nation[']s stock:
The while *pretended patriots*,
    A still more venal race,
With liberty and bawling cant,
    Would fleece them of their place—
90   When a fleecing they, &c.

But cease ye fleecing *senators*
    Your country to undo—
Or know we British *Sans Cullottes* [sic]
    Hereafter may fleece you,
For well we know if tamely thus
    We yield our wool like drones
Ye will not only fleece our backs,
    By God you'll pick our bones—
          When a fleecing ye, &c.

100   Since then, we every rank and state
    May justly fleecers call,
And since Corruption's venal pack
    Would fleece us worse than all,
May we Oppression's out-stretch'd sheers
    With dauntless zeal defy,
Resolv'd fair Freedom's golden fleece
    To vindicate or die.
          When a fleecing they do go.

The Tribune 1, no. 8 (1795): 190–92. This particular song was cited by a witness against Thelwall during his trial. This is one of the best political songs, as the fleecing metaphor is exploited with skill and relish, generating an almost universal sense of social corruption. The special zeal with which he attacks lawyers is perhaps related to his own unfortunate experiences both as a law student (see his "Memoir") and as a combatant against "legal" repression of his political activities. It is also a nice touch that the corruption in the poem begins in the country and works its way to the city, the usual source of social corruption in eighteenth-century literature.

   (l. 14): Rack rents—excessively high rent.
   (l. 50): Mark—venereal disease.
   (l. 69): "Sharpers" were gamblers or tricksters.

The Tribune

A PATRIOT'S FEELING; OR THE CALL OF DUTY. ON QUITTING THE ISLE OF WIGHT. [JOHN THELWALL?]

"Falsus honor juvat, et mendax infamis [sic] *terres* [sic]
"Quem, nisi mendorum [sic] *et medicandum?"*—
                    Hor.

Vecta, farewel—to other scenes I fly,
Far from thy cheerful haunts and genial sky,
Thy fertile vales, thy mountains steep and hoar,
And charms romantic of thy varied shore.
No more along thy level beach I stray,
Nor o'er thy rocky fragments force my way;
Where wrecks of matter in confusion hurl'd,
Wake the wild image of a crumbling world.
No more in *Apley*'s pleasant haunts I rove,
10 Where murmuring surges wash the pendant grove,
O'er *Solent*'s wave while barks unnumber'd glide,
And anchor'd navies float in tow'ring pride:
Nor, turning hence to *Chale*'s tempestuous shore,
The *Blackgang*'s savage horrors I explore—
Terrific chine! whose yawning cliffs arise
From Ocean midway to the azure skies;
While curling clouds, impregn'd with briny dew,
Wrap thy rough summit from the gazer's view!
   These, and a thousand magic scenes beside,
20 Beauteous or wild—where, in luxuriant pride,
Fertility prevails, or where, unbroke,
O'er-rugged Nature spurns the gentle yoke
Of human culture, to our wond'ring eyes,
While rock, bush, brake, in strange confusion rise—
These I forego; and leave with these behind,
Whate'er is dearest to the social mind—
The lisping babe, whose artless smiles impart
Joy's anxious throb to the paternal heart,
And the soft partner, whose kind cares bestow
30 Sweets to each joy, and balm to every woe—
These I forego—the tenderest boons of life!
While I, once more, braving the two-fold strife
Of factious Envy and tyrannic Rage,
Corruption's hydra-headed fiend engage;

Reason's keen sword, once more, indignant wield,
Truth for my helm, and Justice for my shield;
Nor fear, thus arm'd, Oppression's fiercest strife—
The Law's dark ambush, nor the assassin's knife!
For, O what mind of generous frame can brook
To see his country to the galling yoke
Of base Corruption bow? while millions pine,
Condemned each boon of nature to resign!—
To drudge in ceaseless toil, and abject fear,
And ignorance, while Pride, with gripe severe,
Extorts the hard-earn'd produce, to support
The headlong projects of a venal court,
And to unwieldy grandeur lift the crew
Whose crimes undo their country? Who can view
The peasants' starving wretchedness; the woes
Which Labour's palid [sic] progeny enclose
In each proud city; or the village train
Of barefoot, ragged children, who sustain
A vagrant life of penury and pain
By cringing beggary, and dog the wheels
Of passing Luxury—proud fiend! who feels
Nor shame, nor soft compunction, but with smiles
Enjoys their antic tricks and cringing wiles,
And holds such abject homage as his due!
—Who, that has thought, such piteous scenes can view,
Nor feel indignant ardors urge his soul
The cause of wrongs so numerous to controul,
At vile Corruption's o'ergorg'd throat to fly,
And quell the fiend, or in the conflict die!
    Come then,—tho' Calumny, with envious rage,
In league with tyrant enmity engage;—
Tho' base Suspicion, with malignant aim,
Distort my actions, and my views defame:—
Tho' those, for whom, at peril of my life,
I foremost stood to brave Oppression's strife,
To wildest tales the willing ear incline,
And with the common enemy combine
To blast my peace;—yet come, thou godlike pow'r,
To whom full oft, at midnight's solemn hour,
While others sleep, I pour the anxious soul,
That not alone would reach thy glorious goal,
O Liberty! but pants to take along,

The Tribune

>   Freed from vile chains, the renovated throng
>   Long trampled in the dust! Come, sacred pow'r,
>   O'er every sense the enthusiast ardor show'r
> 80   That warms thy favour'd vot'ries. O arise!
>   Flame in my breath, and lighten[lightning?] in my eyes,
>   That I may blast Oppression; rouse mankind
>   To truth and happiness, and lift the mind
>   Above the sordid passions that debase,
>   And fix the fetters of the human race!
>   O, let not private wrongs—let not the pride
>   Of ill-requited services divide
>   Patriot from Patriot, nor in party brawls
>   Plunge him, resentful, while the public calls
> 90   For zeal unanimous. Teach me, blest power,
>   That noble magnanimity to tow'r
>   Above each private feeling. Steel my heart
>   With all the Stoic's firmness; and impart
>   A perservering energy, unsway'd
>   By Passion or Corruption, undismay'd
>   By Pow'r or faction, or the furious hiss
>   Of undeserv'd Suspicion; and be this
>   My sole revenge on those whose sland'rous tongue
>   Taint my fair fame—to show the envious throng
> 100 *Nor wrongs nor favours move his constant mind*
>   *Whose first great object is—to* SERVE MANKIND!

ALDERMOOR,
   27th August, 1795.

The Tribune 2, no. 28 (1795): 297–300. The inscription from Horace, *Epistle*, 16, bk. 1, 39–40: (my translation) "Who is delighted by a deceitful honor or frightened by deceitful slander if not someone morally flawed ?" The poet omits from line 40 the famous last four words, "*Vir bonus est quis?*"—Who is the good man?

If the poet is indeed Thelwall, it indicates that he left London for a summer vacation amid what he perceived were slanderous attacks by fellow reformers. The poem indicates that even before his forced retirement from politics he could articulate the structure of feeling within which he would experience his exile. The Horatian posture here by the beleaguered Thelwall—or someone else—will be assumed by the imprisoned radical, Gilbert Wakefield; see pp. 154–55. The poem was written from Aldermoor, Isle of Wight.

(*l. 1*): *Vectis* is the Latin for Isle of Wight.
(*l. 9*): Apley is an area in St. Helens, Isle of Wight.
(*l. 11*): Solent is the sea channel between Isle of Wight and English mainland.
(*l. 13*): Chale is a village and bay on the southern coast of Isle of Wight.

(*l. 14*): Blackgang is a town on the southwest coast of the Isle of Wight.
(*l. 15*): A chine is a ravine.

Lines written by a Female Citizen!   F. A. C.

    Why slumbers now my Muse? is this a time?
When savage war depopulates each clime?
When dire destruction holds her deadly sway,
And rising horrors blast the face of day?
When the once fruitful field is crimson'd o'er,
And earth's pale bosom stain'd with horrid gore,
While many a weeping peasant's left to mourn,
His harvest trampl'd, and his hopes forlorn,
His kindred slain, and his once happy cot,
10   (Where oft at eve, the day's hard toil forgot,
The rural sport and rustic dance was seen
And joy fantastic trod the neighbouring green)
Wrapt in devouring flames, or prostrate laid
By frantic glory's desolating trade.

    Here as I turn with sympathy oppress'd,
With indignation rising in my breast,
My injur'd country's woes demand my care.
Detested scrowls her ripening fate declare:
Britannia's children droop in galling chains,
20   And lawless Pow'r her boasted annals stains;
With strides gigantic shakes the trembling land,
And lifts aloft oppression's iron hand!

    Strike every chord! apall [*sic*] the guilty breast!
Bid titl'd Pomp his gilded crimes detest;
Bid fell Injustice melt his heart of stone,
Nor dare to triumph 'midst the general groan,
Nor seek fresh plunder from a sinking state,
Where thousands perish for the proud and great.—
The great! in what? in worth and virtue?—no;
30   Virtue must shrink from man's inveterate foe;
From those who honest industry despoil,
Fed by the tradesman's and the peasant's toil—
Their toil who labour for their scanty meal,
Constrain'd the woes of indigence to feel,

The Tribune

While the best produce of their daily gains,
The drones of vice and luxury maintains.

    Ah, wretched land! in every spot is found
Corruption's fatal influence black'ning round:
Here misery and want are hourly seen,
40 With pallid look, and supplicating mien,
Complaint and useless clamour wound the ear,
While Pity drops the unavailing tear!
Unable to relieve, she mourns in vain
Wrongs that the mass of humankind sustain.

    Could our brave sires, who for their country's good,
In Freedom's noble struggle shed their blood—
Could those who dar'd a tyrant to controul,
And shook with coward fear his guilty soul—
Could those, I say, now view our fallen state,
50 View the unnumber'd ills that round us wait,
See each lov'd right and privilege expire,
And Freedom from her native seat retire;
How would each Patriot of those days of yore,
Our abject state and wretchedness deplore!
How would each great and godlike spirit moan,
The glorious object of their toils o'erthrown!
Those sires who dar'd with tyranny contend,
A peoples' [*sic*] dearest interests to defend,
Anxious their charter'd liberties to save,
60 They scorn'd the life that bore the name of slave!

The Tribune 3, no. 38 (1795): 105–6. F. A. C. turns out to be one of the most uncompromisingly militant poets in the periodicals (see her poem in the *Moral and Political Magazine*), as here she stresses class exploitation and contrasts the brave revolutionaries of the seventeenth century with the cowards of the present day. Also notable is her self-awareness as poet, expressing a professional identity.

    (l. 18): Scrowls—scrolls.

PROVINCIAL POLITICAL JOURNALS

1. *The Cabinet* (1795)

Representing provincial radicalism at its best, this Norwich publication, though short-lived, was well written and intellectually sophisticated. Produced by "a Society of Gentlemen," the journal was quite urbane and assumed a moderate position in relation to reform politics. There is a good selection of *Cabinet* verse in Bennett 135–42, 145–46, 165–67. See Walter Graham, "The Authorship of the Norwich *Cabinet*, 1794–5," *Notes and Queries* 162 (1932): 294–95; C. B. Jewson, *The Jacobin City: A Portrait of Norwich in Its Reaction to the French Revolution 1788–1802* (Glasgow: Blackie & Son, 1975); Trevor Fawcett, "Measuring the Provincial Enlightenment: The Case of Norwich," *Eighteenth Century Life* 8 (1982): 13–27; Klancher 42–43.

Sonnet to Winter   N. [Amelia Alderson]

Power of the awful wind, whose hollow blast
    Hurls desolation wide, thy sway I hail!
Thou o'er the scene around can'st beauties cast,
    Superior far to aught that Summer's gale
Can, in the ripening year, to bloom awake;
    To view thy majesty, the chearful tale,
The dance, the festive song, I, pleas'd, forsake;
    And here, thy power and thy attractions own,
Now the pale regent of thy splendid night
10   Decks with her yellow rays thy snowy throne;

Richly her beams on Summer's mantle light,
   Richly they gild chill Autumn's tawny vest
But, ah! to me they shine more chastely bright,
   Spangling the icy robe that wraps thy breast.

The Cabinet (1795) 2: 35. The author, identified by Graham (1932) as Amelia Alderson (1769–1853; *DNB*), later Mrs. Opie, was part of the Mary Wollstonecraft–William Godwin circle in the 1790s and also wrote novels.

2. *The Oeconomist* (1798)

The editor was apparently Thomas Bigge, friend of James Losh (1763–1833; B&G) who was acquainted with Wordsworth (see *WW Letters*, 1: 214 n.1). Joseph Cottle (1770–1853; *DNB*) was one of the journal's publishers. Although only 4 1/2 pence per monthly issue, the journal does not try to appeal to a "town" plebeian audience but rather a farmer readership. It is interesting for its resolute hostility to London and urban culture, its promotion of pastoral values and agriculture, and its affiliation with both the French Physiocrat and the English "country party" ideologies. The journal was printed in Newcastle, the hometown of another pastoralist of a very different sort, Thomas Spence. See Klancher 43–44.

THE COTTAGE
A COMPETENCE AND NOT RICHES
THE SOURCE OF HAPPINESS [Z.]

I ask not for a splendid lot,
Give *me* a neat convenient cot;
Grass for my cow, a nook of soil,
To plough or dig with honest toil:
Of the best books a useful stock,
With Shakespeare, Addison and Locke:
An upright, independent mind:
A reverence for human kind:
A love for just and equal laws:
10   A zeal in holy freedom's cause.
Give me to know the truth, and bold
To speak in spite of pow'r or gold:
To these add cheerful, active health,
I'll envy not the slaves of wealth.
Oh poorly rich and meanly great
Who crowd preferment's slipp'ry gate!
To honour lost, with low-born soul,
Who beg the virtue-barter'd dole,

I envy not your splendid lot,
20   But smile content within my cot.

The Oeconomist (1798), 1: 4. One sees here the myth of the yeoman, independent, proud, educated.

THE HARVEST MOON [N.A.]

The harvest moon gives friendly light
   To finish what has been begun,
While copious dews at morn and night,
   Lessen the fervor of the sun.

The rich reward of toil is nigh,
   The promise of the year is come;
The farmer, now, with grateful eye,
   Beholds his corn brought safely home,

No more he feels the least alarm,
10   No change of weather gives him pain,
No more he fears to suffer harm
   From stormy wind or beating rain.

Remember who it is that gives,
   Nor let your thoughtless hearts forget,
That while your barns are fill'd with sheaves,
   Yourselves should feel the mighty debt.

Distribute to the sons of need,
   Diffuse your charity abroad,
The naked clothe, the hungry feed,
20   Ye are the stewards of your God.

He sees, with equal eye, the case
   Of rich and poor, as Lord of all;
Let then no selfishness disgrace
   These days, which for your bounty call.

The Oeconomist (1798), 1: 326–27. With the poem's emphasis on the moral-religious imperatives of charity to the poor, one can see parallels with Wordsworth's "The Old Cumberland Beggar" (1800).

MONTHLIES

1. *The Moral and Political Magazine* (1796–1797)

According to Mary Thale, the London Corresponding Society's decision to publish a periodical was an unfortunate one in that it was financially disastrous and diverted energy and resources that could have been more wisely allocated (362–64). Each issue cost 6 pence to the public, 4 1/2 pence to members; circulation was between 4,000 and 1,000. In its brief existence (July, 1796–June, 1797), it published twenty-nine poems, at least six of which had been previously published. The magazine's favorite poet was "Tommy Pindar," seven of whose poems, almost all of them lengthy satires filled with topical allusions, were published; his work had appeared earlier in *Politics for the People*. The LCS's most prolific and ambitious poet, John Thelwall, had no poems published.

Song   George Dyer

   While venal bards attempt to sound,
     Through years remote the trump of fame,
   And call the wondering nations round,
     To learn some haughty conqueror's name,
         Justice demands a purer song,
         Let Freedom's sons the strain prolong.

   Let such receive their country's praise,
     Who Virtue's cause undaunted plead;
   And such the poet's untaught lays,
10   Who dare in Freedom's cause to bleed.
         Justice, &c.

   And live there, in degenerate times,
     Men, still to British honour true,

>   Who, blushing for a nation's crimes,
>   Dare yield to truth the honour due?
>   Justice, &c.
>
>   And though a people prove unjust,
>   Nor laurels deck the patriot's head,
>   Genius shall shape the future bust,
>   And future bards their honour spread.
>   Justice, &c.
>
>   Justice shall far extend her reign,
>   And Freedom wave her banners wide,
>   And those immortal honour gain,
>   Who nobly lived or nobly died.
>   Justice, &c.

Moral and Political Magazine (1796), 1: 95. The poet, George Dyer, created a Romantic structure of feeling by imaging the patriotic bard who is devoted to the ideal of justice rather than flattering established power. The poem assumes that posterity will have to redeem the bard's idealism and does not seem to have much hope in contemporary politics which, after the repressive legislation of 1795–96, were not hopeful for the democratic reformers. For Dyer, see Reiman 1979.

SONNET: THE LION   JOSHUA

>   Why grace we the stern lion with the name
>   That marks the chiefs of Europe? More of use
>   To man's assistance do the kine produce;
>   For bulk, behold the elephant's huge frame!
>   For agile beauty see the stately horse.
>   King of the forest HE, and doom'd to reign,
>   Like earthly monarch, o'er the Lybian plain
>   For fierce pre-eminence in brutal force:
>   Before his tyrant rage the fleet horse flies,
>   The patient sheep avoids him, or he dies.
>   Stern bloody beast! they named thee well: thy right
>   Is to this royal title just and good;
>   Thou gain'dst it by thy savage joy in fight,
>   Thy brutal fury, and thy thirst for blood.

Moral and Political Magazine (1796), 1: 192. This blunt anti-monarchical poem illustrates again how important animal analogies were for the imagination of the time. The sonneteer, "Joshua," authored three other sonnets in the periodical, all on biblical themes, and they anticipate the work of Robert C. Fair, a poet whose biblical poems in the 1815 *Theological Inquirer* are much more anti-religious than Joshua's work. Joshua, of course, was Moses' appointed lieutenant who led the Israelites successfully against the Canaanites, and the sonneteer seems to fashion himself as a prophetic figure of triumphant "liberty."

INVOCATION TO THE GENIUS OF BRITAIN A FEMALE CITIZEN F. A. C.

Spirit! brave spirit of a free born race!
Why do'st thou slumber in an evil hour;
E'en now when shame, when ruin, and disgrace,
Are dealt unsparing from the hand of pow'r?
Ah, must the glowing patriot blush to own
A nation thus to every virtue dead!
A land with vice and luxury o'ergrown,
And liberty, its better genius, fled!
Where abject wretchedness is seen around,
10   The wasting form by famine slow consum'd,
That once in decent competence was found,
Now to a sad and happless [sic] pittance doom'd:
Perhaps from charity's cold hand to crave
The scanty morsel nature to sustain,
Or sink unnotic'd to the silent grave,
Borne down by sorrow, misery, and pain!
For 'tis the few, the pamper'd few alone,
Who seize the wealth that thousands ought to share,
Who reap the produce industry hath sown,
20   And leave a barren harvest of despair.
Spirit awake! awake! once more inspire,
With glowing energy each Briton's soul,
Teach him to emulate each god-like sire,
And scorn to stoop beneath a base controul.
For, lo! oppression's giant form is seen
With rapid stride to pace the trembling land,
While abject slav'ry with submissive mien
Stoops low to kiss the terror dealing hand.
Oh shame! oh dire disgrace! shall Britons then
30   Each boasted right and liberty forego,
To seek protection in the lion's den,
Who joys in desolation, death, and woe!
No, rather with a strong and powerful arm

> Arrest the dreaded tyrant on his way,
> Nor, yielding to the terror of alarm,
> The mandates of despotic pow'r obey.

Moral and Political Magazine (1796), 1: 238. The poem's uncompromising ideology adumbrates the radical songs of the Spencean poets and Shelley in its anti-authoritarianism, appeal to will and action, and quasi-socialist critique of illegitimate property relations.

SONNET [N.A.]

> Go place the swallow on yon turfy bed,
> Much will he struggle, but can never rise;
> Go raise him even with the daisy's head,
> And the poor twit'rer like an arrow flies.
> So oft thro' life the man of pow'rs and worth,
> Haply the caterer for an infant train,
> Like BURNS, must struggle on the bare-worn earth,
> While all his efforts to arise are vain.
> Yet should the hand of relative or friend,
> 10 Just from the surface, lift the suf'ring wight,
> Soon would the wings of industry extend,
> Soon would he rise from anguish to delight.
> Go then, ye affluent, go, your hands outstretch,
> And from despair's dark verge, oh! raise the woe-worn wretch.

Moral and Political Magazine (1797), 2: 48. Ideologically, this is a very different poem from the previous one; this stresses the reciprocal relations between rich and poor, and chastises the privileged not for being privileged but for not living up to the duties and responsibilities of privilege. Robert Burns (1759–96) becomes here and elsewhere a figure for the neglected plebeian genius, which in turn becomes a synecdoche for the injustices inflicted upon an entire class.

FABLE. THE ASS AND THE DRIVER. [N.A.]

> A driver of asses from orchard to town,
>   On a time had his panniers so loaded,
> The ass with the burden was near sinking down,
>   Yet his merciless master still goaded:
> Some fine looking apples which hung o'er a wall
>   Caught the eye of this *wealth-thirsting* clown,
> O ho, Master *Johnny!* cried he, by St. Paul,
>   For *a few* you will never lie down.

The ass stagger'd onward with patience and pain,
10   When a pippin the countryman found,
For *one*, cried this worthy, you'll sure not complain,
    But that one sunk the ass to the ground.

Let no man, with inverted glass,
Read Johnny Bull instead of Ass.

Moral and Political Magazine (1797), 2: 240. The revisionary power of the democratic imagination is evident here as Aesop's conservative fable, "The Ass and its Burdens," is completely reframed to produce a story hostile to the interests of the "master."

(*l. 10*): A pippin is a kind of apple.

2. Monthly Magazine (1796–1809)

The *Monthly Magazine*, founded in 1796 by Richard Phillips (1767–1840; *DNB*), edited until 1806 by the Dissenter John Aikin (1747–1822; *DNB*), was the most important middle-class periodical until the *Edinburgh Review* appeared in 1802. It had a circulation of around 5,000 during its most popular period (Altick 392). Phillips, who had been publishing a radical provincial newspaper, the *Leicester Herald*, was imprisoned for eighteen months (1793–94) for selling Paine's *Rights of Man*. The editor's good friend, Gilbert Wakefield, was imprisoned between 1799 and 1801 for the pamphlet *A Reply to Some Parts of the Bishop of Llandaff's Address to the People of Great Britain* (1798) (see Butler 1984, 220). Although the *Monthly Magazine* never promoted the kind of hard-edged radicalism linked with the plebeian movement and found in periodicals like Eaton's and Spence's, the *Monthly Magazine* was radical in its way for representing the concerns of the most insurgent and innovative sectors of the intelligentsia. Relying on the contributions of its readers, it is very different from the pedagogically oriented plebeian journals. It attracted some of the most innovative writers: William Taylor and others introduced to England German philosophy, poetry and literary theory; Coleridge, Southey, Lamb, John Thelwall, George Dyer, and Charles Lloyd (1775–1839; *DNB*) all wrote for it; feminism was discussed sympathetically and some women wrote for it extensively—Lucy Aikin and Fanny Holcroft, the daughters of prominent reformers. Founded after the passage of the repressive Two Acts, it took for granted the circumscribed political situation and focused more on broader cultural issues. The magazine lost its most lively tenor after Aikin left as editor; it reacquired its radical energy much later, in 1824–25, when John Thelwall was editor.

For information, including a bibliography, on the *Monthly Magazine*, see Sullivan 1: 314–19. See also Klancher 39–41.

ADDRESS TO POVERTY   L.

'Tis not that look of anguish, bath'd in tears,
O, Poverty! thy haggard image wears—

'Tis not those famish'd limbs, naked, and bare
To the bleak tempest's rains, or the keen air
Of winter's piercing winds, nor that sad eye
Imploring the small boon of charity—
'Tis not that voice, whose agonizing tale
Might turn the purple cheek of grandeur pale;
Nor all that host of woes thou bring'st with thee,
10 Insult, contempt, disdain, and contumely,
That bid me call the fate of those forlorn,
Who 'neath thy rude oppression sigh and mourn:
But chief, relentless pow'r! thy hard control,
Which to the earth bends low th' aspiring soul;
Thine iron grasp, thy fetters drear, which bind
Each gen'rous effort of the struggling mind!—
Alas! that Genius, melancholy flow'r,
Scarce op'ning yet to even's nurt'ring show'r,
Shou'd, by thy pitiless and cruel doom,
20 Wither, ere nature smiles upon her bloom;
That Innocence, touch'd by thy dead'ning wand,
Shou'd pine, nor know one outstretch'd guardian hand!
For this, O Poverty! for them, I sigh,
The helpless victims of thy tyranny!
For this, I call the lot of those severe,
Who wander 'mid thy haunts, and pine unheeded there!

Monthly Magazine (Feb., 1796), 55. Emphasizing the intellectual and cultural oppression of poverty, this poem, like Thomas Gray's *Elegy* (1751) laments neglected genius. The intellectual emphasis is typical of reformism, which emphasized the "career open to all talents" and opposed arbitrary aristocratic restrictions on free opportunity.

BALLAD [N.A.]

Oh tarry, gentle traveller;
   Oh tarry now at setting day;
Nor haste to leave this lowly vale
   For lofty mountains far away.

Oh tell me what has tempted thee
   Thro' woods and dreary wilds to roam;
Oh tell me what has tempted thee
   To quit thy lot and peaceful home.

Say, hast thou not a partner dear,
    That's constant to thy love, and kind?
And wilt thou leave her faithful side,
    Nor cast one sorrowing look behind?

Yon sun that gilds the village spire,
    And gaily flings his parting ray,
Say, smiles he not as sweetly o'er
    Thy native village far away?

Does mad ambition lure thy steps
    To wander in the paths of strife?
Ah think how swift thy minutes fly!
    Ah, think how short thy span of life!

For life is like yon crimson beam
    That trembles in the western skies;
Full soon, alas! its glories cease;
    It sparkles—glimmers—fades—and dies.

Oh waste not then thy fleeting hours
    In foreign climes and paths unknown;
Return thee to the happy plains
    That bounteous nature made thy own.

For me, nor gold nor princely power,
    Nor purple vest, nor stately dome,
Nor all that trophy'd grandeur boasts
    Shall lure me from my tranquil home.

This rustic cot and silent shade
    Shall evermore my dwelling be;
E'en when my destin'd days are spent
    I'll rest beneath yon aged tree.

Beside the brook, a simple stone,
    Shall serve to guard my cold remains;
And tell the pilgrims, as they pass,
    I died amidst my native plains.

Return then, gentle traveller;
    Return thee with the morning ray;
Nor leave again thy lowly vale,
    For lofty mountains far away.

Monthly Magazine (May, 1796), 316. Two years before the publication of the *Lyrical Ballads,* one finds here a Wordsworthian lyrical ballad celebrating rustic simplicity and domesticity, criticizing the follies of ambition, and developing the central theme of *tempus fugit*—mortality. Poems like this and William Taylor's translations/adaptations of Burger's ballads, which also appeared in the *Monthly Magazine*, are important contexts for the poetic innovations of Wordsworth and Coleridge.

GLEE. (*GLORIOUS APOLLO.*)   J[OHN]. T[HELWALL].

Goddess of FREEDOM, from on high behold us,
   While thus we dedicate to thee our lays;
Long in thy cause hath principle enroll'd us,
   Here, to thy name, a monument we raise.
Thus then combining, heart and voice joining,
   Sing we in harmony to FREEDOM'S praise.

Here ev'ry gen'rous sentiment awaking
   Zeal that inspir'd our patriots of yore;
Each pledge of Freedom giving and partaking,
10   Join we our bleeding country to restore.
Thus then combining, heart and voice joining,
   Send the shouts of LIBERTY from shore to shore.

Monthly Magazine (Aug., 1796), 568. A not-untypical Thelwall poem, this song (and almost-sonnet) is a secular hymn praising freedom in a way similar to what Shelley will do in his "Hymn to Intellectual Beauty" (1817). Also typical of Thelwall—but not of Shelley—is the poem's first person plural as the agent in the verse. This is one of the few *Monthly Magazine* poems that is a song, the most popular by far of all genres in the plebeian journals.

STANZAS, TO THE MEMORY OF ROBERT BURNS   [N.A.]

Portentous sigh'd the hollow blast,
Which, sorrow-freighted, southward pass'd;
I heard the sound, and stood aghast
   In solemn dread:
The mournful truth is told at last,
   And BURNS is dead!

Ah! sweetest minstrel, nature's child,
Could not thy "native wood-notes wild,"
Thy manly sense, thy manners mild,
10   And sprightly glee,
The ghastly tyrant have beguil'd
   To set thee free?

Unfriended, desolate, and young,
Misfortune o'er thy cradle hung;
And penury had check'd thy song,
   But check'd in vain;
Till Death, resistless in his wrong,
   Has clos'd the strain!

Thus, 'midst the cold of winter's snows,
The unprotected snow-drop blows;
Awhile in native beauty glows,
   And charms the eyes;
Till past some ruthless spoiler goes,
   And crops the prize!

But not for thee, O bard, the lot,
In cold oblivion's shade to rot;
Like those, unhonour'd, and forgot,
   Th' unfeeling great,
Who knew thy worth, but hasten'd not
   To sooth thy fate.

Whilst love to beauty pours the sigh,
Whilst genius shall with nature vie,
Whilst pity from the melting eye
   Shall claim regard;
Thy honour'd name shall never die,
   Immortal bard!

But oft, as winter o'er the plain
Shall pour at eve the beating rain,
The hind shall call his little train
   Around the fire,
To listen to some thrilling strain
   Of thy lov'd lyre.

Whether to Heav'n's eternal King
Thou strike the deep-resounding string,
Whilst, rising on devotion's wing,
   Hope soars above,
To happier realms of endless spring,
   And boundless love;

Or whether lighter themes beguile
The moments of relaxing toil,
Bidding, on labour's front, the smile
   Of pleasure sit:

The roof re-echoing all the while
   To genuine wit;

Or if wild fancy seize the rein,
Whilst horror thrills thro' ev'ry vein,
And sprites and elves, an awful train,
   Their orgies keep;
And warlocks o'er the frighted plain
   At midnight sweep:

As works the spell, the list'ning band
Aghast in mute attention stand;
Again thou wav'st thy magic wand,
   Of pow'r so rare,
And all the scene, by Fancy plann'd,
   Dissolves in air.

Thine too the charm of social hearts,
Where wit its vivid light'ning darts,
And Converse keen to age imparts
   The fire of youth,
Whilst, from the fierce concussion, starts
   The spark of truth.

What tho' thy wild untutor'd strain
The Critic's pedant laws disdain,
Not all the wire-cag'd minion train
   E'er pour'd a note
So sweet, as echoing o'er the plain
   The woodlark's throat.

Old *Coila*, first whose brakes among,
Thy infant hands the wild harp strung,
Shall flourish in thy deathless song
   With lasting fame;
And *Ayr* shall henceforth roll along,
   A classic stream.

But thou, O Bard, in silence laid—
Ah! what shall sooth thy pensive shade,
For worth and genius ill repaid,
   With bounty scant;
And hours of sorrow unallay'd,
   And toil and want?

See o'er thy song, as loud it swells,
The lordly Thane delighted dwells;
Or to his fair his rapture tells,
   By thee inspir'd;
His bosom, as the strain impels,
   Or thaw'd or fir'd.

Around him, see, to guard his state,
A train of pamper'd minions wait;
And see, to form his daily treat,
   Each climate join;
While Iceland's frost, and Asia's heat,
   Their gifts combine.

Yet, whilst he revels unconfin'd
Thro' all the treasures of thy mind,
No gen'rous boon, to thee consign'd,
   Relieves thy care;
To Folly or to Vice assign'd
   What Pomp can spare!

For rights withheld, or freedom sold,
Corruption asks the promis'd gold;
Or, in licentious splendor bold,
   Some titled Dame
Squanders, in riot uncontroll'd,
   What Worth should claim!

From hill to hill, from plain to plain,
Wide spreads the Chieftain's proud domain,
That, half a desert, asks in vain
   For culture due;
Whilst cold inaction chills thy vein,
   And rusts thy plough.

Meanwhile thy youthful vigour flies,
The storms of life unpitying rise,
And wounded Superstition tries
   To thwart thy way;
And loath'd Dependance ambush'd lies,
   To seize her prey.

Yet high above thy reptile foes
Thy tow'ring soul unconquer'd rose—

> Love and the Muse their charms disclose—
> The hags retire;
> And thy expanded bosom glows
>   With heav'nly fire.
>
> Go, Builder of a deathless name!
> Thy Country's glory, and her shame!
> Go, and th' immortal guerdon claim,
>   To Genius due;
> Whilst rolling centuries thy fame
>   Shall still renew!

130

Monthly Magazine (Jan., 1797), 53–54. Upon the death of Robert Burns (1759–1796) ensued the "Burns controversy" over exactly how to appropriate the poetry of someone "uneducated," politically democratic, and—at least according to several reports—of dubious morals (Burns was accused of excessive drinking and sexual promiscuity). Burns, then, is a fascinating topic for a periodical like the *Monthly Magazine*. See Donald A. Low, ed., *Robert Burns. The Critical Heritage* (London & Boston: Rutledge & Kegan Paul, 1974).

This particular poem, using the stanza form popularized by Burns, affirms the value of Burns as a genius, "child of nature," victim of poverty which he nevertheless overcame, violator of pedantic poetic rules, and Romantic bard and hero.

(l. 8): The poet is here quoting Milton as he alludes to Shakespeare in *L'Allegro* (l. 134).

(ll. 65–66): The allusion seems to be to Prospero in *The Tempest* act 4, scene 1.

(l. 79): Coila is a river in Ayrshire, Scotland.

(l. 83): Ayr is a river in Ayrshire, Scotland.

(l. 92): A Thane was a Scots baron.

TO STELLA, ON HER BIRTH-DAY, NOVEMBER 1, 1790.   JOHN THELWALL

> November, hallow'd month, and bless'd!
>   Assume, assume young Maia's crown;
> Assume, assume the vernal vest,
>   And cast away thy wonted frown!
> For, lo! to hail the genial day,
>   How all the Sister Graces wait;
> And smiling Loves the shaft display,
>   And lift the playful torch elate.
>
> Why all this joy, November? say—
>   Why smiles the sun, in pomp renew'd?
> Why do the Muses pour the lay
>   To hail thy empire, once so rude?

10

Say, do the Seasons sudden change,
    And second Spring triumphant bloom?
That Nature glows with pleasures strange,
    And Earth and Heav'n the smile assume?

Ah, no—not Spring again appears;
    A brighter image decks the scene!
Whose mien the raptur'd fancy cheers;
20   For mental radiance gilds that mien!

'Tis STELLA, pride of CATMOSE VALE,
    That brightens thus th'autumnal morn!
While gently sighs th' enamour'd gale,
    That fondly hails her natal morn!

Monthly Magazine (Jan., 1797), 55. This particular poem celebrates Thelwall's wife, Cecil Boyle, whom he married in 1789, and whose poetic name is Stella here and in many other poems.

EFFUSION ON THE APPROACHING FAST-DAY   T. S. S.

Ah! what avails it to uplift the eye,
    To bend the knee, and echo forms of pray'r;
Remaining proudly deaf to Mis'ry's cry,
    To Grief's faint moan, and shrieks of loud Despair?
Ye Princes of the Earth, oh! rather yield
    To SUFF'RING MAN this glorious sacrifice:
To chase for ever from th' ensanguin'd field,
    War's horrid crew, and bid sweet Peace arise,
    (Now prostrate bound in mad Ambition's chains;)
10   To wipe away the tear from sorrow's cheek;
To free the debtor, soothe the sick man's pains,
    Fell th' oppressor, and sustain the weak!
Then Angels shall attune their harps to rapt'rous lays,
And Earth's ten thousand tongues shall swell the note of praise,
More grateful far to Heav'n than Fasts or Holy Days.

Monthly Magazine (Feb., 1797), 140–41. This poem is unlike the "fast" poems found in the plebeian periodicals. The protests against the fasts in Eaton's journal, for example, are more bitter and comic, more unapologetically anti-clerical. Here, however, the protest is pitched at an abstract level more idealistic and religious than what one could find in *Politics for the People* or *Pig's Meat*. The decisive factor might not be class but the political repression that effectively shut down the most sarcastic voices of protest.

The Revolutionary Decade

Ode to Terror   S. W.

    Monarch of the gloomy train!
Which haunt the fear-distracted brain;
I feel—I feel, my lab'ring breast,
Grim Terror, by thy potent spells possess'd:
As thy dismal scenes unfold,
The flagging stream of life grows cold;
My trembling limbs, my bristly hair,
My hurried breath, and starting eye,
Fix'd, tho' blasted—all declare,
Tremendous power, thy ghastly form is nigh!

    Upborn by thee, amid the darken'd air,
Now dimly breaks the boiling deep below;
While the livid lightnings glare—
While the raging whirlwinds blow!
Hark! by starts, what mournful cries
'Mid the mingled storm arise!
Some vessel strikes, with sudden shock,
Upon the lurking pointed rock:
    O mercy! hear the dying crew!
See how aloft the straining surge they gain!
'Tis past—the dim discover'd fragments view,
Snatch'd in wild eddies o'er the fiery main.
Their agonizing cries are o'er—
Deep, deep they sink—to rise no more.

    Too well that cruel smile I read,
Turn'd on the spot, where thousands soon must bleed;
Whose bright arms, gleaming from afar,
Now swell the savage pomp of war.
As array'd, on either hand,
Front to front, the squadrons stand;
Ere the shrieks of death resound—
Ere they bite the crimson ground;
See grim Havoc, hot from Hell,
With all the furies in her train,
Hov'ring low, with dire delight,
'Twixt the closing ranks of fight;
Prepar'd the tide of blood to swell,
And scour the groaning plain:
Now the thundering peals arise,
Vengeful shouts and dying cries;

Till Vict'ry waves her purple flag on high,
And echoing triumph rends the tortur'd sky.

    'Tis night! now o'er the silent field,
By the pale moon's light reveal'd,
I see thee steal to view the feast of death!
    To hear the faint expiring groan,
    The mutter'd prayer, the hollow moan,
The parch'd throat gasping hard for breath;
Arm'd with a dagger deep imbru'd,
50   While coward Rapine prowls the slippery plain,
And giant Slaughter, smear'd with blood,
    Reclines his weary limbs on heaps of slain!
But who is she? Misfortune's child,
With hurried step, and aspect wild,
    Who hither seems to move?
And bending oft, surveys each palid [sic] face,
As if she wish'd some friend to trace?
    Alas! she seeks her love!
And, lo! his breathless corpse she spies—
60 She cannot weep—swift frenzy lights her eyes,
She shrieks, she falls, and on his mangled bosom dies.

    Now waving high, in proud disdain,
His broad red pinions o'er the tainted plain,
See savage War exulting flies,
Wafted on a million's sighs,
Where Ambition points the road,
Scenting afar new scenes of blood;
Yet, wherefore lag yon fiends behind,
By earth accurst—by life abhorr'd—
70 Wheeling, like vultures, on the infected wind,
Dreadful followers of the sword?
Famine and pestilence! I know you now,
The country's blasted as you tread;
The groaning city's chok'd with dead,
Your horrid work's complete!
No face is seen, no sounds arise,
Save where some wretch infected flies,
And screams along the empty street!

    Grim power! O spare my aching sight;
80 Nor call thy foul unreal train to light,
By Superstition formed of old,

In sickly Fancy's giant mold!
Yet, lo! they come—along the midnight air
What spectres dire in wild confusion sweep!
See by yon dim and dismal glare,
At once they sink into the yawning deep;
While fainting from the gulf below,
Rise the shrieks of tortur'd woe!

   Now deep within the tangl'd dell,
I hear the wisard's mutter'd spell:
Round him flit a ghastly brood—
The setting moon is turn'd to blood!
Prompt his orders to perform,
Rush the spirits of the storm;
Pitchy darkness veils the skies—
Piping loud the winds arise.
Hark! they howl along the heath,
   While the fiends, with mournful yell,
   To the benighted wretch foretel [sic],
Scenes of woe and death!

   The storm is past! and o'er yon mould'ring tow'r
Steals through yon sable clouds a silv'ry beam:
Avaunt! thou visionary power,
Nor lead me to the haunted stream,
That laves its ivy'd walls.
In vain—its gloomy paths I tread;—
What horrid phantom now my sight appals?
From the green pavement bursts the shrouded dead;
A clear blue flame conducts it through the gloom,
'Mid broken ruins to the fatal room;
And now it points the blood-stain'd bed!
—The firm-built turret shakes, with dismal sound,
'Mid lonely courts that spread their echoes round;
The iron clank of chains I hear,
While shrieks of torture swell more near.
Scarce the crazy boards uphold
The armed spectres that advance;
While one behind, of horrid mold,
Impels them with his fiery barbed lance;
And oft, transfixing each, in fury, cries,
'Thus, every hour, the guilty murd'rer dies!'

    Fearful yawns the dark profound!
Muttering thunders heave the ground!
Down, through her riven entrails, lo! we sweep,
'Till a dim distant light just glimmers from the deep.
    Behold the damned crew—
    O'er the furnace blue;
    By the brimstone's livid flame,
    Doing "a deed without a name:"
130 Around them heavier hangs the cavern'd gloom:
    While summon'd to foretel [*sic*]
    The dark designs of hell;
    In accents dread the monstrous throng,
    Chaunt the strange prophetic song,
And write, in blood, the fated warrior's doom.

Monthly Magazine (June, 1797), 457–58. The "terror" alluded to here is not the Reign of Terror promulgated by the Jacobins in Paris but the European war caused by the counterrevolutionary forces on the Continent and Britain. The poet appropriates the Gothic and the Sublime in ways that run directly against the anti-Jacobin framing of "terror." By bringing in the traditional imagery of hell, the poet also portrays the war against France as unsanctioned by divine authority.

    The poet, S. W., might be the same S. W. who wrote a tribute to Fox upon his death in *Flower's Political Review* (see p. 168).

    (*l. 129*): *Macbeth* act 4, scene 1, line 49; spoken by the witches to Macbeth.

CONSCIENCE THE WORST OF TORTURES   MISS [FANNY] HOLCROFT

'Twas night; mysterious silence reign'd;
    Sleep wav'd his magic wand;
E'en prowling wolves, to mischief train'd,
    Repos'd, a harmless band.

High surging waves, and tempests bleak,
    Were hush'd, awhile to rest;
Fierce Aetna ceas'd in flames to break,
    Nor once disgorg'd her breast:

When, stretch'd on straw, the murd'rer lay,
10   Terrific to behold!
His tott'ring frame spoke sad dismay,
    His eye convulsive roll'd!

His chains he shook with frantic grief;
    Thrice smote his tortur'd breast:

Till fainting nature brought relief,
   And lull'd his limbs to rest.

But fearful visions rack'd his brain;
   His transient slumbers broke:
Before him stood Montalto slain!
   He started, groan'd, and woke.

Yet woke, alas, to mad'ning woe:
   The ghastly form pursued;
With bosom pierc'd, step sad and slow,
   His shroud with blood bedew'd!

Its woe-fraught brow and haggard cheek
   Uprais'd the fiend despair:
A wild and soul-distracted shriek
   Dissolv'd it into air!

"Stay, stay," he cried, "thou damning shade!
   Revenge shall soon be thine.
No more my tardy death upbraid:
   Eternal death is mine!

I'm call'd! The vengeful sword they raise!
   Racks, whips, and fury wait?
The pious brands of torture blaze,
   Ferocious man to fate!

Yet sword and flames I'll dauntless brave:
   No groan shall racks extort;
If blood they thirst, blood let them have:
   Revenge too dearly bought!"

Thus rav'd the wretch, with anguish torn,
   Pursu'd by fell despair,
Till soon the sanguinary morn
   Bad him for death prepare.

With well-intention'd vengeance fraught,
   The fearful cohort meet:
Their mind to holy terror wrought;
   Their brow with ire replete.

Yet unappall'd their victim stood,
   Death's threat'ning pangs defied;
"Montalto, lo! here's blood for blood!
   Behold, and quaff," he cried.

Then dauntless met each fearful stroke,
  No pangs could force one groan;
His threatning eye defiance spoke,
  Till sense and life were flown.

Monthly Magazine (April, 1798), 289. Fanny Holcroft, poet and novelist, daughter of Thomas Holcroft (1745–1809; *DNB*), has written here a Gothic poem ideologically consistent with her father's in that the "natural" conscience does a far more efficient job chastising and correcting evil social behavior than do social institutions. In typical Romantic fashion, the truth appears and is experienced at night, in dreams.

ON MISS LINWOOD'S ADMIRABLE PICTURES IN NEEDLE-WORK   L[UCY]. A[IKIN].

When Egypt's sons, a rude untutor'd race,
Learn'd with wild forms the obelisk to grace,
And mould the idol God in ductile earth,
The loom and polish'd needle took their birth.

When doom'd to dull obscurity no more,
Fair Science reign'd on each surrounding shore,
And stretch'd her arm o'er Greece and early Rome,
Still in her train appear'd the labours of the loom.

When Gothic night o'erwhelm'd the chearful day,
10   And sculpture, painting, all neglected lay,
And furious man, creation's savage lord,
Knew but the hunter's spear, the murd'rer's sword;

Our softer sex emboss'd the 'broider'd vest,
In flow'ry robe the blooming hero drest;
Or rang'd in tap'stry's glowing colours bright
The mimic crests, and long embattled fight.

Now Learning's better sun-beam shone anew,
And Gothic horrors, gloomy night, withdrew;
Again Prometheus wak'd the senseless clay,
20   Grace, beauty, order, leapt to second day.

Most did the manly arts its influence feel,
The pencil chas'd the housewife's humbler steel;
Rent was the aged tap'stry from the wall;
Exulting genius gloried in its fall;

To monstrous shapes, and hydra forms uncouth,
Succeeded nature fair, angelic truth;
The artist man awoke the victor's lay,
And woman's labours crumbled in decay.

Then LINWOOD rose, inspir'd at once to give
30   The matchless grace that bids the picture live;
With the bold air, the lovely lasting dye,
That fills at once, and charms the wond'ring eye.

Hail! better Amazon, to thee belong
The critic's plaudits, and the poet's song:
To thee may fame no barren laurels bring,
But flow'ry wreaths, that bud each rising spring!

Monthly Magazine (April, 1798), 287. Lucy Aikin, daughter of John Aikin, was a serious writer and until the 1832 Reform Bill was a proponent of reform. The Miss Linwood referred to here was Mary Linwood (1755–1845; *DNB*) from Birmingham, who embroidered pictures of paintings with such skill she had various exhibitions of her work, the most famous of which was in 1798. Linwood was also a composer. Making the claim that traditional "women's" art is as valuable as any other art, deserving the highest honors, Aikin anticipates later feminist arguments. Indeed, in terms of human evolution as she portrays it, women's art was the first thing to "soften" the dominant masculine brutality.

(l. 21): "Prometheus," an important Romantic figure, alludes here to the Renaissance or the Reformation.

(l. 23): The rent tapestry alludes to the rent veil of the Temple after Jesus's crucifixion (Matt. 27: 51).

OWEN PARFET*   [N.A.]

There lived, in Shepton Mallet late,
    Of unrecorded fame,
A taylor, born to luckless fate,
    And Parfet was his name.

His race from Cambrian mountains wild,
    First issued, but few know when;—
His parents, therefore, gave their child
    The christian name of Owen.

---

*The circumstance on which this ballad is founded, actually took place at Shepton Mallet, in Somersetshire, between twenty and thirty years ago. Many persons who are now living, attest the fact; nor has any plausible account of the unfortunate man's disappearance ever been given.

He plied his trade both late and soon,
10   By honesty to live;
And happy was from morn to noon,
    From noon to setting eve.

Good credit long he well sustain'd,
    By profits small and few;
Nor would, tho' all the world he gain'd,
    A deed dishonest do.

Six days he labor'd in the week,
    With unremitting care;
The seventh, he would duly seek
20   The public place of prayer.

When Owen at his calling sate,
    Upon his outspread carpet,
A busy sister's harmless chat,
    Well pleas'd her brother Parfet.

No wife had he, or ever strove
    Fair maiden's heart to gain:
And she,—no favorite of love—
    Ne'er captivated swain.

Was Owen pleased?—his sister too,
30   Well pleased the house would range;
Was Owen dull?—again she knew
    A sympathetic change.

But happiness is seldom found
    To be of lasting date;
Nor live there one on mortal ground,
    Secure from adverse fate.

The wind blew keen one winter night,
    And fast came down the rain;
Then Owen in unguarded plight,
40   Was drench'd upon the plain.

Now, pains rheumatic writh'd him sore,
    And piteous 'twas to see
Poor Owen now, unable more
    To live by industry.

To him relief his sister dealt,
    At early hour and late;
And every wish, that Owen felt,
    Strove to anticipate.

No weekly profits now were told,
    And poor became his lot;
His implements of trade were sold;
    And customers forgot.

The savings of his former days
    Were all expended soon;
No maintenance he then could raise,
    And craved the Parish boon.

But now, what fain I would not tell,
    My story must unfold—
To Owen Parfet what befel,
    When he grew faint and old.

His sister, on a summer's day,
    Remov'd him from his bed;
And placed him near the public way,
    Fast by his humble shed.

There in his chair, at nine o'clock,
    The morning bright and clear,
Did Owen sit;—while kindly flock
    His old acquaintance near.

They speak him fair, but little reck
    Never to see him more:
Departing then, their business seek,
    And leave him at the door.

But there, poor Owen did not stay;—
    Yet how he went, or whither,
Nor mortal, ever, from that day,
    By search or wit could gather.

The alarm is spread both far and near,
    The townsmen stand aghast;
In vain they seek,—and pale with fear,
    Believe that day, the last.

His fate, they ponder'd with concern,
    Themselves from earth might sever;

Again they seek—but home return
  At night, as wise as ever.

They drain next day each pond and well,
  Each nook and corner spy;—
They ransack thicket, brake, and dell,
  And long on Owen cry.

The busy search next day they plied,
  Thro' town and hamlet near;
And ten miles round the neighbours ride,
  Nor tale nor tidings hear.

'Twere ludicrous, I fear, to tell
  What all the town said then;
How he was borne, by wicked spell,
  To some infernal den.

Just as he vanish'd, some declare,
  As gaping crouds stand round—
They heard a tumult in the air,
  And wonder'd at the sound.

Some dreamt of late strange things at night,
  But others grew more bold;
And Owen saw, they said out-right,
  Fast in a demon's hold.

But some this vile aspersion quick,
  Indignantly withstood;
And said, that Owen, for old N____k,
  Was certainly too good.

More like they said, some hand unseen
  Had loosed each mortal fetter;
And kindly whipp'd him off this scene,
  To place him in a better.

Let those that will, at Owen's cost,
  Be wickedly diverted;
Yet, that he thus was strangely lost,
  Remains uncontroverted.

To tell his fate, I've no pretence;—
  Conjecture none I make;—
But if the D____l took him hence,
  He made a great mistake.

The Revolutionary Decade

Monthly Magazine (July, 1799), 480–81. This literary ballad could have found its way easily into *Lyrical Ballads* without anyone sensing something dissonant. Indeed, one cannot discount a direct influence on the poem by *Lyrical Ballads*. Founded on something true, focused on a blameless tailor who gets too sick to work, sinks into poverty, and disappears mysteriously, giving rise to a narrator's surmise and a folkloric narrative of the supernatural, "Owen Parfet" resembles "Simon Lee" (1798), "The Thorn" (1798) and "Goody Blake and Harry Gill" (1798)—to name only three. Other than the German ballads translated by William Taylor, the *Monthly Magazine* typically did not publish ballads.

(l. 107): Satan or the Devil (l. 119).

Female Education at Two Periods [N.A.]

May I some small attention share,
    If seniors grant me leave,
Their education to compare
    With that we now receive?

Observe then: first they learn'd to read,
    I do not say *how well*;
And learn'd to write, and some, indeed,
    Some few, *once learn'd to spell*.

No grammar at their schools was taught,
10   Such knowledge was debar'd her;
As useless in the kitchen thought,
    As useless in the larder!

Who never from her duty swerv'd,
    But work'd th' appointed skreen,
Her *virtue* and *ripe fruit preserv'd*,
    And *pickl'd what was green*.

These homely merits wou'd alone
    A choice of lovers bring her;
Palm of her hand as hard as stone,
20   And *lacerated finger*.

The *finger* shew'd, by *needle torn*,
    One *prudent occupation*;
The other prov'd the *broom had borne*
    Its part in *education*.

But now, that hand that "wou'd be woo'd"
    Must be *as soft as cygnet's down*;

Not with *industrious tokens rude*,
   As it had spun the russet gown.

Let me remark; while we compare—
   The chief objection made is,
Our ancestors *good housewives* were,
   The present race, *fine ladies*.

The system shou'd be new-arrang'd;
   Some faults there are remov'd;
But *those* for *other faults* are chang'd;
   'Tis alter'd, not improv'd.

Best specimens of what I treat,
   In middle rank we find;
For there the Graces oft we meet
   With Industry combin'd!

Now let me introduce—*Good la*!
   I drop my pen; description fails—
Miss—come home wiser than *mamma*,
   Prepar'd to tell *surprising* tales!

Thinking such talents shou'd be known,
   She through the peaceful village fends,
With Miss's *congees*, and her own,
   Invites her kins-folk and her friends.

Miss on her mother passes jests,
   Who comes with sauce-boat in her hand,
And prays the pardon of her guests;
   "*Her maid*," she says, "*don't understand*:"

"*She never was before in place.*"
   "*Law, Ma!*" says Miss, "*that is so funny!*
"*Before I wou'd so burn my face!*
   "*You might have any thing for money.*"

Miss laughs, when Mother's at a loss,
   And *pertly* tells her, she is wrong;
Each has *connection* with *the sauce*,
   The *mother's hand*, the *daughter's tongue!*

And while she sees *her* opening mind
   By novels ev'ry day enriching,
To culinary arts confin'd,
   She triumphs in the kitchen!

John Bull then thought her richly grac'd
    (Of learned women wond'rous shy),
Who cou'd, with economic taste,
    Hash *your calf's-head*, or make a pye!

Had we liv'd in those days of eating,
    I own my project wou'd be baffl'd;
My book of *other science* treating
    I close; and *study Mrs. Raffald*.

How much refin'd is now the mode
    Of this once *eating nation*;
What gravies, sauces, soups, were stow'd
    In *ev'ry corporation*!

"No riot dooms the lamb to bleed,"
    No fish forsakes the silver tide,
No cormorants are there to feed;
    Lord, no! *all that* is laid aside.

Does any doubt this truth? Why, then
    My character is undone;
Ask the Lord Mayor and Aldermen,
    And Livery of London.

And drinking too! how fam'd was he,
    That *upright* man, with pride elate,
If bumper ply'd, his *eyes cou'd see*
    Each *sinking friend* his *chair vacate*.

But in this age of genuflexion,
    We from such things disgusted turn;
To eat and drink's out of the question,
    What do we now? "We live and learn."

"And learn? what learn the ladies, pray?"
    Sir, did you want a wife? "Why—yes"—
They learn to draw, to sing, to play,
    To march, to skip, to dance, to dress.

While men are studying classic rules,
    Immers'd in grave recess at College,
Our sex are taught, at boarding-schools,
    Most superficial knowledge.

Ever, with sylphic lightness they
    Twine, where the loves and graces blend;

Nor e'er explore that nobler way,
   Which does to heav'n-born science tend.

Some men of sense there are advance,
   The softer sex may be too wise;
Wou'd rather wed fair ignorance;
   A blank preferring to a prize!

Hear Osmyn cry, "What! shou'd the fair,
110 "Abstrusely educated then,
"Profoundly deep researches share,
   "Study with scientific men?

"Forbid it all ye softer powers,
   "Ye Loves forbid it—Cupid—Venus!
"What! no advantage still be ours,
   "No difference, ye gods! between us!

"Your genius soaring such a height,
   Cannot descend to household stuff;"
That *female*, Sir, who *acts not right*,
120   Believe me, *does not know enough.*
She who your learn'd researches shares,
   Who "sees the work in sense sublime,"
Will not neglect domestic cares;
   She knows "for all things there's a time!"

Monthly Magazine (Dec., 1799), 888–89. Written apparently by a woman, this poem explores some of the ambiguities of one of the momentous and historic transformations among the "middling classes": the "improvement" of middle-class manners and culture, and the emergent norm of "respectability." Francis Place (1771–1854; *DNB*) writes extensively on this movement towards respectability affecting the laboring class as well (see Mary Thale's *Autobiography of Francis Place (1771–1854)* [Cambridge: UP, 1972]). Austen's novels, like *Mansfield Park* (1814), by criticizing aristocratic manners in particular ways, seem to argue for a similar improvement in morals and manners among the wealthiest classes. In short, the movement towards "respectability" in the nineteenth century seems not to have been restricted to any one class.

  This particular poem represents that within living memory a wife's duties included a large amount of manual labor, particularly in the kitchen, whereas the new norm established a more genteel role for the middle-class wife. The poet does not sneer at the older way of life and does not idealize the new, maintaining a fairly balanced perspective on modernity, including a feminist protest against the superficial education of women somewhat along the lines of Mary Wollstonecraft. The poem's sarcastic wit is especially effective in lines 16–17, on preserving virginity and fruit, and lines 61–64, contrasting the daughter's novel-reading and the mother's cooking.

(l. 14): See Austen's *Pride and Prejudice* (1813), book 1, chapter 8, where covering screens is cited as one of the "accomplishments" of genteel women.

(l. 26): Down of a young swan.

(l. 46): Congees—curtsies.

(l. 72): Elizabeth Raffald (1733–81) wrote the popular and often reprinted—even into the nineteenth century—*The Experienced English Housekeeper* (1773).

HORACE, BOOK I.
EPIST. 18. VERSE 96. TO THE END.
GILBERT WAKEFIELD.

'Midst all thy cares, some hours of respite find,
With stores of science to enrich thy mind:
Her votaries ask, those votaries only know,
How clear and calm the stream of life must flow;
Lest fears and fruitless hopes destroy thy rest,
Or craving passions rankle in thy breast:
Ask them, if learning virtue's robe impart,
Or nature weave the tissue in our heart:
What boundaries, ask, care's wide excursions end;
10   What lore will make thee to thyself a friend:
If that pure bliss, compos'd affections know,
In the rank soil of wealth and grandeur grow;
Or in the still sequester'd vale alone,
Where winds the path unnotic'd and unknown.

   Sooth'd by the waves, that cool Mandela's swain,
'Midst the full glories of my rural reign;
Say, friend! what thoughts engage my bosom there?
What the fond project, and the secret prayer?
Without one wish to make my substance more,
20   Tho' time impair the pittance of my store,
E'en thus my future days, if Heaven should give
Those future days, I to myself will live.
May year by year of food its portion find,
And books, the nobler banquet of the mind;
Lest my loose purpose, sway'd by fortune's power,
Float on the balance of each wavering hour!
For life, and life's support, to Jove I pray:
Those his high will, or grants, or takes away.
Those if he give, myself supplies the rest,
30   Curb'd passions, fix'd resolve, and tranquil breast.

Monthly Magazine (Aug.,1800), 44. Wakefield, a good friend of the editor John Aikin, was a prominent reformer and classical scholar who was in jail when this translation was published. His being jailed for two years for a relatively innocuous "seditious libel" indicated that the government was not going to tolerate any radical dissent from anyone, even people from the most well-educated class (see Butler 1984, 220–21; Thompson 1969). That Wakefield would find Horace's gently stoic epistles so relevant at this time is perhaps a commentary on the overall ideology of the intellectuals at the time who were passionately committed to the Enlightenment values of reason, dialogue, and intellectual development.

(l. 15): Mandela was a town in Horace's (65–8 BCE) Sabine country.

To Gilbert Wakefield, A. B. on his Liberation from Prison   J[ohn]. Aikin

    Pure light of learning, soul of generous mould,
    Ardent in Truth's great cause, erect and free,
    Welcome, O welcome! from thy prison gloom,
    To open air and sunshine, to those boons
    Which Nature sheds profuse, while tyrant Man,
    "Drest in his brief authority," and stern
    In all the little jealousy of pow'r,
    Restricts the bounty of a Father's hand,
    And scants a Brother's bliss.—But now 'tis o'er,
10   And social friendship and domestic love
    Shall pour their healing balm; while conscious worth
    With noble scorn repels the sland'rous charge,
    That brands imprudence with the stamp of guilt.

       Meantime disdain not, learned as thou art,
    To scan this world's great lesson: high-raised hopes
    Of Justice seated on the throne of Pow'r,
    Of bright Astrea's reign reviv'd, and Peace,
    With heavenly Truth and Virtue by her side,
    Uniting nations in a band of love,
20   Have faded all to air; and nought remains
    But that dire law of force, whose iron sway
    The sons of men through every blood-stain'd age
    Has ruled reluctant. When that sage benign,
    The Man of Nazareth, preach'd his gentle law,
    And listening crowds drank honey from his tongue—
    When Mars, Bellona, and the savage rout
    Of Gods impure and vengeful, shrunk to shades,

And rescued Man adored a common sire;
Who could restrain to hail the blessed time
30 Of swords to sickles turn'd, of general good
Pour'd in full streams through all the human tribes,
And shared alike by all? But ah! how soon
The glorious prospect darken'd! When the cross
Gleam'd direful 'mid the host of Constantine,
And took the eagle's place—when mitred priests
Mimick'd the flamen in his mystic pomp,
And proudly bent around a despot's throne;
Then, whilst the name at Antioch first rever'd
Ran conquering thro' the world, it lost its sense,
40 And join'd in monstrous league with all the crimes
That force, and fraud, and lawless lust of sway
Inspir'd to plague mankind. Then, Gospel-rules
Were held an empty letter; and the grave
And specious commentator well could prove
That such an holy, humble, peaceful law,
Was never meant for empire. Thus relaps'd,
The human brute resumed his native form,
And prey'd again on carnage.

    Cease then, my Friend, thy generous hopeless aim,
50 Nor to unfeeling Folly yield again
Her darling sight, of Genius turn'd to scorn,
And Virtue pining in the cell of guilt.
Desert no more the Muse; unfold the stores
Of fertile Greece and Latium; free each gem
From the dark crust that shrouds its beauteous beams,
And fair present them to th' admiring eye
Arranged in kindred lustre. Take serene
The tranquil blessings that thy lot affords,
And in the soothing voice of friendship drown
60 The groans, and shouts, and triumphs of the world.

Monthly Magazine (June, 1801), 422. Written by the editor and Dissenter John Aikin, good friend of Wakefield's, this poem celebrates Wakefield's liberation from prison in 1801. Urging Wakefield to "Desert no more the Muse" and to forsake political activism, Aikin asserts that political hope is now foolish as French liberty has turned into French imperialism, just as—and here his Dissent background becames apparent—the early hopes for Christian renewal of societies were dashed by the institutionalization of Christianity and its attendant compromises with principle for the sake of secular power. The poem nicely particularizes that historical moment of political retreat and consolation by the liberal reformers.

(l. 17): Astrea is the goddess of Justice.

(l. 26): Mars and Bellona are Roman gods of war.

(l. 34): Constantine (272–337) was the first Christian Roman emperor.

(l. 36): Flamen—ancient Roman priest.

(l. 38): The Council at Antioch (341) consecrated Constantine's church organization.

To John Aikin, M. D.   Gilbert Wakefield

Next to the first of comforts to the soul,
The plaudit of conscience self-approv'd,
AIKIN! I deem the gratulation sweet
Of sympathysing friendship, and a Muse
Terse, uncorrupt, ingenuous, bold and free;
A Muse from whom nor titled grandeur bribes,
Nor pamper'd wealth, a sacrificial strain.
Hence with sensations bland of conscious pride
I feel the manna of thy tuneful tongue
10   Drop medicinal influence on my breast,
Ruffled, not torn, by Persecution's blast.
Thus, after chilling frost, morn's genial ray
Invigorates, cheers, expands, the shrivell'd flower:
Thus the broad mountain flings his cooling shade
O'er the faint pilgrim in a thirsty land.
Oh! may thy friend, as in the noon of life,
Responsive to the calls of truth and Man,
Self in benevolence absorb'd and lost,
Thro' the short remnant of his closing day.
20   With brave defiance, or with calm disdain,
Front the grim visage of despotic power,
Lawless, self-will'd, fierce, merciless, corrupt;
Nor, 'midst the applauses of the wise and good,
Lose the fond greetings of a Muse like thine!

Monthly Magazine (July, 1801), 513–14. In response to the previous poem by Aikin, Wakefield's epistle, dated June 19, from Hackney, cleverly plays upon Aikin's message of "leave not the Muse" for politics by politicizing the Muse: the Muse here is defiant, independent, and resisting of "despotic power." It is a gracious reply, but it is also a subtle disagreement with Aikin's emphasis on retreat.

To the Memory of the Rev. G. Wakefield

L[ucy]. A[ikin].

    Friend of departed worth! whose pilgrim feet
Trace injured merit to its last retreat,
Oft will thy steps imprint the hallow'd shade,
Where Wakefield's dust, embalm'd in tears, is laid;
"Here (wilt thou say) a high undaunted soul,
That spurn'd at palsied caution's weak controul—
A mind by learning stor'd, by genius fir'd,
In Freedom's cause with gen'rous warmth inspir'd—
Moulders in earth; the fabric of his fame
10 Rests on the pillar of a spotless name!"
    Tool of corruption—spaniel slave of power!
Should thy rash steps in some unguarded hour
Profane the shrine, deep on thy shrinking heart
Engrave this awful moral, and depart!
That not the shafts of slander, envy, hate,
The dungeon's gloom nor the cold hand of fate,
Can rob the good man of that peerless prize
Which not pale Mammon's countless treasure buys—
The conscience clear whence secret pleasures flow,
20 And friendship kindled 'mid the gloom of woe,
Assiduous love that stays the parting breath,
And honest fame, triumphant over death.

    For you, who o'er the sacred marble bend,
To weep the husband, father, brother, friend,
And, mutely eloquent, in anguish raise
Of keen regrets his monument of praise—
May Faith, may Friendship, dry your streaming eyes,
And Virtue mingle comfort with your sighs;
Till Resignation softly stealing on,
30 With pensive smile bid ling'ring Grief begone,
And tardy Time veil o'er with gradual shade
All but the tender tints you would not wish to fade!

Monthly Magazine (Oct., 1801), 220–21. This tribute to Gilbert Wakefield by Lucy Aikin was published shortly after his death. That he died so shortly after his release from prison was interpreted as his having been killed by prison, by the political repression.

The Condemned Sailor   Fanny Holcroft

'Twas mine to watch the dreary night,
    The threat'ning storm to brave;
'Twas mine to view the morning light,
    "And hail myself a slave."

But now sweet sleep shall not deny
    A respite to my grief:
"My former wrongs I now defy;"
    Oh death, thou bring'st relief!

I hail thy sad yet welcome shore,
10   Where mis'ry finds repose;
Where coward-boys shall strike no more
    Who struck his country's foes.
My indignant soul, by wrongs inflam'd,
    Receiv'd a mortal wound:
A boy my veteran-locks defam'd!
    I fell'd him to the ground.

Nor could the captain's wrathful eye
    The burst of passion quell:—
Tyrant, behold your minion lie;
20   Thrust by this arm to hell!

Now bind these limbs; the scars efface,
    By honour proudly worn:
Nor chains, nor whips, can brand him base,
    Whose wrongs are nobly borne.

Monthly Magazine (Nov., 1801), 328. A poem like this one by Fanny Holcroft indicates how much the nature of the war has changed since the rise of Napoleon. This poem does not protest impressment, mindless slaughter of the innocents in an unjust war against French liberty; it does not focus on the war's power to separate lovers and destroy families. Rather, the poem's focus is a proud veteran who is about to die for killing the captain's "boy," whose cowardly behavior enraged the protagonist. As a poem about laboring-class pride, it presents being a sailor as a job—quite unlike the anti-war poems of the early 1790s.

The Revolutionary Decade

Part of an Inscription Designed for a Garden   J[ohn]. T. R[utt].

Thou who shalt mark this spot with pensive eye,
Where mem'ry claims affection's frequent sigh!
Whate'er the intrusted [sic] talent, wouldst thou raise
From gifts divine the Giver's holy praise?
The Christian's hope eternal wouldst thou feel,
The patriot's energy, the martyr's zeal?
And, scorning tyrant-pow'r, delighted prove
Each social blessing, each domestic love?
Then linger here, to rouse the sacred flame,
10   And teach these echoes Wakefield's honour'd name:—
But wouldst thou, heedless of the destin'd hour,
Inglorious dream in pleasure's fairy-bow'r?
Or does ambition prompt thy vain desires,
Lur'd by each magic form the world admires?
Haste, ere these hallow'd scenes dissolve the spell!
Yet, first to virtue bid a long farewell!

Monthly Magazine (Nov., 1801), 328. Another tribute to Wakefield the liberal martyr, Rutt's poem emphasizes the Christian aspects of Wakefield as well as the defiantly patriotic. It is also interesting to see another poem by Rutt, whose work appeared in many periodicals.

A Picture and a Prophecy   A. R.

———"The wrongs that are,
The rights that shall be, the futurity
Miraculous in good that is begun." Goethe.

When sanguine youth, in fond Utopian dreams,
    First launches on the troubled sea of life,
He trusts to sail on pleasure's smoothest streams;
    Alas! he wakes to woe, and scenes of strife!

The fair illusion fades before his sight;
    Around he sees a war of fraud and force,
Where every finer feeling meets a blight,
    And every act betrays a selfish source.

With generous purpose fraught, and glowing heart,
10   He seeks to heal the wounds which man inflicts;
But Falsehood speeds, and flings her poison'd dart:
    His quivering heart the shaft of Slander hits!

Yes! 'tis a scene where Man "erect and tall"
    Bows his base neck at each usurper's nod!
And while he vaunts, the would-be lord of all,
    Kisses the tyrant's soul-subjecting rod!

There reasoning Man pursues a phantom-form
    That still eludes his grasp, and brings him woe;
He looks for bright sereneness in the storm.
    He seeks for bliss in toys and senseless show!

There Cunning, veil'd in Wisdom's borrow'd dress,
    Shared the respect which Wisdom fails to find;
There Pride and Power unbending Worth oppress,
    And Prejudice still clips the wings of Mind.

There icy Caution chills the soul that glows
    With sweet Enthusiasm's generous fire!
Blasts all the joys Benevolence bestows,
    And snaps the thrilling strings of Transport's lyre!

There black Suspicion, "green-ey'd monster," reigns,
    Quick to conceive a word—a look, amiss;
Broods, gloomy, o'er his self-created pains,
    And poisons at its source the stream of bliss!

And there Injustice, fiend gigantic! stalks,
    With Want, and Woe, and Havoc in his rear!
There Ignorance, with twin-born Evil, walks,
    And deems the source of virtue, idiot fear!

There, oh, what scenes to wound th' unpractis'd sight!
    Pale Virtue droops, a persecuted guest;
And millions toil, condemned to mindless night,
    That one may riot in unhallow'd waste!

'Tis objects such as these that steel the heart,
    And make short-sighted Man his race's foe;
Too soon quick Youth feels Disappointment's dart;
    He sinks; or, world-school'd, feeds on others' woe!

Yet, let not scenes like these, soft-bosom'd youth!
    Thy all-susceptive soul 'gainst feeling steel:
Hope smiling comes! and soon shall mighty Truth
    Humanity's unnumber'd sorrows heal!

And the dark clouds, that blur the beauteous face
    Of Nature, all shall vanish into air!

Nor long shall man, striving in error's chace,
  Be doom'd to disappointment and despair!

Then worship Truth, and scorn base Falsehood's wrongs,
  And leave foul Calumny to feast and gorge!
Nor join the selfish woe-inflicting throngs,
  Nor sink beneath the World's life-with'ring scourge!

Lo! Truth appears! and brighter scenes arise!
  The clash of arms and interests shall cease!
The past alone shall claim soft Pity's sighs,
60 And renovated Earth shall rest in peace!

Monthly Magazine (Jan., 1803), 518–19. The poet, from "W———r, Northumberland," writes in a now familiar Romantic vein, lamenting the destruction of one kind of idealism and searching for a consolation that can rescue some of the idealism and hope. The abstract diction and personifications are not in the Wordsworthian manner, but the concerns are those of *The Prelude* (1850), *The Triumph of Life* (1824), and *Fall of Hyperion* (1857). One can also see the kind of psychological analysis that will inform *Prometheus Unbound* (1820) or that informs Blake's poetry, namely, a concern with contraries and warring human faculties. The ultimate recuperation of idealistic allegiance to "Truth" and to faith in "renovated Earth" is also not unlike the various Romantic resolutions to the problem of initial disillusionment.

[NO TITLE]   ANTHOCLES

Burdett!—who 'young in years, in counsels old,'
  Utterest a warning voice to those who sleep
Forgetful of their country's weal, be bold
  In that good cause: with thunders loud and deep,
Break thou their fatal slumber: we our eyes
  Bend on thy lonely virtue, ev'n as they
Who struggle with the waves, explore the skies
  For that safe star, that shall direct their way:
Thou art the beacon of our sinking land,
10 A senator unspotted: thou art he,
Who in the desert with uplifted wand,
  Dost point the health of nations—Liberty,
That we may gaze and live: the lisping praise
Of children shall be thine, in distant days.

Monthly Magazine (Sept., 1809), 191. Sir Francis Burdett, Radical MP, friend of Horne Tooke, was partially responsible for reviving the reform movement during the Regency period. The dramatic action that stimulated the dormant reform movement was his proposal for parliamentary reform in 1809 and then his imprisonment in the Tower in 1810 for "slandering" the House of Commons. For a number of years following, he was the most prominent reformer. This tribute, a Shakespearean sonnet by "Anthocles," represents that moment of exhilaration and hope when the reform movement seemed once again alive due to the courage and principled action of a reformer.

(l. 1): The exact wording in Shakespeare is "young in limbs, in judgment old": *Merchant of Venice* act 2, scene 7, line 71.

3. *Athenaeum* (1808)

Edited from 1807 to 1809 by the Dissenter John Aikin, who also edited the *Monthly Magazine* (1796–1806), this periodical has very little poetry usually and is designed for a well-educated readership quite remote from the radical artisans for whom the plebeian periodicals were intended.

NECESSITY [N.A.]

Yes, I, too, mark with anxious eye
The world's great pageant passing by!
Breathless I catch the mighty name
That swells, that fills, the trump of fame;
On wings of speed, with eye of fire,
He hastes—I shudder, and admire—
The battle roars, the day is won—
Exulting Fortune crowns her son:
Sick'ning I turn on yonder plain
10 To mourn the widows and the slain;
To mourn the woes, the crimes of man,
To search in vain the eternal plan,
In outraged nature claim a part,
And ponder, desolate of heart.

But, restless long, the wanderer Thought
Returns at length with comfort fraught,
And thus, with air benign, serene,
Would moralize the mortal scene.
Weep'st thou the dead? and who are *they*?
20 Those powerless limbs, that senseless clay?
Weep'st thou the dead? and can'st thou read
The spirit's doom, the spirit's meed?
Go, fold thine arms, and bow the head
In rev'rence o'er their lowly bed,
Then lift thine eyes, and calmly trust
The Wise, the Merciful, the Just.

The widow'd?—Yes, they claim a tear,
Yet comfort meets us even here:
'Tis but the fate of one short span
That lies within the gripe of man;
Whate'er of joy the oppressor steals,
Whate'er of woe the victim feels,
The lapse of ages in their course
Shall bring a compensating force,
Succeeding worlds atone the past,
And strike our balance right at last.
—Unclench thy hand, subdue thine eye,
Recal [sic] those curses deep and high;
Tame thy rude breast's vindictive swell,
Nor rave of everlasting hell!
"I hate the oppressor!" say'st thou—hate
A poor blind instrument of fate?
Does not the tyrant's self obey
Some feller tyrant's lawless sway?
See Anger goad his fiery breast,
Remorse, Suspicion, kill his rest;
And rather say—"Thou suffering soul,
Doom'd for a time, beneath the pole,
In guilt, in fear, short breath to fetch,
A hated, solitary wretch—
May Death his friendly stroke extend,
And soon thy hard commission end,
And bear thee hence, O sweet release!
To taste of innocence and peace."

For human woe, for human weal,
Man will, man must, man ought to feel;
And while they feel, the untutored crowd,
With clamours vehement and loud,
Will rend the skies, and wildly trust
God shall *avenge*, for God is just!
They see not a resistless might
Still guide us on, and guide us right;
Foreseen our passions' utmost force,
Foredoom'd our most eccentric course,
We *seem* to will, nor cease to be
Slaves of a strong necessity.
This knows the sage, and calmly sees
Vice, matter's weakness or disease;

The eternal Mind, the first great cause,
70 A power immense, but bound by laws,
Wise all its ways, contriving still
The most of good, the least of ill,
Redressing all it can redress,
And turn'd to pity and to bless.
Touch'd by this faith, his mellowing mind,
From terror and from wrath refin'd,
Light from the scene upsprings, and wrought
To tender ecstacy of thought,
Sees a just God's impartial smile
80 Relieve the opprest, restore the vile,
Pour good on all—With joy, with love,
He looks around, he looks above;
And vies no more with *anxious* eye
The world's great pageant passing by.

Athenaeum (July, 1808), 52–53. The contrast in these tetrameter couplets between the stoic sage who accepts "necessity" and the "untutored crowd" (l. 57) ruled by prejudice situates this poem firmly within Enlightenment culture. The Necessitarian emphasis will appeal later to Shelley in some of his writings.

4. *Flower's Political Review* (1807–1808)

Edited by the same man who edited the *Cambridge Intelligencer*, Benjamin Flower, this monthly periodical (1807–11), like the *Athenaeum*, is aimed for the more genteel liberal reformer.

Monday's News, at Bath; In the month of January, 1807.   T. P.

On Sundays, like good christians, we prepare,
For solemn duties in the house of prayer;
The public papers into corners hurl'd,
We turn our backs upon this wicked world.
The mind is like a pendulum, its powers
Drawn one way to the highest pitch, for hours,
Will, when the strong suspending force is past,
Swing to the opposite extreme as fast.
Thus after Sunday comes a lounging day,
10 In which we're less inclined to work than play;
Though of the week-days it has least to boast,
Because no information comes by post:

It thus becomes a literary blank,
Yet well supports its dignity and rank;
For curiosity, like hunger, will
By moderate abstinence, grow keener still;
And ready wits on Mondays always try,
To indulge our taste with some appropriate lie.

When Monday comes, impatient of delay,
The stated question is, What news to day?
"The French are beat, huzza! the French are beat,"
Resounds with transport through the crowded street.
I meet a man, whose happy features speak,
The joy with which he has commenc'd the week;
Friend, what's the news? "Why Sir, thank God, the Russians,
"Have drubb'd the French, and quite aveng'd the Prussians."
But is it true? "I can't say much about it;
"All that I know is, no man dares to doubt it."
I next accost one of superior cast,
With, we have glorious news, I hear, at last;
Pray is th' intelligence to be believed?
"Beyond dispute Sir, papers are received,
"Brought by the mail, but what I deem much better,
"By the same post, I've seen a private letter."
I beg your pardon Sir, by *post to day*?
"It must have come then by some other way;
"The writer's high in office, and of course,
"Gets information from the purest source;
"He says, it is a credited report,
"And deem'd unquestionably true at court."
I thank you Sir, well, 'tis a strange reverse
Of fortune surely, and forebodes much worse.
Ambiguous words startle a strong believer,
And so we part, when each has touch'd his beaver.
Saunt'ring, perhaps, the breadth of one good house;
Musing upon the *Mountain* and the *Mouse*,
Another greets me, trying, prudent elf,
By bold assertion to convince himself:
"NAPOLEON Sir, is covered with disgrace,
"And reach'd Berlin with only half a face!"
And do they say who found the other half?
"'Twas shot away in battle, why you laugh!"
My laughter friend, you know, implies no grief,
I'm thinking how his face looks in relief!

Flower's Political Review

    All are loquacious, eager to diffuse
    The rapture kindled by the recent news;
    And every one, in politics well vers'd,
    Acquires some merit, if he tells you first.
    "Why such a victory was never won,
60 "The French are now eternally undone!
    "They've lost, the different accounts concur
    "In stating, more than eighty thousand, Sir!"
    Another tells me, "Why *them* monstrous Croats,
    "Can take a meagre Frenchman down their throats;
    "And *them* fierce Cossacks in a battle thrive,
    "For they can eat their enemies alive!"
    Why that's cheap living friend, howe'er they carve,
    I see they are not likely soon to starve.
    This coarse intelligence, scarce worth a smile,
70 Gives place to something in a higher style:
    "A messenger from Petersburgh, by ship,
    "After a very expeditious trip,
    "Brings a full confirmation of the news:
    "Brave ALEXANDER still the foe pursues;
    "Poland is clear'd, and at Berlin 'tis known,
    "They wait for FREDERICK to resume his throne:
    "The Austrians too have thrown off all disguise,
    "And butcher every Frenchman as he flies;
    "The Arch-duke, the finest General of the age,
80 "Brings up his veteran troops, enflam'd with rage:
    "NAPOLEON thus hemm'd in on every side,
    "Is wand'ring, none knows where, without a guide:
    "And, take the subject up in any shape,
    "It is impossible he can escape."
    But where's Lord Hutchinson? does he not write?
    "Oh! he's engag'd in council day and night;
    "They follow'd his advice you may be sure,
    "And thereby render'd victory secure."

    Where's the Gazette? Can you Sir, guess the sense,
90 Why government thus keeps us in suspence?
    "They wait for regular official letters."
    Well then, for once, I'll imitate my betters:
    My patience, though this morning sorely tried,
    Will hold, till mad credulity subside;
    Till time with steady pace the fact supplies,
    And truth shall put to flight this host of lies.

Flower's Political Review (Feb., 1807), 145–47. This breezy couplet satire on bourgeois manners and perceptions pokes fun at a group of which the author and implied reader are members. The complacent rich in the poem need nevertheless the comforting illusions that their enemies are near collapse and that victory in the war is imminent. The poem represents the unreliability of "news" and how rumor becomes information during an especially bleak period for Britain in its war against Napoleon, who at this time was having great success on the battlefield.

(ll. 9–10): St. Monday was observed not just by laborers and artisans.

(l. 44): Beaver hat.

(ll. 49–50): In fact, Napoleon, fresh from victories over Prussia at Jena and Auerstadt in October, 1806, issued the Berlin decree announcing, among other things, the economic blockade of Britain in November, 1806.

(l. 74): Alexander I (1777–1825) was still fighting Napoleon but he would shortly make a peace treaty (Tilsit, 1807).

(l. 76): Frederick William III (1770–1840), Prussian ruler.

(l. 79): Francis II (1768–1835) appointed the Archduke and general, Charles Louis (1771–1847) to treat with Napoleon, and the result was the December 26, 1805, Treaty of Pressburg.

(l. 85): Lord Hutchinson (1757–1832; *DNB*) was a general and diplomat, sent by the British government in November,1806, on a unsuccessful mission to the Prussian and Russian courts.

To the Memory of the Right Honourable Charles James Fox   S. W.

Patriot renown'd!—rever'd, and lov'd afar;
'Twas thine to smooth the rugged front of war;
To calm the raging storms of wrathful strife,
And woo the charities that sweeten life.
O skill'd in intricate debate to shine,
'Twas thine to charm with eloquence divine,
While crowded senates wrapt in wonder hung
With silent awe on thy commanding tongue.
Man's powerful friend, whatever skin he wore;
10 Where'er he suffer'd, on whatever shore,
To whatsoever sect, or tribe allied,
Thy energetic voice was on his side.
Of honest heart, of word, and look sincere;
'Twas never thine the power of man to fear.
Though some apostatiz'd, and few remain'd
Faithful and firm when PITT the tyrant reign'd,
And like a comet shot his baleful blaze,

Flower's Political Review

That struck mankind with terror and amaze!
So Providence permits the whirlwind's breath
O'er summer isles to spread dismay and death;
Or sees awhile some angry mountain throw
Its burning lava on the plains below.
Yet thou wert found in terror's dreadful hour
To dare the haughty insolence of power;
Still foremost thou in freedom's sacred cause,
To plead man's rights, and liberties, and laws.

Allur'd by thee—lo! she of heavenly birth,
Long absent PEACE, look'd down upon the earth,
To stay the thunder by mad passions hurl'd,
And heal the wounds, and miseries of the world.
Beneath thy smiles that GOD-LIKE pilgrim bless'd,
So little by the sons of men caress'd!
GOOD-WILL came forth to harmonize mankind,
And hostile chiefs in bonds of love to bind.
Too soon alas! the stranger guests withdrew,
And bade with thee a suffering world adieu!
O wail *his* death—the *pilot* skill'd to guide
The lab'ring state-ship o'er the boisterous tide.
In evil times, by love of country fir'd;
He brav'd the storm, and at the helm expir'd!
Weep sons of Peace! *Cains* of the world rejoice!
For silent now that once prophetic voice;
Oft lifted up, but lifted up in vain,
And like that faithful *Seer's* in *Ahab's* reign,*
Against the war-whoop's yell unequal found,
For priests, and rulers rais'd the madd'ning sound,
And murder prowl'd the peopled earth around.
O wail *him* then with patriot grief sincere,
The *man of peace*, whom e'en his foes revere:
Still for his death let suffering empires weep,
And man's best friends long hallow'd vigils keep.

The vain *Ahithophel* of modern days,
Let folly's sons *his* memory blast with praise;
The great in words—of serpent cunning proud,

---

*Micaiah:—To be acquainted with whose faithful conduct, and that of the time-serving priests, and *Pittites* of his day, and with the fatal consequences that followed the rejection of the word of truth, consult the last chapter of the 1st. book of Kings.

Prompt to deceive the undiscerning crowd.
For ever sunk—whose fame would quickly fade,
But for the ruins which his crimes have made.
In future times, great FOX! shall live thy fame,
Men yet unborn will venerate thy name;
60 More lasting honours consecrate thy grave
Than e'er to PITT the *saints* of Cambridge gave.
Let them heap offerings at their idol's shrine;†
All Europe's praise, great friend of man! is thine.
Besides her Fox, his country mark'd with pain
Her great men fall, her chiefs untimely slain,
For *Abercromby* sigh'd, allow'd no more
To win renown on Egypt's burning shore:
Wept for *Cornwallis*, fallen on India's plains,
Where prowls the tiger, and the lion reigns;
70 Where man, than cruel beasts more cruel far,
At ruin smiles, and drives the storm of war;
Mocks the loud thunder, and the lightning's fire,
More fierce his wrath, more terrible his ire!
These Britain mourn'd, but never known to fame,
Alas! what multitudes of meaner name,
Have fought, and perish'd on a foreign shore?
Struck off life's muster-roll for evermore!
Where rest their bones within the sea-beat strand
No muse informs, or artist's skilful hand;
80 Nor graven brass, nor sculptur'd marble tell
How brave in honor's lap the veterans fell;
Or how disease, tainting air's sultry breath,
Their squadrons smote, and thinn'd their ranks by death;
Winds howl their requiem to the surf-spent waves,
No tears but heaven's bedew their lonely graves!
Thy victims, war!—But what are thy train'd bands?
Like locusts swarming o'er devoted lands,
In devastation's dreadful work employ'd;
Oft by the famine they create destroy'd.
90 Turn Britain then, from prostrate heroes turn,
To bathe with tears thy last great statesman's urn;
Of all thy sons *he* claims thy sorrows most,
A tower *his* wisdom, and *his* name an host!

---

†Alluding to the subscription monument to be erected to the memory of Mr. Pitt by the University of Cambridge.

Fresh warriors may succeed to warriors slain;
Another Fox will never rise again!
Let war's spent thunderbolts in silence rest;
His name will live—*his* memory shall be bless'd!

Foil'd friends of peace lament your champion's death;
Expir'd your hope with his departed breath!
100 Fall'n are the brave—their dreadful work is o'er;
And Fox man's long tried friend, can plead for man no more!

At time's eventful period, thus the sun,
His long career of peerless glory run,
To darkness turn'd, and quench'd his mighty fire,
Shall 'mid the wreck of lesser orbs expire!

Flower's Political Review (March, 1807), 227–29. Written in Bath, Feb. 26, by S. W. shortly after Fox's death (Sept. 13, 1806), this tribute to Charles James Fox celebrates the most famous hero of the liberal Whigs. The heroic couplets portray Fox as a great statesman for peace and "liberty," the antithesis of Pitt the "tyrant." Compared to the Hebrew prophets and even Jesus, Fox is elevated to the highest level of political fame. Fox's death is more tragic than the events befalling unfortunate military leaders like Sir John Abercromby (1772–1817; *DNB*) (l. 66) who was imprisoned by Napoleon from 1803 until 1808, and Admiral Cornwallis (1744–1818; *DNB*) (l. 68) who was relieved of his command in 1806, and the anonymous soldiers lost in battle or to disease.

(l. 9): Fox supported abolition of the slave trade, and shortly after his death, and in part because of his efforts, an abolition bill passed (March, 1807).

(l. 28): Long an advocate of peace with France, Fox supported the Peace of Amiens (April, 1802-May, 1803).

(l. 40): At his death he was part of the Ministry of All the Talents formed in January, 1806.

(l. 44): 1 Kings 22, Micaiah the prophet's words anger King Ahab, who punishes the prophet but who is killed in battle shortly thereafter.

(l. 52): The story of Absalom, David, and Ahitophel is in 2 Samuel 15–19, and retold in Dryden's *Absalom and Achitophel* (1681) as contemporary political allegory. Pitt is depicted as the Ahitophel figure, the advisor to the rebel Absalom.

HOLY ANTICIPATION;
FOR A FUTURE
THANKSGIVING DAY.   [N.A.]

THANKSGIVING DAY all hail! I love thee well,
Quoth the fat priest, with corporation vast;
Not like thy hungry brother, daemon fell.
All hail thanksgiving day! welcome at last!

The Revolutionary Decade

It is a long time since I saw thy phiz;
Long since thy pudding smoak'd upon the board:
Ah! say, dear friend, what the sad reason is,
That thou'rt so shy with people of the Lord!

I love thy plump round face, thy copious grin,—
10 Thy *new morality*,—indeed I do;
And when thou shak'st thy greasy double-chin,
I glory that I feel—I feel like you.

Perish our enemies whoe'er they be,
Let them all sink beneath the briny wave,
Like Pharoah's host o'erwhelm'd by Edom's sea,
Where'er they dwell soon may they find a grace.

Let cannon roar, let arrows, fire and death
Destroy the world, and every face make pale;
Let war and famine stop each caitiff's breath
20 That dares from our old house to draw a nail.

We joy to know that thousands have been slain,
That still the work of blood and slaughter speeds:
Many thousands more fall on the goary plain,
And British heroes glory in such deeds!

Perish the *swinish herd*! What are their lives,
A little air in dull and vulgar clay.
The constitution lives, the church still thrives,
And I have liv'd to see this glorious day!

My tythes are duly paid, my game secure,
30 My table richly spread, no want I know:
I leave all fasting to the hungry poor,
My fleece is warm,———the rest[,] old friend[,] may go.

Flower's Political Review (Feb., 1808), 119–20. This anti-clerical satire touches upon some of the usual points of reference: clerical hypocrisy, complacency, insensitivity, corruption, and moral obtuseness. The poet turns the Anglican divine into a follower of the devil, worshipping all the things associated with evil. Here, as usually elsewhere, the anti-clerical focus is also anti-aristocratic, as there is an emphasis on the social aspects of "the fat priest" 's existence.
  (l. 5): Phiz—face.
  (l. 10): The New Morality here probably refers to the ideas of moral reform associated with the Evangelical wing of the Church; in the 1790s, the New Morality referred to English "Jacobin"—reformist—ideas.
  (l. 15): Exodus 14.
  (l. 19): A caitiff is an evil person.

PART TWO

The Rebirth of Radicalism, 1815–1824

1. *The Theological Inquirer* (1815)

A freethinking journal, edited by "Erasmus Perkins," who was actually George Cannon, began publishing in March and stopped in September of 1815. The journal's connection with Shelley (1792–1822) remains mysterious as we do not yet know the exact extent of cooperation between Shelley and Cannon or between Shelley and the journal's principal man of letters—poet and reviewer of *Queen Mab*—"F." See Newman I. White, *Shelley* (NY: Alfred A. Knopf, 1940), 1: 409–10; 696–97; and Louise Boas, "'Erasmus Perkins' and Shelley," *Modern Language Notes* 70 (1955): 408–13. There is recent information on George Cannon and F.—Robert Charles Fair—in Iain McCalman's *Radical Underworld. Prophets, Revolutionaries and Pornographers in London, 1795–1840* (Cambridge: UP, 1988). Cannon was a Spencean radical and a pornographer, while Fair was "a young shoemaker-poet, formerly on the fringes of the LCS who joined the Spenceans shortly before Spence's death [in 1814]" (19). Fair evidently knew Robert Wedderburn, Allen Davenport, and Edward J. Blandford, other artisan poets who were Spenceans. For the Spencean poets, see Chase ch. 4 and 5; McCalman ch. 3 and 7; Hone ch. 6. Fair was a Spencean leader for the Bethnal Green tavern club in 1817 (McCalman 124). Concerning the *Theological Inquirer*, McCalman writes: "Even aside from Shelley's contributions, the *Theological Inquirer* was an impressive rationalist production and one that deserves attention from literary and social historians" (81).

The militant freethinking and anti-religious zeal we find in this periodical represent an aspect of radical culture that was never a mainstream current but was nonetheless important. Anti-clerical sentiment and resentment against the privileges of the Anglican Church were, however, very much a part of mainstream Reform sensibility.

ODE TO RELIGION   F. [R. C. FAIR]

What art thou, phantom of caprice,
   Veil'd in the rolling clouds of Doubt,
Now singing to the lute of Peace,
   Now trumpeter to War's wild rout?
How shall the magic skill be mine,
   Thy art, thy nature, to define,

Rebirth of Radicalism

To view, by truth's bright lamp, thy inmost cave?
    O! that I could thy riddle solve,
    Then, like the Sphinx, thou mightst involve
Thy power mischievous in Destruction's grave.

How vast a scope thy spells engross!
    How wild and strange thy deeds have been!
Thou didst erect the bloody cross,
    Where died the far-famed NAZARENE.
Thy rancor wove the webs of flame
    That mantled round SERVETUS' frame,
And hoary CRANMER's aged limbs encas'd;
    And, in a more enlighten'd age,
    For EATON rais'd Scorn's public stage,
And in Oppression's dungeon HOUSTON plac'd.

Are not these THY demoniac glooms?
    Or is there some impostor sprite,
Who thus thy specious robe assumes,
    And wields the mace of earthly might;
Whose rage drove Emigration's host
    To people vast Columbia's coast,
And rais'd at Nantz the persecuting storm;
    Who on Bartholma's eve accurs'd
    His stiff'ning knees in blood immers'd,
And scowls his bloodshot eyes on Erin's woe-worn form[?].

Where dost thou most delight to dwell?
    Close in some woody mountain's side,
Embosom'd in the hermit's cell,
    Or in the rich cathedral's pride?
Dost thou behold with Pleasure's smile
    The widow'd Hindoo's burning pile?
Or ride and revel on the vesper's note?
    Are sleeves of lawn thy favorite wear?
    The mitred cone or tonsure bare,
The Rabbi's vest, or Quaker's modest coat[?].

Or are those fond enthusiasts right,
    Who see thy visionary shade
Enrob'd in weeds of purest white,
    Contemplative in Virtue's glade?
And whether at the morning's beam,
    At noon reposing by the stream,

Or musing on the golden hills at eve,
   Revolving plans of human weal,
   To teach the wayward heart to feel
50 Its own defects, and others' to relieve[?].

Ah! didst thou act this generous part,
   Didst thou with this pure lustre shine,
Then shouldst thou find no human heart
   A warmer devotee than mine;
But in thy gathering shades confin'd
   Truth can no certain pathway find,
And Reason vainly tries, amid the gloom,
   To lift on high her beacon torch,
   Construct her vast exalted porch,
60 And lift to other spheres her well-proportion'd dome.

Theological Inquirer (1815), 142–43. The poet distinguishes between the institutional and spiritual qualities of religion, protesting against the violence and coercion of the one and wistfully praising the other (ll. 41–50), in much the same way as Shelley did. The last stanza identifies the poet as a deist.

(l. 16): Michael Servetus (1511–1553) was a Spanish theologian and physician executed as a heretic.

(l. 17): The first Protestant Archbishop of Canterbury, Cranmer (1489–1556; *DNB*) was burned at the stake for his religious views.

(l. 19): Daniel I. Eaton, editor and publisher of the 1790s periodicals *Politics for the People* and the *Philanthropist*, was sentenced by Lord Ellenborough (1750–1818; *DNB*) on May 15, 1812, to the pillory and eighteen months in prison for publishing Thomas Paine's deist essays, even though Eaton was in poor health and sixty years old. Shelley wrote his *Letter to Lord Ellenborough* (1812) in protest of this sentence.

(l. 20): Lord Ellenborough sentenced George Houston in 1814 to two years in Newgate for translating Holbach's *Ecce Homo!*, which had recently been published by Eaton. Houston was the publisher in 1814 of William Cobbett's *Political Register*. He fled to America after his release from prison and started a career there as a radical publisher (see Houston's very interesting newspaper, the *Correspondent*, published from New York starting in 1827).

(l. 27): The 1598 Edict of Nantes declared the official toleration of the Huguenots; the Edict was revoked in 1685.

(l. 28): On St. Bartholomew's Eve, 1572, many Huguenots were slaughtered.

Scripture Soliloqu[i]es.
Our blessed Saviour on
Mount Calvary.   F. [R. C. Fair]

Why am I here? Nailed to the cross of shame,
Scourg'd and insulted by a rabble vile,

Rebirth of Radicalism

    Pierc'd by the hired assassin's reeking spear,
    Set, ev'n below Barabbas in the scale
    Of popular esteem, and doom'd to die
    The death of thieves? What deed have I committed?
    What thought conceiv'd, that I, the son of God,
    The merciful, the just, and the almighty,
    Should thus by his decree in suffering writhe,
10 And feel Death's ice collecting round my heart?
    O bitter cup! that his lov'd only son
    A father's power to save has thus forsaken!
    And yet how needful! when th' Almighty God
    Ev'n by these means can only save *a few*
    From him who rules the fiery domes of Hell.
    How just, that he who suffered man to sin,
    Should suffer to redeem him; that his son,
    On whom his best affections should recline;
    An exile from those fields of radiant glory,
20 Where Heav'n expands her choir-resounding porch,
    To meet perpetual morn's enlivening smile;
    Should roam, while more than thirty years have heap'd
    Their load on time's broad shoulders; that his life
    Burthened with hard reviling and contempt,
    Without a home to chear his weariness,
    Should lead to unjust death and all its horrors.
    Oh! how these pangs must rend a father's soul!
    Yet only thus could He, whose boundless power
    No limit circumscribes, effect his will.
30 No more: I faint; 'tis finish'd. Consciousness
    Recedes: yet through the vista of the future,
    I see the priest of ages yet unborn,
    Deck'd in the robe and diadem of might.
    Lifting my cross in sight of multitudes,
    And (threatening torture to the unbeliever,)
    Demanding faith; receiving at my shrine
    The layman's costly gift; and whispering
    Despotic maxims in the ears of kings.
    Oh! glorious prospect! happy consummation!
40 Death's draught becomes a cordial; and I fall
    Content to do the will of him who sent me.

Theological Inquirer (1815), 144. This is the first of the poet's four "Scripture Soliloquies," dramatic monologues focusing on Jesus, Moses, Noah, and Solomon. Until line 32 the poem is fairly unremarkable in its imagining the crucifixion scene, but from that point on, it articulates a version of Jesus that only the most radical of freethinkers could accept. The more common attitude among radicals was the one Shelley adopted in *Prometheus Unbound* (1820) and elsewhere: that Jesus was an ethical paragon whose ideas were turned into oppressive institutions. Even Shelley, however, in a footnote to *Queen Mab*, viewed Jesus as interested more in power than in virtue (Oxford *Shelley* 820 n.1). One of Shelley's early writings that has been lost was something he referred to as "Biblical Extracts," portions of the Bible suitable for framing in a radical way and for a popular readership. Shelley too was attracted at times to the Manichean-like dualism articulated in lines 14 and 15.

ON SECTARIAN PERSECUTION. S.

From bitter reflection some moments to spare,
I take up the pen to address my friend —— [Fair.]
Believe me, my friend, mine's a desperate case,
No wealth, no employment, no pension, no place;
To leeward I'm running, from squalls unprotected,
With adversity burden'd, by fortune neglected;
Scoffed, contemned, and despised by connexions at home:
Ah! whither for comfort, for peace can I roam,
At home called a *Christian*, abroad scorned a *Jew*,
10 Charybdis and Scylla both frown on my view.
How strange! in a country where liberty dwells,
Which in art's useful glory triumphant excels,
That the merchant, the artist, should shut fast their doors,
Because for employ 'tis a Jew that implores;
Yet this my endurance for bigotry rules,
The convenience of knaves, and the reason of fools,
But my soul feels its pride, and to honor is true,
And remains, my dear friend, your devoted—Adieu.

Theological Inquirer (1815), 417–18. The prefatory note by "F." identified the poet as "born a Jew, but detested bigotry," so that presumably he was not a religious Jew—which explains line 9. Radical culture at this time was not especially sensitive to anti-Semitism, and this is one of the few poems that protests against it at all. More typical was Cobbett's "populist" anti-Semitism. See Todd M. Endelman, *The Jews of Georgian England, 1714–1830* (Philadelphia: Jewish Publications Society, 1979).

THE RUINED CITY F. [R. C. FAIR]

Bellowing with fury from his cloudy car,
To call the hosts of elemental war,
The god of storms his sable flag unfurls,
And through the air his gleaming falchion whirls;

This strikes electric flashes on the earth,
And *that* impels the hurricane to birth;
Awful the thunder of his chariot-wheels,
Nature an universal horror feels;
The sky dissolves in cataracts of rain,
And beats resounding on the smoaky plain;
Here desolation builds his gloomy seat,
And holds his undisputed sway complete;
Far to the east the desert waste extends,
And, gradual with the misty distance blends.
Impervious forests south and west surround,
And ridgy hills the northern prospects bound:
No cottage roof my straining sight descries,
No human visage meets my longing eyes;
A seeming outcast from the social zone,
Regret's expressive tear I shed alone.
Thus, (as those records, dear to the devout,
Tell fond credulity and cautious doubt,)
When Heav'n's fierce fit of rage dissolved to peace,
And God's repentance bade the deluge cease;
As from the wondrous ark the patriarch stept,
He view'd Destruction's wanton deed and wept.
Sure this wild spot existence never blest!
By art improved, by cultivation drest!
Yes, here her golden fanes a city rear'd,
And vegetation's wholesome stores appear'd;
Here Delma's marble piles to Heav'n aspir'd,
Delma, whose eagle fame the world admir'd;
Riches and glory wreathed her noble brow;
Where are those riches? where that glory now?
Where are the sceptered tenants of her throne,
Whose sweetest music was a vassal's groan?
Where are those vassals, dead to freedom's heat,
On whom he trampled, yet who kissed his feet?
Her heroes, ardent for the wreath of fame?
Her merchant's [*sic*] bold in traffic's mighty aim?
Her sages, versed in law and reason's ways?
Her minstrels, tuneful in their country's praise?
Where are all these?—Beneath oblivion's blot,
Their words, their actions, ev'n their names forgot;
No record of their days can now be found,
Here mutilated columns strew the ground,

And mouldering piles with moss and weeds o'ergrown,
At each rude gust in heaps come tumbling down.
Hoar, silent Time, whose unrelenting sway
50   Loads all things with the pressure of decay;
         ****

62   Nought can NECESSITY'S decree dissolve,
That only certain, bids *all else* revolve.
Amid the physical and moral world
The wheel of change incessantly is whirl'd,
And matter must the Protean law obey,
68   A jewel now, and now a lump of clay.
         ****

108 Onward, yet slow, I course the wide forlorn,
And as the paths, half-choak'd with weeds, I trace,
Once trod by population's busy pace,
Oft the full sigh comes bursting from my heart,
To see the mutilated works of art,
That once so proudly tower'd above the ground,
114 In sad confusion scattered all around.
         ****

127 All, all are hushed:—the blaze of Delma's might
Scarce glimmers on oblivion's thick'ning night.

     Read on yon mouldering monument of death
130 What should inform who fills the grave beneath;
"Here lies immortal."—Who? No name appears;
Lost in the gradual ravages of years;
Placed to commemorate a hero's fame,
This stone is powerless, even to keep his name.
Perhaps some warrior; who, in valour's prime,
Great only by the magnitude of crime;
Blew glory's bubble through the trump of war,
And spread the terror of his name afar.
Villain obnoxious! to the world a pest;
A petty robber I would less detest;
This hard necessity may drive to prey,
142 But *that*, false glory and the love of sway.
         ****

189   Here, hid by lofty walls, in solemn gloom,
Religion's prison stood; a living tomb;
Whither, by tyranny compelled to go;
By love unfortunate; by hopeless woe;

Or by mistaken piety inspir'd;
The spotless vestal from the world retired;
Her silent reign here melancholy kept,
And in the dreary cloister'd echo slept;
Save when the deep-toned bell for vespers rung,
Or choral sisters early matins sung;
Here many a sweet enthusiast hid those charms,
200 Designed by nature for a lover's arms;
Here lost its lustre many a brilliant eye,
And many a blooming cheek its healthful dye.
Thinkst thou, recluse, true faith thy bosom warms?
Reason and truth despise restrictive forms.
Or thinkst thou, fool, 'tis glory to renounce
The cares and pleasures of the world at once?
Far greater his who braves the storm of life,
Through all temptations stems the billowy strife;
Still holds his course undaunted by the blast,
210 And guides his vessel safe to port at last.

    Fair was Estella, she was beauty's prize,
The power of feeling glistened in her eyes;
Dwelt in her heart, and sanctioned every thought.
—Ah! had that heart been fashioned as it ought!
But 'twas from childhood superstition's slave,
The nurse's tales an early bias gave;
Legends of saints and angels fann'd the flame,
And priesthood saw, and urged his artful claim;
Till, by the visionary toil ensnared,
220 Her tongue the world-renouncing vow declar'd.

    One fatal night the crackling noise of fire
Awoke the lovely nun to terrors dire.
Her chamber, filled with suffocating smoke,
And shrieks without, the dreadful truth bespoke;
Faint with dismay, life flitted from her thought,
And when the tenement again it sought,
Recumbent in a bower she lay, perfumed
With all the richest scents that ever bloomed;
A lovely youth hung fondly o'er her form,
230 Whose ardent gaze called forth the blushes warm;
Such blushes might a hermit's coldness melt.
Ah! then Estella first love's impulse felt;
Then to her conscious feeling first was known,

That woman lives not for herself alone;
And chilled, indeed, that apathetic breast,
Where Cyprian's image had no mark imprest.
Estella saw him, rich in manhood's pride,
Bright were his eyes; his cheeks by beauty dyed;
Sweet were the accents of his rosy breath;
And more—his valor rescued her from death.
The past, the present, and the future lot,
All but the other's presence each forgot;
Calm was the night, and quiet ruled the hour;
Luxuriant breezes floated through the bower;
Gay pleasure shook her incense in the air,
And love resigned to joy the happy pair.

    Bright rose the orient morn, but that bright beam
Dispersed the lover's soul-entrancing dream;
Remorse recalled Estella's vestal vow,
And superstition scowled with heavy brow;
In vain fond Cyprian, with persuasive tongue,
Strove to dispel the consciousness of wrong;
Eternal constancy he swore in vain,
Estella's mind peace entered not again;
Secluded in a wild romantic hut,
'Mid woody tufts and craggy mountains shut;
Twelve moons they lived, their bliss with sorrow mix'd,
For in the fair one's soul remorse was fix'd:
Oft an hereafter fear's dark pencil drew,
And hope, at times, pourtray'd a brighter view.
Ah! foolish fear! repugnant to the mind!
Ah! weak unfounded hope! to reason blind;
The mental conflict tore Estella's frame,
Love could no longer feed life's quivering flame;
Death stole her latest sigh with gentle kiss,
And Cyprian wept the ruin of his bliss.
Poor, beauteous victim of Religion's dream!
No more for thee arose the morning's beam;
Thy sighs, thy smiles, thy tears, thy joys were o'er,
And consciousness to thee returns no more.
        DIRGE.
No tolling bell; no weeping crowd;
No vaulted tomb; no fringed shroud;
No plumy hearse; no blazon'd shield,

    Their honors to thy burial yield;
    Yet chorus'd birds thy dirge attest;
    Green earth receives thee to her breast;
    Sweet flowers thy passive limbs enwreathe,
    And one fond heart, with bursting breath,
                Laments thee, lovely corse.

280 Not long that heart will life desire,
    But lose it in the battle's ire;
    Till then, its thought will not desert
    Thine image pure;—for pure thou wert.
    Say, cynic, moralist, or saint,
    Is nature's dictate crime's foul taint?
    Or if such beauty error wears,
    Who but must prize it, and with tears
288   Lament thee, lovely corse?
    * * * * * * * *

529 Thee, Public Virtue, in the trying hour
    Hope rests on; Oh! be thine unbounded power.
    Light up thy beacon with that glorious flame
    That beams on Washington's immortal name;
    That crown'd with radiance Cato's dying brow,
    That shone on Hampden, shines on Stanhope now,
    Upheld by thee let innocence appear;
    Bring moderation, calm, yet strange to fear;
    Assume no frown but shrinking guilt's desert,
    And that let anxious mercy half avert:
    Then shall the pure-soul'd patriot bravely urge
540 His res'lute prow though Faction's foaming surge,
    Attack Corruption, manned with pirate ranks,
    And ride triumphant o'er her scattered planks,
    Till, anchored safe in Renovation's bay,
    He sees th' encircling shores with freedom gay;
    Sees peace reposing on the fertile plain;
546 And Virtue loosed from Superstition's chain.

Theological Inquirer (1815), 140–42; 220–24; 300–303; 376–79. The poem's speaker finds himself among the ruins of "Delma," a fictional empire with a glorious past. The first part (ll. 1–188) develops a number of related themes: the vain desire of tyrants for immortality, the superior power of time and Necessity, the fragility of social liberty, and the evils of war and a bellicose religion. The second part (ll. 189–300) emphasizes the destructive power of religion somewhat by direct comment but more by the story of Estella and Cyprian. The third part (ll. 301–486), which I have left out entirely, criticizes the courts, courtiers, and luxury of Delma, while speculating on the more general principles by which a society disintegrates. The final section (ll. 487–546) turns from Delma to Britain, whose decline is compared to Delma's, and excoriates the principal evils of trade, war, and religion. Hope is figured as a patriotic public virtue that will attack Corruption and initiate social reform.

This very ambitious "ruins" poem was to have been published with other "F." poems, but if it was I have discovered no trace of it. A famous "ruins" literary work with a revolutionary ideology was Volney's *Ruins* (1791), one of the most frequently reprinted radical texts which also influenced P. B. Shelley. The poem is so strikingly Shelleyan that I once thought Shelley was indeed the author. One at the very least wonders how close the relationship was between Fair and Shelley. The references to Lord Stanhope—the LCS's favorite establishment politician—and (in a section I did not include) Georgiana, Duchess of Devonshire (1757–1806; *DNB*), indicate that Fair formed his ideological bearings in the 1790s, even though he was a Spencean later. Although the poem could have been written in or close to 1815— Georgiana's famous poem, "Passage of the Mountain of St. Gothard," was reprinted in 1812, and Lord Stanhope was still a radical leader in the Regency—*The Ruined City* might have been written in the 1790s.

2. *The People* (1817)

One of the ephemeral periodicals of 1817, a year of widespread protests even during the suspension of Habeas Corpus between March 4, 1817, and January 28, 1818, this journal's fifteen issues ran from April 19 to July 19. Aimed at a popular audience (priced only 2 pence), the journal was published by William Butler and William Wilks, printed by Hay and Turner, and edited by "P. R." There was considerable Spencean participation in the journal, including a letter by Robert Wedderburn (see Chase ch. 4 & 5; Hone ch. 6; McCalman ch. 3 & 7). The journal's motto, "The Safety of the People is the Supreme Law," was aggressively Jacobin, in that the Terror was carried out under the auspices of the Committee for Public Safety.

Spontaneous Verse P. F. P——

On the death of a much beloved child, by his afflicted parent; now living indeed in a "VALE OF TEARS."

In him malignant passions found no place,
But all was sweetness, intellect and grace.

"Take him for all in all, I ne'er shall look upon his like again.["]

Oh! for an hallowed muse of sacred fire,
That well could paint the bitterness of woe
Which parents['] hearts in agonies endure;
When death arrests the progress of their child;
Yet takes no bail to stay his ruffian hand;

But, fierce to judgement, carries on his suit,
In closest custody the prisoner keeps,
And mocks at those, who, deeply in their hearts
The cruel separation bathe in ceaseless tears[—]
10 Ceaseless, till time has mellowed down their grief
To calm dejection, often then renewed,
By causes which excite memorial of their grief.
Oh, for an hallowed muse for such a work!
That they who read may feel as he who writes;
That sympathetic suff'ring touch those chords,
Which vibrate in responsive tones with those,
The fond, fond parents so accutely [sic] know.
Oh, my dear boy, the memory of *thee*,
Can never be effaced, while here I breathe
20 A weary pilgrim seeking for his rest,
Thy beauteous beaming face, thy well turned limbs,
Those clear blue eyes, that Cherub's mouth,
Those lips e'er clad in witchery of smiles,
In their first efforts to express thy wants:
The pointed finger of that lovely hand,
Which never did an act not fraught with good,
But often us'd to shew thy want of words,
When pleas'd with diet, or affection place,
And cry "poor, poor," to child, or doll, or cat;
30 That intellect so logically true,
Which never false conclusions rashly drew;
That power of imitation strong and clear,
When scarce thy baby-clothes were laid aside;
These, and a num'rous list of little charms,
Thy hand, thy eyes, thy mouth, have oft express'd,
Can never be eras'd from his fond soul,
Who now in all the misery of tears,
Before thy corpse is to the earth convey'd,
Describes the merits, thou canst show no more.
40 Oft did the minstrel's pipe delight thine ear,
And beams of joy would lighten in thy looks;
Accordant then thy pliant limbs would move
And prove to harmony thy soul was form'd.
Oh! my dear boy, that ever fatal night,
Which told me of thy dissolution near;
Those pains thy tender hearted mother saw
Thy tender breast endure, in closing gasps,

The People

    Ere thy sweet soul departed its abode,
    (Not resident therein for two full years)
50 That fatal night, and that last hour of day,
    When thy dear body will be borne away,
    To find interment near the Abbey-pile;
    These two sad periods, oft as they recur,
    In annual repetitions, during life,
    I trust, sincerely trust, will be to me,
    Times which, in meditation, will be spent,
    Reflecting on the progress of my course,
    With resolutions to amend what's wrong;
    And striving to become, in heart like thee,
60 Pure and untainted by the deeds of guilt:
    That what the Saviour of the world once taught,
    In words benevolent and truly sweet;
    "Who enters heaven's kingdom must come there,
    "A little child," clear inf'rence may afford,
    To all pure, honest, and candid minds, that sin
    Is not imputed to the human race,
    For Adam's lapse from righteousness, beyond
    The imputed righteousness of Christ.—
    Hence, my dear boy, I'll consolation find
70 From faith, that thou art blest; and further hope
    That yet I'll see thee number'd with the just,
    Where grief and sorrow shall be known no more.
    "To thee, my love, the bitterness of death
    Is pass'd; to me, I feel 'tis present now,
    And ever will be, when I think of thee.
    The sable ever round my heart I'll wear,
    When outward signs of woe are all withdrawn.
    Oh, my lov'd boy! 'twould be an impious act,
    An act which God and nature both forbid,
80 To hasten on life's close, by violence;
    Or else, I should not wait the ebbing tide,
    To pass the gulph that separates our shores!
    But would be with thee, ere another night,
    But there compress thee to my ardent soul.
    Oh, my dear boy, hadst thou but longer liv'd,
    Till reason o'er thee had more pow'rful sway,
    O, how delightful would have been the task
    The rule of duty rapturously fulfill'd,
    To pour, upon thy soul, religion's law,

90 The waters taken from the fount of life;
With other maxims drawn from other source:
But all the projects which of late I'd plann'd,
Of talk, and rural walk, warm-hand in hand,
Are now delusions, phantoms, like a dream;
To prove the vanity of human hopes,
Which Death can turn to gloom—to deepest gloom,
To deepest, blackest gloom, with instant touch,
As now, O now, I too severely find.
Oh, that the thing itself were but a dream!
100 That fancy only made me thus regret
The loss of thee, my sweetest lovely boy!
But, for my future peace of mind, alas!
The thing indeed is far too true; 'tis one
Among "the sad realities of life,"
Which, till life ends, I ever shall deplore.
No time can ever change my thoughts on thee,
Perhaps, no time can mitigate my grief.
Of all afflictions I have ever felt,
(Nor stranger I to many of life's woes,)
110 By far the most severe is loss of thee.
The loss of friends, of property, of books:
(Of books, the solace of my studious life,
With care, collected during many years,
But seiz'd by ruffians, for a paltry debt,—
For a poor, paltry debt—and in a land
Where labour toils in vain for scanty food;
Where effort, genius, merit—all are vain;
Where Industry pines out his wearied day;
And where his sinking limbs Exertion strains.
120 Even to exhaustion, worse than Afric slave,
Dragging a ling[']ring death of famish'd life;
Where nought but weeds of noxious growth can thrive:
The spy, the informer, the blood-money villain;
Corruption[']s agents, fiends,[—] worst fiends of hell,
Luring to crime, and then, incarnate devils,
Betraying and exaggerating acts
Of desperation, which themselves have caus'd:
And offering up the victims of their schemes
To that insatiate monster, that most dread
130 Of tyrants, that arch-demon fell,
Corruption, 'neath whose curs'd, whose direst sway,

The People

    Earth groans oppress'd, and virtue, happiness,
    And ev'ry hope of human life expire.)—
    Yes loss of friends, of property, of books,
    From mean soul'd spirits and malicious wrath,
    I've firmly borne, without a tear; though not
    Without some feeling—feeling too most keen[,]
    But tears have flowed in torrents since thy death,
    Nor do few fall, while yet I pen these lines.
140 My dear, dear boy, if spirits such as thine,
    When disembody'd [*sic*] are allow'd to roam,
    And view what's passing in this nether world;
    This world of follies, miseries, and vice,
    Chequer'd with virtues to bate those ills;
    If such thy privilege, do thou descend,
    And, on my pillow, often take thy seat;
    There whisper in my ear those accents sweet,
    Which oft have thrill'd my soul with pure delight,
    When sounding interjective "Oh!" or else
150 "Papa, mama," and other tender words,
    Of easy utterance to an infant's tongue.
       If no such privilege belong to thee,
    Then let me hope that Fancy will supply
    Thy spiritual presence, and the joy of night
    Yield consolations for the woes of day:
    For woeful ever will the time appear
    Which took thee hence to move in other sphere.
       My darling boy, thy name I shall not state,
    But ne'er forget thee till the day of fate.
160 If sense be perfect, in the hour of death
    Thy name I'll utter, with my latest breath;
    And say, "I come, to join thee with the bless'd,
    "In scenes of bliss; pure, everlasting rest."
       A father's feelings rapidly thus penn'd,
    In hopes of doing good; he here must end.

The People (1817), 305–308. An unusual poem in any context but especially in a radical journal at a politically explosive moment, this is a long and moving lament of a father for his dead child in blank verse, for the most part; it has a political protest section (ll. 116–33), which is perhaps why the editor included the poem—unless, of course, the poet and the editor are one and the same.
    Take him for all in all, I ne'er shall look upon his like again (inscription): *Hamlet* act 1, scene 2, line 187.
    (ll. 63–64): Matt. 18: 1–6.

Rebirth of Radicalism

An Englishman's Domestic View of his Political situation, Addressed to the Partner of his Bosom.   R. W[edderburn].

O! not a kiss!—not one be giv'n
Till joy those eyes can raise!
Go, change thy love—go, vow to heav'n,
Till earth sees happier days!

When first that hand in mine,
The mutual help was there;
And when this heart I pressed to thine,
It throbb'd not with despair.

But now no help—no toil can serve;
Some Demon's touch is here;
Industry shrinks through every nerve,
And withers in its sphere.

And O! this heart feels th' icy shaft;—
'Tis sick, it's full tide's o'er;
And Slavr'y's [sic] bitter, bitter draught
Chills curdled at its core.

Yet when Reflection tells, who chain,
Who our high hopes controul,
The hot blood boils through ev'ry vein,
And scalds this recreant soul.

O how I loathe their mean command,—
My own base, abject fall!
*The vile fool's word—the coward's hand
Have stript us of our all.*

Earth's fairest gifts once kiss'd thy side,
Once made profusion thine;
And honor—independence—pride—
All freemen hope—were mine.

But now whole ages' toils we lose;
With *birthright* all are fled,
And he who weds a maid now woos
Dishonor to his bed.

The People

What! shall we bring new slaves to light—
New creeping, cringing souls,
That mark'd—that badg'd shall glut the sight
Of lux'ry, as it rolls?

Shall innocents of us be born—
Cast where seduction leads—
To beg that charitable scorn
40 *That poisons, as it feeds?*

Shall I on mine, so lov'd, instil
What slaves and despots teach—
To learn that *Law* which Tyrants will,
That *God*, whom Courtiers preach?

Fathers! ye gave me blood—not chains,—
Blood free thro' ages past;
And it shall down through freemen's veins,
Or mine shall be the last!

For this, thee, Fair! he leaves who loves,
50 Love more than slaves dare feel—
I seek the car, thro' tears[,] that moves,
That crushes with its wheel.

Should I sit smiling at the board
'Neath our new robe of shame,
And loll like Helen's guilty lord,
'Till Ilion's wrapt in flame?

Rouse!—rouse! we all! O, swell the blast!
O Home!—Oh Country dear!
The Rubicon's long pause is past,
60 And Caesar's bands are here.

For this did England's voice implore,
When wing'd with her alarms,
We fled our homes—we throng'd the shore,
And slept but on our arms?

Was it that while we stay'd the hand
Arm'd with a Xerxes' might,
At home should rise a *trait'rous* band
To rob us of each right?

Rebirth of Radicalism

    While pow'r impell'd—while wealth decoy'd
70 This pow'r—this wealth to serve,
    Ours have been plunder'd—ours destroy'd,
    And we turn'd forth to starve.

    Our blood-bought compact traitors tore,
    And will and pow'r unchain'd;
    Nor home, nor hearth is sacred more—
    Our homes, our hearths are stain'd.

    Crouch we beneath the venal tribe?
    Crouch we the lofty wing?
    Ask we the perjur'd for his bribe,
80 The serpent for his sting?

    Deep is the grave where traitor's [sic] fall;
    High is the block prepar'd—
    O! Hampden—Russell—Sydney—all!
    Your manes shall be heard.

    Freedom!—no more—go, voiceless bleed,
    Ye abject, suppliant, meek!
    Again we meet at Runimede,
    Where more than tongues shall speak.

    Till then farewell the festive board;
90 Each joy—each social pow'r!
    Can Freemen when enslav'd afford
    For mirth one tainted hour?

    For me while law—while freedom sleeps,
    No friend henceforth I know:
    No friend henceforth but him who weeps,
    But him who feels his woe.

    Th' applauding theatre—the stroll—
    The feast—the shew's decoy—
    The pipe—the dance—th' inspiring bowl—
100 The thoughtless, fruitless joy—

    These are the toys which tyrants give,
    The badges slaves admire,
    The despot gaudes, which freemen grieve—
    For tyrants which conspire!

    Since but for these—these all in all,
    True spoils of prostrate France,

The People

    The tyrant arm would nerveless fall,
    And wither at a glance.

    But ye who will be friends indeed,
110 Who hate this gilded keep;
    Come, let our hearts their fulness plead,
    And o'er our country weep.

    Yet *country!*—that's a name prescrib'd;—
    Come not in public stare;—
    Day and it's thousand eyes are brib'd,
    And perjury is there.

    But come ye, when the slavish crowd
    Sleep on and dream their woes,
    Come mantled in the midnight shroud,
120 And cloak'd from midnight foes!

    With silent tread and cautious pause;—
    Whisper not to the air,
    Lest the dark hand that near us draws,
    Should catch us in the snare!

    Our fathers' spirits guard the way—
    Now to our shrine repair;
    And let us ere th' approach of day
    On Britain's altar swear,

    Swear not by heav'n or broken creeds,
130 Less heav'n consume our tongues;
    Like Brutus! swear by her who bleeds!—
    Swear by your country's wrongs!

    Will ye for her?—for England dear,
    Her laws—her ev'ry good—
    'Tis treason dark—some Reynold's fear—
    Let's sign us in our blood.

    And O! may *her* deep, crying wounds—
    Hers, whose dread hour is nigh,
    Whose freedom this dark deed re-founds,
140 Be heal'd without a sigh.

    But if no balm—if still the crest
    Be raised of scorpion pow'rs,—
    May we then never, never rest,
    'Till all her shrines be ours.

S[t]ill may we toil—still fly repose
'Till ours the patriot meed;
Nor think this blood too freely flows
Our country's rights to feed.

The scaffold thrones the Freeman bold;
150   Let wrath—let bolts be hurl'd;—
Him nations from afar behold;—
He dies before a world.

His blood for prostrate man he sheds;
'Tis shar'd from pole to pole;—
His spirit thro' the nations spreads,
And rises with his soul!

The People (1817), 423–26. The militance, anti-religious views, and socio-economic radicalism all would seem to indicate that R. W. was Robert Wedderburn, Spencean radical, son of a black slave. (For Wedderburn, see McCalman ch. 3 & 7; Chase ch. 4 & 5; Hone ch. 6.) The Stoic repudiation of ideologically tainted pleasures was part of the structure of feeling current in French Revolutionary Jacobinism, something still creditable with Wedderburn. A different, shorter version of this poem was published in *Sherwin's Political Register* (1817), 1: 238–40.

(*ll. 55–56*): Helen of Troy's "guilty lord" was Paris, who stole Helen from Menelaus, starting the Trojan War.

(*ll. 59–60*): Julius Caesar (100–44 BCE) crossed the Rubicon as he attacked the Roman Republic.

(*l. 66*): Xerxes (d. 460 BCE) was the Persian king who invaded Greece.

(*l. 83*): John Hampden, Lord William Russell (1639–1683; *DNB*), and Algernon Sidney were all republican heroes martyred in the struggle against absolute monarchy.

(*l. 87*): Runnymede was where King John (1167?-1216) reluctantly accepted the Magna Carta.

(*l. 103*): Gaudes are worthless ornaments.

3. *The Forlorn Hope / Axe Laid to the Root* (1817)

This ephemeral, inexpensive (1½ pence) periodical of 1817 was printed by A. Seale, and published by C. Jennison until Robert Wedderburn took over as publisher (see McCalman 69–72; 126–27). There is a poem, usually by Wedderburn himself, at the end of each issue of this Spencean journal whose flamboyant militance can be glimpsed from the periodical's full original title: *The "Forlorn Hope," or A Call to the Supine, To rouse from Indolence, and assert Public Rights*. This was later changed to the no less uncompromising *Axe Laid to the Root, or a Fatal Blow to the Oppressors*. "Axe Laid to the Root" is a biblical allusion (Matt. 3: 10; Lk. 3: 9), and Horne Tooke's slogan for radical reform in 1796 was to put an axe to the Tree of Corruption (M. Dorothy George, *English Caricature. 1793–1832* [Oxford: Clarendon P, 1959], 230). For Wedderburn, see Chase ch. 4 & 5; Hone ch. 6; McCalman ch. 3 & 7.

THE DESPONDING NEGRO   R. W[EDDERBURN].

On Afric's wide plains where the lion now roaring,
When freedom stalks forth the vast desert exploring,
I was dragg'd from my hut and enchain'd as a slave,
In a dark floating dungeon upon the salt wave.
                CHORUS.
Spare a half-penny, spare a half-penny,
O spare a half, [sic] penny to a poor Negro boy.

Toss'd on the wide main, I all wildly despairing
Burst my chains, rush'd on deck with my eye balls wide glaring,
When the light'ning's dread blast, struck the inlets of day,
10   And its glorious bright beam sent for ever away.
                Spare, &c.

The despoiler of man his prospect thus losing
Of gain by my sale, not a blind bargain chusing,
As my value compar'd with my keeping was light,
Had me dash'd overboard in the dead of the night.
                Spare, &c.

And, but for a bark, to Britannia's coast bound then,
All my cares by that plunge in the deep had been drown'd then,
But by moonlight deferred was dash'd from the wave,
20   And reluctantly robb'd of a watery grave.
                Spare, &c.

How disastrous my fate, freedom's ground though I tread now,
Torn from home, wife and children, I wander for bread now,
While seas roll between us which ne'er can be cross'd,
And hope's distant glimmering in darkness is lost.
                Spare, &c.

But of minds foul and fair, when the judge and the ponderer,
Shall restore light and rest to the blind and the wanderer,
The European's deep dye may out-rival the foe,
30   And the soul of an Ethiop prove whiter than snow.
                Spare, &c.

Forlorn Hope (1817), 26–27. The poem comes at the end of a political essay by Wedderburn who protests against, among other things, slavery and religious hypocrisy. Wedderburn himself was a black from Jamaica, son of a slave. The poem is probably modelled on William Cowper's "The Negro's Complaint" (1789), the often reprinted anti-slavery poem. On blacks living in England in the early nineteenth century, see Walvin.

THE NEGRO BOY SOLD FOR A WATCH   R. W[EDDERBURN].

When thirst of gold enslaves the mind,
   And selfish views alone bear sway,
Man turns a savage to his kind,
   And blood and rapine mark the way,
        Alas! for this poor simple toy,
        I sold the weeping negro boy.

His father's hope, his mother'[s] pride,
   Tho' black, yet comely to their view,
I tore him helpless from their side,
   I gave him to a ruffian crew,
        To fiends that Afric's coast annoy,
        I sold the weeping negro boy.

In isles that deck the western waves,
   The unhappy youth was doom'd to dwell,
A poor forlorn insulted slave.
   A beast that Christians buy and sell,
        And yet for this same simple toy,
        I sold the weeping negro boy.

May he who walks upon the wind,
   Whose voice in thunder's heard on high,
Who doth the raging tempest bind,
   And wings the lightening thro' the sky,
        Forgive the wretch, who, for a toy,
        Could sell the guiltless negro boy.

Forlorn Hope (1817), 27. This poem was printed below the previous poem. Like much other anti-slavery verse, this appeals to the sentimental pathos of the broken-up family and redefines key words like "savage" and "Christian," and key concepts like humanness and property. As in the previous poem, blackness is revalued positively, with biblical echoes (ll. 7–8).

THE AFRICAN[']S COMPLAINT ON BOARD A SLAVE SHIP   R. W[EDDERBURN].

Trembling, naked, wounded, sighing,
   On dis winged house I stand,
Dat with poor black man is flying,
   [F]ar away from his own land.

Forlorn Hope/Axe Laid to Root

Fearful water all aronnd [*sic*] me!
    Strange de sight on every hand,
Hurry, noise, and shouts confound me,
    When I look for Negro land.

Every thing I see affrights me,
    Nothing I can understand,
With de scourges white man fight me,
    None of dis in Negro land.

Here de white man beat de black man,
    'Till he's sick and cannot stand,
Sure de black be eat by white man,
    Will not go to white man's land.

Here in chains poor black man lying,
    Put so tick, dey on us stand,
Ah! with heat and smells wer'e [*sic*] dying,
    'Twas not dus in Negro land.

Dere we've room and air and freedom,
    Dere our little dwellings stand,
Families, and rice to feed 'em,
    Oh! I weep for Negro land.

Joyful dere before de doors.
    Play our children hand in hand;
Fresh de fields, and sweet de flow'rs,
    Green de hills in Negro land.

Dere I often go when sleeping,
    See my kindred round me stand,
Hear 'em toke—den wak in weeping,
    Dat I've lost my Negro land.

Dere my black love arms were round me,
    De whole night, not like dis band,
Close dey held, but did not wound me,
    O! I die for Negro land.

De had traders stole and sold me,
    Den was put in iron band,
When I'm dead they cannot hold me,
    Soon I'll be in black man land.

Forlorn Hope (1817), 32. This, like the two prior poems, utilizes the dramatic monologue form for the anti-slavery message. This is even more clearly modeled after William Cowper's "The Negro's Complaint" (1789), as Wedderburn uses the same metrical form. Unlike Cowper, Wedderburn tries to represent the speech of the captive black.

[NO TITLE]   [R. WEDDERBURN]

1.
Britons! who have oft contended
   'Midst the fields of victory,
All your glorious duties ended,
   Claim your birth-right——to be free.

2.
Will you see those charters perish,
   Bought by many a patriot's grave,
Those just rights no longer cherish,
   Which your fathers died to save.

3.
Shall the land where Sidney flourish'd
   Bend beneath oppression's rod,
Shall the land which Ham[p]den nourish'd
   Bow before a tyrant's nod.

4.
Here our Swiss their rights asserting,
   'Neath oppression scorn'd to bow;
Shall their sons their cause deserting,
   Basely quail to tyrants now.

5.
See! your fathers' shades approach me,
   Bid me lead you forth to fight;
See their frowning brows approach me,
   Thus to yeild [sic] their well-earned right.

6.
Shades revered! no more I linger——
   Haste the glorious call obey;
Britons see! with gory finger,
   Favouring spirits point the way.

7.
They who fell in fields of glory,
   They who died to make you free,

They who live in deathless story,
  Point the way to victory.

8.
'Midst the fight shall they attend us,
  Who for freedom fought and fell,
Hovering near, from harms defend us,
  Guarded by a sacred spell.

9.
They who burst the chain enslaving,
  They who curb'd the tyrant's power,
They who died their country saving,
  Gaurd [*sic*] their sons in battle's hour.

10.
Tyrants tremble! Freedom call us,
  Justice lifts the awful scale,
The tyrant's frown no more appals us,
  Justice—freedom—must prevail.

Axe to the Root (1817), 46–48. The poem is introduced by a "C. T.," who writes that the poem was supposed to have been written by the younger James or "Dr." Watson (1766–1838; B&G), with the intention of "reciting them at the head of the rioters, when about to lead them from Spa-Fields to the Tower." The Watsons were leaders of the Spencean Philanthropists, the ultra-radical group centered in London, formed in 1814, and very active even into the 1820s. The Watsons were the leaders of the left-wing of the Spenceans, with Thomas Evans (1763–?; B&G) leading the moderate wing. The Spa Fields riot was a turning point, in that it exacerbated the breach in the Reform movement between radicals and moderates, and precipitated government repression. However, since the poem is so like Wedderburn's "An Englishman's Domestic View of his Political Situation," in the *People*, it seems likely the poem's author is Wedderburn. For the Spa Fields riot of December, 1816, see Thompson 1963, 633–36; Hone 264–66.

Even a radical Spencean song, whose intention is to arouse a revolutionary crowd, appeals to the past for its authority to rebel.

(st. 3): Algernon Sidney; John Hampden.

4. *Sherwin's Political Register* (1817–1818)

One of the major popular (selling for 2 pence) journals of the Regency, the *Political Register* ran from April 5, 1817, until August, 1819, when Richard Carlile took over the journal from W. T. Sherwin (1799–18??; B&G) and changed its name to the bolder *The Republican*. The journal was generally Painite in orientation, and Sherwin kept the focus from becoming narrowly sectarian or exclusively the mouthpiece of the editor. For Sherwin, see Hone 284–86. For Carlile, see Wiener.

On the New and Unconstitutional Legislative Acts passed by the Lords, the Commons, and the Regent

H. W.

O injured Land! that Englishmen must call
Their country still—how I lament thy fall!
Shrunk from the splendour of thy ancient fame,
Thy ancient freedom, even freedom's name.—
Not nobly vanquished by a foreign foe
Victorious, but by many a doubtful blow;—
No,—thine it was the mighty to subdue,
As well thy field attests, fam'd Waterloo!
By native force, dishonoured art, alone,
Thy rights are crush'd, thy glory overthrown;
And those thou seest depart like beams of light
Fast waning in the shadows of the night;
With scarce a struggle of the heart to save,
The laws our fathers lov'd, and nature gave.

But yet the page of history remains,
And those who read it will not breathe in chains;
The page of Britain! where in cherish'd lines
A host of patriot names, immortal shines;
Where Alfred, Hampden, Sidney, Russel, Penn,
Still bid us live or die—a race of MEN!
And O shall we, who call such men our Sires,
Disgrace their memories, and renounce their fires?
Shall we, to please some petty Lordlings, lie,
With prostrate necks, a recreant progeny?
Shall we by no high-soul'd example teach
Mankind—that freedom is within their reach?
Or are we now both slaves and tyrants grown,
Despoiling others['] rights to lose our own?
'Tis even so,—our breaths we now must draw
According, not to Nature, but to Law.
If thou art not immured in some dark cell,
But in the open face of heaven may dwell,
Praise, duly praise the great Omnipotent!—
But thank L——d S——m——h too or his consent.
Yet while we thus in mean existence crawl,
Have we no prowess? speak Iberia! Gaul!
Why rules a Ferdinand? a Louis, why?

       Beneath what star? what baleful destiny?
       Oh! slaves ourselves, congenial tasks we find,
40   And hope to fetter UNIVERSAL MIND!
         Beloved England! take that name once more,
       It tells me of a land I did adore;
       A spot of earth how dear in my esteem!
       Like the reality of blessed dream!
       But now such dark and hideous change is wrought,
       I almost spurn thee from my very thought—
       Yet that can never be—thou dost remain
       Too close about my heart-strings and my brain.
       No more!—but, mark, in one convulsive hour,
50   Shall perish both the system and its power;
       And thou again both lov'd and honour'd be,
       The fairest land that rises from the sea.

Sherwin's Political Register (1817), 1: 79–80. The passage of the repressive legislation of 1817 provokes H. W. to protest in ways that are typical of radical culture and that can be viewed as paradoxically conservative: the government is violating the true nature of the national identity, which is rooted in a libertarian tradition (from Alfred to Penn). The ruling order, then, and not the radical reformers, has rebelled against the true "constitution" of the country. The poem is idealistic, hopeful, patriotic—tonal qualities we will not see much in the verse written after the Peterloo Massacre two years later.

(l. 19): The only unusual member of the sacred patriots is William Penn (1644–1718; *DNB*), who is actually more famous as the Quaker leader and settler of Pennsylvania. The others are conventional patriotic heroes: King Alfred; John Hampden; Algernon Sidney; William Russell (1639–83; *DNB*). I suppose it is interesting who gets left off these typical lists: Oliver Cromwell (1599–1658; *DNB*), John Lilburne (1614?–57; *DNB*), Gerrard Winstanley (fl. 1648–52; *DNB*), Wat Tyler (d. 1381; *DNB*). That is, the lists are usually not as radical as they could be. Although sometimes included, John Milton is not mentioned very often.

(l. 34): As Home Secretary, Sidmouth (1757–1844; *DNB*) was responsible for the details of the repression and was accordingly unpopular.

(l. 37): The poet evokes recent monarchs who had been returned to power after revolutions had failed: Ferdinand VII (1784–1833) of Spain and Louis XVIII (1755–1824) of France.

On seeing in a List of New Music *The Waterloo Waltz*   R. S[HORTER].

A moment pause, ye British Fair,
    While pleasure's phantom ye pursue;

And say, if sprightly dance or air
   Suit with the name of Waterloo?
      Awful was the victory!
      Chasten'd should the triumph be;
      'Midst the laurels she has won,
      Britain mourns for many a Son.

Veil'd in clouds the morning rose;
   Nature seem'd to mourn the day
Which consign'd before its close,
   Thousands to their kindred clay;
      How unfit for courtly ball,
      Or the giddy festival,
      Was the grim and ghastly view
      Ere evening closed on Waterloo!

See the Highland warrior rushing
   Firm in danger on the foe,
Till the life-blood warmly gushing,
   Lays the plaided hero low!
      His native pipe's accustom'd sound,
      'Mid war's infernal concert drown'd,
        Cannot soothe his last adieu,
      Or wake his sleep on Waterloo.

Chasing o'er the Cuirassier
   See the foaming charger flying,
Trampling in his wild career
   All alike, the dead and dying.
      See the bullets through his side
      Answer'd by the spouting tide;
      Helmet, horse and rider too,
      Roll on bloody Waterloo!

Shall scenes like these the dance inspire?
   Or wake the enlivening notes of mirth?
O! shiver'd be the recreant lyre
   That gave the base idea birth?
      Other sounds, I ween were there,
      Other music rent the air!
      Other waltz the warriors knew
      When they *closed* on Waterloo.
Forbear till time with lenient hand,
   Has sooth'd the pang of recent sorrow;

And let the picture distant stand,
  The softening hue of years to borrow!
    When *our* race has passed away,
    Hands unborn may wake the lay,
    And give to joy alone the view
    Of Britain's fame at Waterloo.

Sherwin's Political Register (1817), 1: 303–4. Publisher of the *Theological and Political Comet* (1819), Shorter was a radical and a deist. This particular poem protests against the moral callousness of the genteel in their appropriating Waterloo for trivial purposes.
  (l. 25): A cuirassier is a French cavalryman with cuirass (breastplate).

MONOPOLY   ALFRED

Crown Patronage has so increas'd,
And has so much the people fleec'd;
That, starved and naked, millions moan,
While Crown dependants feast alone;
Who in the very face of day,
Their spoils exultingly display,
While police officers attend,
The glittering plunder to defend,
Lest starving subjects should be led,
10 To ease the pamper'd and well fed,
Of what they might and ought to share,
With those who're driven to despair:
How different this from Alfred's reign!
When purses safely might remain
In public highways, night and day,
Without their being stol'n away:
But now another scene appears;
Behold a Nation drown'd in tears!
By the abuse of power and wealth,
20 By official fraud and stealth,
By the gross vices of the great,
By foreign bloodsuckers of state,
By robbing many of their due,
To satiate a vicious few;
By pensions undeserved, and spent
'Mong strangers on the continent.
By sinecures withheld by peers,
While thousands starve, absorb'd in tears;

By lack of commerce and of trade,
30 By the sad havoc vice has made,
By undue influence of the Crown,
By state affairs turned upside down,
By the rapid augmentation
Of the *poor* of our own Nation,
While we're generous to excess,
To foreign Despots in distress;
Thus to *Monopoly* we owe
Our present unexampled woe:
St. Stephen[']s gave this monster birth,
40 Whose presence chased away all mirth;
Thus those who held the Nation's purse,
By treachery proved our greatest curse.

Sherwin's Political Register (1817), 1: 320. "Alfred" could be the *Medusa*'s Thomas Davison (d. 1826; B&G), who published after Peterloo the short-lived *London Alfred; or People's Recorder*. The post-war economic crisis was often interpreted in terms like these, putting the blame on the indulgence of the most wealthy and powerful.

(*l. 39*): St. Stephen's was the locale for Parliament.

Appeal to Englishmen   S. R.

The cause which nerved a Brutus' arm,
To strike a tyrant with alarm;
The cause for which brave Hampden died,
For which the gallant Tell defied,
A tyrant's insolence and pride.
The mighty cause of Sparta's glory;
And Athens, far renowned in story;—
O may that same cause steel our hearts,
To act the Grecian, Roman parts;
10 Undaunted may we claim our right,
Though toiling hard in glorious fight;
And if we firm, united be,
No power on earth 'gainst liberty,
Can aught avail, or chain the free.
  Shall we unworthy of our race,
The contest shun and meet disgrace;
Far o'er the ocean see the palm,
Won by Columbia's infant arm:
Yet tamely bear th' outrageous sway,

20 Of that arch-demon C——!
    No! rather bravely let us all
    With sword in hand, undaunted fall,
    Be firm, and never quit the field,
    Nor unto K——'s our Freedom yield.
    But trust the force by nature given
    And leave the issue unto Heaven!
      And though some years Oppression's chain,
    May bind the world and freedom's flame;
    Yet still the destined hour is nigh
30 When o'er the earth her name shall fly,
    And tyranny beneath her feet subjected lie.

Sherwin's Political Register (1817), 2: 64. The poet gathers authority and validation for revolutionary violence from a variety of sources, Classical, English, even American (l. 18). There is no appeal whatsoever to religious authority, which is in keeping with the general deist outlook of the journal.

(*l. 1*): Lucius Junius Brutus (fl. late 6th century BCE) was a famous figure in republican writing for deposing the last Tarquin, instituting the Roman republic, and showing his republican fervor by condemning to death his own sons who conspired to restore the Tarquins.

(*l. 3*): John Hampden.

(*l. 4*): William Tell was a legendary thirteenth/fourteenth century Swiss hero who resisted Austrian oppression and who became a figure in nationalist ideologies. Schiller's 1804 play, *Wilhelm Tell*, was typical.

(*l. 20*): Robert Castlereagh was the much-loathed, at least by radicals, Foreign Secretary.

(*l. 24*): Kings.

THE TOPIC   A. D[AVENPORT].

When the National Debt, which is ten hundred millions!—
  Shall all be rubbed off like a public-house score;
When vile placemen shall cease, and all pensioned villains,
  The land of Great Britain shall sorrow no more.

When the Pitt-coined paper* on which we have stranded,
  Abolished shall be, and illusion be o'er;

---

*Mr. Pitt, by causing the Bank to stop cash payments, created that enormous amount of paper money that is now in circulation, and which has principally contributed to the ruined state we are now in. I would recommend to the Ministry, in order to prevent a National bankruptcy, to cause so many bank notes to be issued as would amount to the value of the whole National debt,—pay the fundholders their whole demand, both principal, and interest, and then stop paper payments. This would at least be paying them in their own coin!

> When the armies of war shall in peace be disbanded;
>   The land of Great Britain shall languish no more.
>
> When reform shall have purged that base House of Commons,
>   And the purchase of seats in the Senate be o'er!
> When power to the standard of Justice is summoned,
>   The land of Great Britain will murmur no more.
>
> When the long Civil List, shall be somewhat curtailed,
>   And useless expenditure gave to the poor;
> When reason, and truth, have o'er folly prevailed,
>   The land of Great Britain shall wish for no more.

Sherwin's Political Register (1817), 2: 106. "A. D." was the often used signature for Allen Davenport, shoemaker, poet, and radical activist. Publishing his first poem in 1814, familiar with Spence's "system" from 1805, Davenport belonged to the Evans or "respectable" wing of the Spencean socialists, was active in trade union activities, and first entered politics in 1818–19. His poetry was widely published in the radical periodicals from the Regency to the Chartist period; indeed, he was an active Chartist, too. See his *The Life and Literary Pursuits of Allen Davenport* (London: G. Hancock, 1845; rpt. NY & London: Garland, 1986); Chase ch. 4 & 5; McCalman ch. 9.

Davenport's analysis in this poem follows fairly closely that of William Cobbett in linking war, domestic oppression, the national debt, and paper currency. The cure-all is parliamentary reform. In fact, however, Davenport was more radical than his Cobbett-like analysis would indicate.

ODE ON THE ANNIVERSARY OF THOMAS PAINE'S BIRTH-DAY, JANUARY THE 29TH, 1818

CLIO RICKMAN

> Shall laureate Bards, in fulsome strain,
> Applaud the mad, the base, the vain,
>   And sing of EMPERORS and KINGS;—
> Apostate Bards—the SOUTHEYS vile,
> The dire disgrace of Britain's isle,
>   Like those they hail—detested, hateful things.
>
> Shall knaves praise knaves—and we not laud
> A name the good and wise applaud,
>   Of every land and clime;
> 10 Shall we not raise the heartfelt strain
> To sing of Thee, immortal PAINE,
>   In head and heart sublime.

Shall the fell troublers of mankind,
Who live to scourge us and to blind;
   Who wade in sin and blood,—
Shall such find knaves to sing their worth,
The curse of man and plagues of earth,
   Reverse of all that's good:
Who live to afflict their fellow-men, and throw
20   Around them crime, oppression, want, and woe.

And shall not HE, whose truth-fraught pen,
Employed to serve his fellow-men,
   Produced the "RIGHTS OF MAN,"
Whose principles, unerring, true,
Were meant CORRUPTION to subdue,—
   Justice alone his plan.

Shall HE not claim the votive lay,
Who gave COLUMBIA perfect day,
   Whose precepts—wise, discreet,
30 Would drive injustice from the earth,
Would give its children a new birth,
   And make their bliss complete.

Yes, ONE FREE BARD!—though he not soars
Those heights sublime which he adores,
   By TRUTH alone inspired;
Thy natal day, great PAINE shall hail,
Who feels that VIRTUE will prevail,
   And rear on earth her throne;
That throne, whenever reared, and Man is free
40 The world shall owe, immortal PAINE, to THEE!
Yes, ONE FREE BARD, who loved thee well, and long
Shall give thy natal day the heart-dictated song.

The time will come, when thy illustrious name
   Shall loved and reverenced be throughout the world;
When grateful Nations shall, with loud acclaim,
   Hail their deliverer PAINE! who hurled
Priestcraft and Kingcraft down,—who led the way
To incorruption—oped the glorious day
Of light and life to man, and made him be,
50 A creature blest, beneficent and free!

Shameless or ignorant must be that breast,
   Which dares abuse the man who proudly stood;
Of every talent every worth possest,
   Immutable, and just, and wise, and good!

Is wit a quality to charm the soul?
   Is genius dear? is science to be loved?
Is reason, whose omnipotent controul,
   Man's highest, noblest boast, to be approved?

Is all divine philosophy, held forth
   As every good dispensing to our race,
Spread philanthropy and taste on earth,
   And raising man above the vile and base?

Are strong, romantic, rich poetic powers,—
   Fancy, that scatters all the graces round—
And anecdote, that gilds convivial hours—
   Talents acute, impressive, and profound?
Are these held dear, and by the Bard and Sage[,]
   Reverenced[,] esteemed, and praised, from pole to pole?
Then PAINE must live in every future age,
   And IMMORTALITY his name enroll.

Such were the qualities of heart and head
Of him who stemmed Corruption, and instead,
A system planned with every blessing fraught,
Beyond what other Sages reached in thought;
For all, however great, to PAINE must yield;
They fade like stars that quit Heaven's azure field,
When bright the beams of morning blaze o'er earth,
And nature hails the day with songs of mirth.

The "AGE OF REASON" yet shall be—
Justice shall rule, and error flee,
Before his pure philosophy;
And crime and cant shall pass away,
And TRUTH emit her glorious ray;
Then unblasphemed the GREAT SUPREME shall shine
His BOOK CREATION!—holy, clear, divine.
Right thinking shall promote a conduct true,
And individuals rectitude pursue;
Then through the world this maxim shall be shewn,
"That Peace, O VIRTUE! Peace is all thy own."

90   The time will come, when led, great PAINE, by THEE!
     WISDOM, and LIGHT, and LIFE shall begin below;
When man, led on by COMMON SENSE, shall be,
From vile, from wicked erring systems, free,
     From slavery, superstition, crime and woe:
Then happiness alone shall reign on earth,
And every heart and tongue declare thy worth;
Man's grateful sons with rapture shout thy name,
And hand it down to EVERLASTING FAME!

Sherwin's Political Register (1818), 2: 184–86. Clio Rickman was a bookseller, poet, political writer, biographer and popularizer of Paine.

   Rickman, in the poem's last section, makes of Paine's deism something much more religious than Paine ever did. Sherwin's periodical frequently advertised Paine's works, so this tribute is hardly accidental.

   (l. 23): *The Rights of Man* (1791–92) was Paine's answer to Burke's *Reflections on the Revolution in France* (1790).

   (l. 79): *The Age of Reason* (1795; 1807) articulated Paine's deist views.

   (l. 92): *Common Sense* (1776) defended the American Revolution.

TO ENGLISHMEN   M.

When the dark-visaged thunders the welkin deform,
And the red-pinioned lightnings are leading the storm,
No motion of terror my Spirit can break,
Though the heavens recoil and the universe quake!

Let the "Tyrants of Man" strew the continent o'er,
With the wreck of all nations, and bathe it in gore!
Let their swords glow with death 'neath the curtains of night,
Still my *Spirit* should feel no sensations of fright!

Though son against father erect a foul hand,
10   And a civil commotion rush fierce through the land,
Unshocked at the scene, still my Spirit would rise,
Leave the world to its guilt, and inherit the skies!

Were nature to sicken, and all the things give way,—
Were the stars and the lights of the world to decay,—
Were this fabric sublime, circumvented with fire,
Still my Spirit would smile, mounting higher and higher!

'Tis not the dark picture of slaughter and woe,
Nor the deathly career of the continent-foe,
That excites in my breast those sensations of dread,
20   Which the tyrants at home so industriously spread!

But when I behold a brave people recoil
From the duties of man, and relinquish the soil
To a horde of State-jugglers, who laugh at their guilt,
Can the mind be astonished if blood should be spilt?

When the highways attest that Corruption's abroad,—
When the patriots themselves are detected in fraud,—
When the strumpets of ROYALTY roll through the town,
Where the beggar scarce finds him a seat to sit down!

Then, indeed, could my vision, with savageness fired,
Delight in beholding the People inspired!
Then, indeed, could mine arm, growing furiously warm,
Lead the chariot of death o'er the wrecks of the storm!

Woe, woe to that country where Liberty's hushed,
Where the People are Slaves, and their genius is crushed,
Trampled down by the feet of a blood-thirsty race,
To Religion,—to Reason,—to Brutes, a disgrace!

Yes, woe to that land wheresoever it be,
Where Corruption is nursed, and the Press is not free!
Whether England or France can these frailties deny,
Let those who can judge of the question—reply!!

Sherwin's Political Register (1818), 2: 330.

England, At the commencement of the Reign of George III. 1760. [N. A.]

(*Tune, "Nancy Dawson."*)

Sixpence a gallon was the bread,
When first our crown graced George's head,
And good ox-beef was sold, 'tis said,
   At three ba-bees a pound sir;
Fat pigs and poultry, calves and sheep,
Were then so very—very cheap,
A jubilee poor folk could keep,
   Aye, just the whole year round, sir!

Nine weekly bobs paid lab'rer's hire,
For turf and wood nought cost for fire,
And such as did pit-coal desire,
   For bushels thirty-six sir,

But sixteen shillings had to pay,
And with the measure then, they say,
They might as well be hanged as play,
   Their little dirty tricks, sir.

Each workman, then, with candle-light
Could cheer his humble cot at night,
For, with five half-pence then he might,
   A pound of candles buy, sir!
A Sunday's hat one shilling cost,
His shoes but half-a-crown at most,
And all of good warm clothes could boast,
   And beer to drink, when dry, sir!

Then trade was brisk and taxes few,
Mechanics had enough to do,
And so had every tradesman too,
   In every occupation;
In every clime, on every coast,
Great Britain could of commerce boast,
And of the nations happiest most,
   Most happy was this nation!

Then snug small farms o'erspread the soil,
And plenty crowned Britannia's isle,
For providence did kindly smile,
   On England and her cause, sir;
Her happy people heart and hand,
Formed one united patriot band,
And swore to guard their native land,
   Their *liberties* and *laws*, sir!

Though British soldiers were but few,
They always did her foes subdue;
And beat them one to ten ('tis true,)
   Nay, twice that odds, her tars, sir!
They fought to conquer or to die,
No power on earth could make them fly,
For tars and soldiers then did vie,
   To shorten bloody wars, sir!

Sherwin's Political Register (1818), 3: 63–64. This song ends so abruptly that perhaps the editor left out a section. Interesting as social history, the poem represents a William Cobbett-like lament for the Old England that has passed away.
  (l. 4): Ba-bees: if "bob" is signfied, the price would be three shillings.

Sonnet.
Written with a Pencil upon one of the Pillars of Covent Garden Church, after the late Election for Westminster.

CLIO RICKMAN

No more the scene of folly, guilt, and noise,
    The balderdash harangue, and lying speech:
Of madding PARTY's wild disordered joys,
    And all the crimes that Faction's agents teach.

Here one may safely wander;—but the soul,
    With horror contemplates the spot of strife;
And inly asks, if REASON's bright controul
    Shall ne'er to man give liberty and life?

Shall ne'er PHILOSOPHY lay ERROR low,
    And man enlightened, dignify the name;
Truth each despot system overthrow,
    And Virtue, only, constitute his fame?

Yes! when the PRESS shall give, without control,
PAINE and CONDORCET's works, from pole to pole.

Sherwin's Political Register (1818), 3: 159. The election to which Rickman refers is probably the 1818 Westminster election which was won by Sir Samuel Romilly (1757–1818; *DNB*) and Sir Francis Burdett, but the divisions between radical and moderate reformers almost resulted in a Tory victory (see Hone 279–88). The sonnet suggests that Rickman's own political commitments were made in the 1790s, and that he had a difficult time identifying with the mass politics of the Regency, far removed from the Godwinian emphasis on reason and philosophy.
    (*l. 14*): Thomas Paine was Rickman's political hero; Condorcet (1743–94), a philosopher and revolutionary politician, whose particular interest was public education, was imprisoned by the Jacobins, and died in jail.

Distress of the Poor;
A New Song.

G. TAYLOR

Tune—Derry Down.

The spinners of Manchester loudly complain
How toilsome their labour, how trifling their gain;
The hatters, the dyers, the weavers also,
Are starving with hunger you very well know.
        Derry Down, &c.

We fondly did hope when the wars were all o'er,
That hunger and thirst we should never feel more,
But woeful experience shews us the reverse,
That the peace only served to complete our distress.

10 The widows' salt tears often dropp'd for the dead,
May now flow afresh for the loss of her bread;
Her fatherless children are starving also,
Is this a fit recompence, tell me, or no!

An adequate price for our labour we want,
But this our proud gentry never will grant;
So far they from striving our wrongs to redress,
They laugh at our sufferings, and mock our distress.

Your cringing, soliciting, never will do,
Too oft it has proved unsuccessful to you;
20 I could tell you a way to relieve your distress,
But I can't bring the words in to metre my verse.

But a word of advice I would give to you all,
Let no party spirit your bosoms enthral;
Religious divisions, forget them likewise,
Unite in the cause, and you're sure of the prize.

Sherwin's Political Register (1818), 3: 336. The Manchester poet records an early instance of industrial working-class discontent that finds political articulation. During the Regency this was a small aspect of the overall radicalism but by the 1830s it was much more signficant.

A Hint to the Congress   A. D[avenport].

Ye mighty monarchs! lords of all below!
We need not much enquire what made you so;
Legitimacy, and a right divine,
Makes all your councils and your actions shine;
Your awful voice is heard through every land;
Both peace and war await your dread command,
And, while like Gods you sit in high debate,
From you, the Nations round expect their fate;—
The task is yours to settle each dispute,
10 'Tis ours to bow,—to tremble, and be mute:
What would be wrong had plebeians been appointed
Is right in you, who are the Lord's anointed!

Should you decree that we 'gainst freedom fight,
Who can deny that you possess the right?
You have a right to order and ordain
That South Columbia shall submit to Spain;
And should the rebels set you at defiance,
And brave the thunder of the "holy alliance;"
Then you are further priviledged [sic] to command
20 That the Atlantic shall be turn'd to land!—
That without ships you may send armies over,
Meantime dispatch the Noble Lord to Dover,
With orders not to stop for tide, or weather
Till he has brought the Sovereigns* all together;
While this is going on, his lordship's agents
May first collect and then ship all the Regents;†
Should all this argument and wisdom fail,
The boroughmongers‡ must get under sail.
The Bank may issue out more bales of paper,
30 In order to prevent things getting cheaper.
You§ have a right to make those requisitions,
While People are content with your conditions.
But we possess one right;—pray do not jeer,
We have one little right, the thing is clear;
Should we resist the taxes!—yes, should we!
Then, after all, the Nations must be free;
Your pardon, mighty Kings, I see you tremble,
But we are not yet quite the *tout ensemble*;
I did not mean to put you in a fright,
40 I only said we have that little right,
To exercise it should we e'er incline,
Down goes your "holy leagues" and right divine!

Sherwin's Political Register (1818), 3: 383–84. This is typical Allen Davenport verse in that the colloquial diction is direct, clear, and succinct, while the political argument is carefully thought out. The occasion for the poem is the Congress of Aix-la-Chapelle where the so-called Holy Alliance engaged in diplomacy designed to suppress any moves toward democratic change anywhere, including South America (l. 16). The play on sovereigns and money, and the emphasis on paper money, reflect to an extent the influence of William Cobbett. For Davenport, see p. 206.

---

*The gold Sovereigns.
†The half Sovereigns, commonly called Regents.
‡The Five Shilling pieces, sometimes called Boroughmongers.
§The Sovereigns now assembled at Aix la Chapelle.

5. *The Mirror of Truth* (1817)

This Owenite publication was a one-shilling fortnightly periodical with hardly any poetry, dedicated as it was to promoting Owen's "plan." Later Owenite periodicals, most notably the *New Moral World* in the 1830s, were seriously engaged in literary and cultural matters. For Robert Owen (1771–1858; *DNB*) and the Owenite movement, see Gregory Claeys, *Citizens and Saints. Politics and Anti-Politics in Early British Socialism* (Cambridge: UP, 1989).

THE DEVIL'S THOUGHTS
PROFESSOR PORSON [S. T. COLERIDGE]

From his brimstone bed, at break of day,
    A walking the Devil was gone;
Just to look at his snug little farm the earth,
    And how his stock went on.

Over the hill and down the dale,
    He strutted along the plain;
And backward and forward he switched his long tail,
    Just as a gentleman switches his cane.

He saw a lawyer killing a viper,
    On a dunghill beside his stable;
"Ah! ah!" quoth the Devil, "this puts me in mind
    Of the story of Cain and Abel!"

He saw an apothecary, on a white horse,
    Ride by on his avocations;
Which put him in mind of his old friend
    Death in the Revelations.

He saw a cottage with a double coach-house,
    A cottage of gentility;
The sin of all sins which the Devil loves best,
    Is the pride that apes humility.

As he passed by the prison in Cold Bath Fields,
    He peep'd into a solitary cell;
And the Devil was pleased, for it gave him a hint
    For improving the dungeons of Hell.

He saw a turnkey in a trice,
    Fetter a troublesome blade;
"Numbly," quoth the Devil, "the fingers move,
    When a man is pleas'd with his trade."

He saw the same turnkey unfetter a man,
    With but little expedition;
Which put him in mind of the long debates
    On the Slave Trade Abolition!

He popp'd into a rich bookseller's shop—
    "Sir," says he, "you and I are of one college:
For myself, like a cormorant, once
    Sat perch'd on the tree of knowledge."

He saw a pig right rapidly,
    A down the river float;
The pig swam well, but every stroke
    Was cutting his own throat.

Old Nicholas groan'd, and switch'd his tail
    With joy and admiration,
As he thought of his own child, Victory,
    And her darling babe, Taxation!

General G——e's fiery face,
    He view'd with consternation;
And back to hell his way did take,
For the Devil he thought by a slight mistake,
    'Twas the general conflagration!!

The Mirror of Truth (1817), 2: 67–68. Richard Porson (1759–1808; *DNB*), the famous Cambridge classical scholar, did not write this poem, which was written by Samuel Coleridge, first published in the *Morning Post*, September 6, 1799, as "The Devil's Thoughts," and first included in Coleridge's collected works in 1828. (For the poem and a history of the text, see E. H. Coleridge 319–23.) This is particularly interesting because the *Morning Post* version had 14 stanzas and this one has 12, while the 1828 and 1829 versions have only 10, and the final version in 1834 has 17. There are variants in the text of the poem in this version that do not seem to have been recorded before.

(*ll. 9–12*): Whether this is a specific or general satire on lawyers is unclear.

(*ll. 13–16*): Medical satire is rare in radical verse, although bitter criticism of professionals was commonplace.

(*l. 21*): Cold Bath Fields prison was located in London.

(*l. 32*): The slave trade was finally abolished in 1807, but there were years of agitation and debates over the slave trade before that, especially in the 1790s.

(*l. 45*): General Isaac Gascoyne (1770–1841; *DNB*) was acting major general for the troops suppressing the Irish rebellion in 1798; see E. H. Coleridge 323 n. 1.

6. *The Theological and Political Comet; or, Free-Thinking Englishman* (1819)

One of the ephemeral periodicals of 1819 to appear shortly before (July 24) the Peterloo Massacre (August 16) and to disappear shortly before (Nov. 13) the introduction of the repressive Six Acts (Nov. 29), this inexpensive (1½ pence) journal was intended for a popular audience and was edited by "Sir John Falstaff," a pseudonym probably for Robert Shorter, who was unquestionably the publisher. The journal was militantly anti-religious and emphasized Paine's deism, showing support for Richard Carlile, the frequently imprisoned follower of Paine. It added "and Political" to its title after the Peterloo Massacre.

[NO TITLE] [R. SHORTER?]

Let preachers waste their breath on aged fools,
To hoary sinners, lay down *gospel rules*;
In canting rapture, dwell on Jesus' pow'r,
To pardon guilt e'en at the elev'nth hour.
With tedious sermons, strive the *soul* to save,
Just as the body drops into the grave.
Be mine the task to fix REASON, FREEDOM, TRUTH,
WISDOM, and VIRTUE, on the mind of youth;
To guard from *nonsense*,—*folly* to prevent,
And teach the value of a life *well spent*.

Theological Comet (1819), 5. This and the following poem are embedded in an anti-religious polemic, "To the Deluded People of England." The poem assumes that its targeted audience will have already been a "victim" of religious indoctrination, probably Methodist, so that it appropriately emphasizes last-minute confessions and offers an alternative set of esteemed qualities for the idealistic person.

[NO TITLE] [R. SHORTER?]

When Babylon's notorious wh——re
No longer rest could find,
She, in great haste, made her escape,
And left her smock behind.
Oxford and Cambridge, *priestly sons!*,
For to adorn their trade,
Divided it among themselves,
And, of it, aprons made:
But, the few rags which did remain,
10   The more refined sects,

Of academics, fondly claim,
And wear about their necks.

Theological Comet (1819), 5. The whore of Babylon refers to Revelation 17: 4–5, one of the favorite texts for the millenarian Christians. The anti-clerical satire is directed also at the dons of Oxbridge, so that it expresses an overall class enmity for the elite's illegitimate power.

THE BLOODY FIELD OF PETERLOO! A NEW SONG.   R[OBERT]. S[HORTER].

Hero[e]s of Manchester, all hail!
    Your fame the astonish'd world shall know;
Th' immortalizing bard can't fail,
    To sing the *deeds* of Peterloo!

The Muse shall soar on daring wing,
    And her ecstatic numbers flow;
But Pindar's muse wou'd fail to sing
    Your *glorious deeds* at Peterloo!

You all shall live in deathless fame,
10   For chivalry you there did show;
Children shall lisp the Yeomen's name,
    As Hero[e]s all of Peterloo!

How on that memorable day,
    Ye did with martial ardor glow;
And such heroic zeal display,
    All on the plains of Peterloo!

How swell'd your breasts with rapture high,
    To meet the *well arm'd*, banner'd foe;
What courage teem'd in Yeoman's eye,
20   When dashing on to Peterloo!

Methinks I see the mettled steed,
    Trampling the mangled corses low,
Whilst charging round, in furious speed,
    The *bloody field* of Peterloo!!

Methinks I hear the cries, the groans,
    (And view their fatal overthrow)
Heart-rending sighs, and piteous moans,
    Rise from the field of Peterloo!

Methinks I see the crimson flood,
And mark the well aim'd fatal blow,
The Yeoman's sabre dy'd in blood,
Reeking on far fam'd Peterloo!

Wives, mothers, children, on the plain,
In one promiscuous heap, I view;
The husband, son, and father slain,
Stretch'd on the field of Peterloo!

But Yeomen's hearts are form'd of steel,
Ardent to fields of blood they go;
Their gallant souls disdain to feel,
Whilst dealing death at Peterloo!

My muse the truth shall ne'er deny;
The good, the wise, the just, we know,
Think you deserve promotion high,
In *iron case* on Peterloo!!

Theological and Political Comet (1819), 85–86. Shorter, the publisher of the journal, wrote this poem with its contemptuous sarcasm, embodied in the very folkloric designation for the Manchester massacre, sustained and elaborated in its mock heroism of the soldiers who are "celebrated" for attacking an unarmed crowd of working-class families.

On August 16, 1819, at "Peterloo"—a sarcastic pun fusing Manchester's St. Peter's Fields, where the massacre took place, and Waterloo, the decisive battle in the defeat of Napoleon—an unarmed crowd of laboring-class demonstrators (men, women, and children) who numbered near 100,000 and who advocated parliamentary reform, was attacked by soldiers, killing between six and eleven people, injuring perhaps hundreds. Although Peterloo led ultimately to the repressive Six Acts at the end of the year, the massacre inspired the reform movement to hope for victory because of the public revulsion against the government. Some—including P. B. Shelley—thought England was on the verge of a civil war. See Shelley's own poem on Peterloo, *The Mask of Anarchy*, written in 1819, not published until 1832. See Thompson 1963, 681–91; Marlow; Scrivener 196–210.

(*l. 7*): Pindar (522?–443? BCE), Greek poet, noted for odes.

A PSALM, TO THE PRAISE AND HONOR OF LIBERTY [R. SHORTER?]

Why do the zealous bigots rage,
    To lead us in a string?
And why do preachers of the age,
    Imagine a vain thing?

Our hearts unequal to the pain
  Of precepts were created:
David talks quite another strain,
  Or we are strangely cheated.

He tells us, to be brought to court
10   In finery, is our duty:
And that the KING himself shall sport,
  And solace in our beauty.

Then let us break these bonds in two,
  And cast their words behind us;
Indulge each pleasure old and new,
  Lest age or sickness find us.

Theological and Political Comet (1819), 96. This satirical poem is embedded in an anti-religious satirical dialogue between "Parson" and "Miss," a genteel young woman who is the speaker of the above verses. The satire here is double-edged, against simultaneously superficial and hypocritical genteel mores and Christian asceticism, so that it combines social and theological radicalism. Genteel hypocrisy seems to be a favorite topic for Shorter, so that is why I assign the poem to him. Cf. "On seeing in a List of New Music The Waterloo Waltz," (201).

There are numerous biblical echoes: *(l. 4)* Psalms 2:1; Acts 4: 25; *(ll. 7–12)* 1 Samuel 16; Isaiah 33: 17; Isaiah 57: 4.

THE WANTON WIFE OF BATH   [R. SHORTER?]

In *Bath* a wanton wife did dwell,
  As *Chaucer* he doth write;
Who did, in pleasure, spend her days,
  In many a fond delight.

Upon a time sore sick she was,
  And at the length did die;
Her soul, at last, at Heaven's gate,
  Did knock most mightily.

Then *Adam* came unto the gate,
10   'Who knocketh there?' quoth he;
'I am the wife of *Bath*,' she said,
  'And fain would come to thee.'

'Thou art a sinner,' *Adam* said,
  'And here no place shalt have;'

The Theological and Political Comet

'Alas, for you, good Sir,' she said,
   'Now gip, you doating knave.'

'I will come in, in spight,' she said,
   'Of all such churls as thee;
'Thou wast the cause of our woe,
20   'Our pain and misery.

'And first brok'st God's commandments,
   'In pleasure of thy wife:'
When *Adam* heard her tell this tale,
   He run away for life.

Then down came *Jacob* at the gate,
   And bade her pack to hell;
'Thou false deceiver! why,' she said,
   'Thou may'st be there as well.

'For thou deceiv'd'st thy father dear,
30   'And thine own brother, too.'
Away went *Jacob* presently,
   And made no more ado.

She knocks again with might and main,
   And *Lot*, he chides her straight;
'Why then,' quoth she, 'thou drunken ass,
   'Who bid thee here to wait?

'With thy two daughters thou didst lye,
   Of them two bastards got!'
And thus most tauntingly she chast
40   Against poor silly *Lot*.

'Who calleth there,' quoth *Judith* then,
   'With such shrill sounding notes?'
'This fine minks surely cannot hear,'
   Quoth she, 'for cutting throats.'

Good lord! how *Judith* blush'd for shame,
   When she heard her say so:
King *David* hearing of the same,
   He to the gate did go.

Quoth *David*, 'who knocks there so loud,
50   'And maketh all this strife?'

'You were more kind, good Sir, she said,
  'Unto *Uriah's* wife.

'And when thou caused'st thy Servant,
  'In battle to be slain,
'Thou caused'st then more strife than I,
  'Who wou'd come here so fain.'

'The Woman's mad,' said *Soloman*,
  'That thus doth taunt a king!'
'Not half so mad as you,' she said,
60   'I know in many a thing.

'Thou haddest seven hundred wives,
  'For whom thou didst provide,
'Yet, for all this, three hundred whores,
  'Thou didst maintain beside.[']

Theological and Political Comet (1819), 100–101. This satire was "to be continued" but unfortunately never was. The poem has a critique of Christian asceticism with an anti-religious counter-interpretation of figures in the Hebrew Bible, which would ordinarily be read according to Christian typology. It was a standard tactic for freethinkers to emphasize the immorality and brutality of biblical heroes and heroines, usually for the purpose of discrediting Christian authority but occasionally for anti-Jewish purposes as well. Note, for instance, the numerous instances in Shelley's anti-religious writings where he focuses on "Old Testament" immorality. Freethinkers could exploit barely latent anti-Semitism by portraying vicious Jewish behavior, which a mostly Christian audience might accept, and then using that as a stepping-stone to get at the much more difficult target, Christianity.

"The Wife of Bath" narrative is one the *Canterbury Tales* by Chaucer (1340?-1400). The biblical allusions are as follows: Genesis 3 (Adam); 25; 27 (Jacob); 19 (Lot); Book of Judith; II Samuel 11 (David); I Kings 11 (Solomon).

[NO TITLE]   ["COUNTRY CORRESPONDENT"]

Blush, *Christian*, blush with guilty shame;
Or own no more that SACRED name!
Go, hide thy persecuting head!
Where is thy vaunted meekness fled?
Why did'st thou raise thy front, and boast
That Hell, with all its powerful host,
'Tho oft it should thy gates assail,
'Gainst thee ne'er would, nor could prevail?
And yet, thou shrink'st with dire alarm,
10   When man but lifts his puny arm;

The Theological and Political Comet

And fear'st that e'en a mortal foe,
Thy stately frame can overthrow;
That e'en the breath of man can shock,
'Tho' built on *Truth's* eternal rock!
Hast thou not said, the eternal power
Will guard it to the latest hour?
Yet shew'st the Mighty void of sense,
By fearing for omnipotence!
Thy faith thou prov'st an empty plea,
Thou wilt not trust the Deity,
But fliest for help to human laws,
To prop thy weak—thy tottering cause!
To pains, to penalties, and fine,
To uphold a cause thou call'st divine!
Presumptious [sic] man! must thy weak arm,
Protect the Almighty's cause from harm?
Thine is the unbeliever's part,
An Infidel to heaven thou art!
Think'st thou that chains and fetters bind
Th' all aspiring human mind?
Can dungeon glooms obscure its light,
Or stop it in its daring flight?
As well might'st thou *impotent* say—
'My hand shall check the solar ray!
I will arrest its bright career,
And turn it backwards from our sphere!'
As strive to check, by fraud and force,
SCIENCE and KNOWLEDGE in *its* course
O'er errors and murky clouds *'tis* ris'n,
Aspiring to the highest heav'n;
Through Truth's bright sphere, THEY wing *their* flights,
Scatt'ring around *their* heav'nly light;
While Reason's pure and piercing eye
Sees all the mist and shadows fly,
And hails, with infinite delight,
The constellation's glorious height:
Nor long shall SUPERSTITION BASE,
The noble mind of man disgrace,
But banish'd thence to HER OWN HELL
With Persecution there to dwell:
And Bigotry upon her throne,
A Trinity of Hell shall own.

Rid of *their* influence dire, the Earth
Shall hail, at length, the second birth
Of *Paradise* again restor'd,
And Nature's God *alone* ador'd.
Impartial Justice there shall reign,
And Man's long injur'd rights maintain.
OPPRESSION, FRAUD, and CRIME shall cease,
60   And all be LIGHT, LIFE, LOVE, and PEACE.

Theological and Political Comet (1819), 114–15. The tetrameter couplet satire was inserted after an article protesting Richard Carlile's trial for blasphemous libel (October,1819; see Wiener ch. 3). The first half of the poem exploits a contradiction between the theological assumptions justifying repression of blasphemy and the theological implications of that same repression: if the Almighty were as powerful as the Christian says, then repression of blasphemy would be hardly necessary; therefore, the act of repression seems to indicate some lack of faith on the part of the supposedly faithful and pious. The second half of the poem asserts the poet's own faith in a natural religion and brings the deism to a nearly millennial triumph at the end. In terms of structure of feeling, this kind of deism is intended to compete with popular, emotionally accessible religion, like Methodism; it is very remote from the deism of gentlemen, the kind William Blake (1757–1827) found so distasteful.

SAINT ETHELSTONE'S DAY   A. D[AVENPORT].

A Manchester parson, to church and king staunch,
Much fam'd in the pulpit, but more on the bench,
Resolv'd to be *sainted* without more delay;
And the SIXTEENTH OF AUGUST was fixed for the day.

To contrive the best means, all his genius was bent,
How to celebrate such an auspicious event;
When he saw the Reformers, in marching array,
Move on to the field on SAINT ETHELSTONE'S DAY.

Then, the oath of his office, inform'd him, 'twas good,
10   That the vest of a saint should be sprinkl'd with blood;
When his Counsellors whisper'd, "'Twill be the best way,
"The Reformers to crush on SAINT ETHELSTONE'S DAY."

He took the advice, and, to make all things sure,
Read the riot act o'er, on the step of his door;
When the yeomanry Butchers all gallop'd away,
To do some great exploit on SAINT ETHELSTONE'S DAY.

The Theological and Political Comet

They hack'd off the breasts of the women, and then,
They cut off the ears and the noses of men;
In every direction they slaughter'd away,
20 'Till drunken with blood on SAINT ETHELSTONE'S DAY.

"Cut away, my brave fellows, you see how they faint,
"They are BLACKGUARD REFORMERS!" exclaimed the new *Saint*,
"Send them to the Devil, my lads, your own way,
"And, no doubt, they'll remember SAINT ETHELSTONE'S DAY."

Theological and Political Comet (1819), 125. Allen Davenport's introduction to the song included the information that the tune—"the Prince's favorite"—was to be "Gee-up Dobbin." The fifth stanza's highly charged sexual imagery is congruent with the popular reaction to Peterloo (see Scrivener 196–210). Another "A. D." poem appeared in the same periodical earlier (p. 21) *Ethelstone*: The Rev. Charles Wicksted Ethelston (1767–1830) was one of the three important Manchester magistrates (see Marlow). For Peterloo, see the note on p. 219. For Davenport, see p. 206.

A NEW SONG [N.A.]

Tune—"Hearts of Oak."

Rouse, rouse, loyal Britons, your fame to maintain
Nor tamely submit to wear Slavery's chain;
Like Britons stand firm in Humanity's cause,
Asserting with spirit your rights and your laws,

   Chor. Thus united and free,
    May we ever agree;
   And man view each other
   As friend and as brother;
   And may Britons be happy, as happy can be!

10 By Justice supported, with rapturous eye,
See the banners of Liberty waving on high;
Her sons are all rallying round at her call,
Resolv'd by her standard to stand or to fall.
   Chor. Thus united, &c.

To the traitors' perdition, whose merciless plan
Is, by Tyranny's force, to destroy Rights of Man,
Your freedom to shackle, your rights to invade,
And, by state-craft and trick, make religion a trade.
   Chor. Thus united, &c.

20 Not long shall the demons o'er Britain have sway,
    Not long on her vitals these vultures shall prey;
    United and firm all their efforts withstand,
    And Oppression and Anarchy chase from our land.
        Chor. Thus united, &c.

    While Nature, in plenty, her riches doth pour,
    And Providence kindly is blessing the store,
    With the feelings of Britons, how shall we endure
    To see Pride and Cruelty starving the poor?
        Chor. Thus united, &c.

30 Old England, my country, may Heaven thee defend,
    On each patriot heart all thy blessings descend;
    Thy foes all confounded, thy triumphs secur'd,
    That the sun of thy glory be never obscur'd!
        Chor. Thus united, &c.

Theological and Political Comet (1819), 131–32. Written not long after the Peterloo Massacre, this song can be compared to Shelley's *Mask of Anarchy* (1819 written; 1832 publ.), in that both try to provide some morale-boosting for the reform movement, both emphasize unity against the oppressor, both allude to the "Old England" myth of liberty, and both see the established powers in terms of "Anarchy." Also interesting is line 21, an allusion to the Prometheus myth. All the parallels suggest how much material was not the product of individual authors but in the public domain, so to speak, of common frames of reference, ideology, and symbolism. For Peterloo, see the note on p. 219.

7. *The White Hat* (1819)

One of the ephemeral publications that surfaced after Peterloo (Oct. 16, 1819) and disappeared in the government repression (Dec. 11, 1819), this journal appealed to a popular audience (costing only 2 pence), was printed and published by "C. Teulon," and ran for nine issues. Its particular angle was to support radical parliamentary reform from a Christian perspective at a time when Painite deism had considerable sway among the radical reformers.

SONNET [N.A.]

Muse of old Albion! in whose deep ton'd lyre
    Dwell the recording songs of lasting fame,
Thou that dost cleanse by thy celestial fire
    From earthly dross, the patriot's holy name,
And lift it into glory! wake! arise!
    Sing of our fathers—their bold manly words,

The Medusa

    Their still more manly daring, and the prize
        Of freedom, won by their victorious swords—
    For the old beldam tyranny is rife,
10   And shall our lip turn slave, and kiss the rod?
    Ours, of the land that gave a Milton life,
        The land of Sydney's heart, and Hampden's strife?
    No, muse of Albion! tread we as they trod,
        And our high cause confide in our protecting God[!]?

White Hat (1819), 96. The poet might be the same "T. A. T." who authored the next poem, which appears on the same page in the journal, and the classical republicanism is much like "R. W."'s. This poem and the following illustrate clearly that after Peterloo on August 16, 1819, many, including P. B. Shelley, expected further violent conflict and anticipated civil war. For Peterloo, see the note on p. 219.

    (ll. 11–12): John Milton, Algernon Sidney, and John Hampden are republican heroes.

IT IS LOVELY TO DIE FOR OUR COUNTRY.   T. A. T.

    Should we on cross or scaffold die,
    Or in the field of honour lie,
    Delightful is the patriot's death
    Who for his country yields his breath.
    Freedom his narrow house shall trace,
    And tread with reverence the place.

    Though on that spot there be no stone,
    The seed of virtue there is sown,
    From thence a holy flame shall rise,
10   Ascend and spread o'er earth and skies,
        Whilst proud of his devoted fate,
    Myriads his fame shall emulate.

White Hat (1819), 96. Other poems by "T. A. T." appeared in the *White Hat* and also in the *Black Dwarf*. Again, there is the expectation of violence and the generation of an appropriate idealism to sustain heroic conflict. For Peterloo, see the note on p. 219.

8. *The Medusa* (1819)

One of the most radical periodicals, the one-penny *Medusa* was a weekly edited and published by Thomas Davison from Feb. 20, 1819, to Jan. 7, 1820. Davison published also the *Cap of Liberty* and the *London Alfred*. For information on Davison and his journal, see Thompson 1963, 676, 702. The journal's motto declared its position clearly: "Let's die like Men, and not be sold like Slaves!" A journal like this was of course closed down after the Six Acts.

The journal had a lot of poetry and the favorite poets were Allen Davenport and "E. J. B."—Edwin—or Edward—J. Blandford, hairdresser and Spencean poet and activist who wrote also for *Sherwin's Political Register*. For Blandford, see Chase ch. 4; Hone ch. 6; McCalman ch. 7–9. Davison provocatively reprinted Coleridge's "Fire, Famine, and Slaughter," changing the scene from France to England, changing the subtitle from "A War Eclogue" to "A Civil War Eclogue," and making a few other changes (93–94).

Majesty in the Shades [T. Davison?]

'Tis said that a lady who died t' other day,
    In her road to a place—but I may not say where;
Met some wandering sprites who had journey'd that way,
    Allow'd by their keepers to taste the fresh air.

The first that she saw and remember'd, was Tooke,
    And though here she detested him worse than the devil,
And though he was neither a Prince or a Duke,—
    Being dead, she believ'd she had better be civil.

So she said, "my dear Horne, have the kindness to tell me,—
10   That is, if the terrible secret you know,—
If those traitorous wretches are going to sell me
    To him who reigns Prince of the darkness below?"

"Old woman!" he answered, "I fancy you're going,
    Where Satan is monarch by right most divine,—
"Oh, hold!" she exclaimed, "no such fate can be owing
    To virtues so high,—so exalted as mine!"

"Old woman! thy virtues"—he would have said more,
    But Bosville that moment caught hold of his arm,
And hurrying out by an adjacent door,
20   They left the old lady brimful of alarm.

She was then hauled along *sans ceremonie*,
    Past Tom Paine, and Voltaire,—and more than enough
To fill her with anger—but none could you see,—
    While they turned up their noses, she turned up her snuff.

At length she beheld, or imagined she saw,
    A very large man, with a very large wig;

The Medusa

And she bawl'd pretty loud, "is that you Mr. Law;"
   For she knew he no longer with titles was big.

"Yes, 'tis I, Mistress ———" he answer'd her quick,
30   "But how comes it that you are still lingering here?—
By heaven! I think I see into the trick,
   They intend us to *go in together* my dear."

And, perhaps, he was right—for that moment was heard
   A wonderful roaring and hissing around;
But of all that was said, I could catch not a word,
   So I crept from the abyss, and got above ground.

Medusa (1819), 11–12. This comic satire employing the same conceit Byron was to use in his *Vision of Judgement* (1822) might have been written by Thomas Davison, at the end of whose essay this poem appears. Horne Tooke, Thomas Paine, and Voltaire (1694–1778) were well-known freethinkers.

  (*l. 18*): Friend of Horne Tooke, Francis Burdett, and William Cobbett, William Bosville (1745–1813; *DNB*) was a well known radical at the time.

  (*l. 27*): Edward Law, the Chief Justice, Lord Ellenborough (1750–1818; *DNB*), notoriously hostile to reformers and radicals.

THE WRONGS OF MAN. OR, THINGS AS THEY ARE.
SPENCEAN PHILANTHROPIST

O Heaven and Earth, and all therein,
   Your wonder high express,
While *bounteous* nature yields such store,
   That man should know distress;
Ye Muses, your assistance grant,
   That I may here unfold
The cause of *human misery*:
   Then let the truth be told.

Man nothing less than lord was meant
10   Of all things here below;
But then 'twas giv'n to *all* mankind,
   All records plainly show;
But in despite of heaven's decree,
   There is a *lordly* race,
That from the Pagan world has sprung,
   And usurp'd the Maker's place.

For *Lords*, and *Gods*, they *needs must* be,
    To whom we all must bow,
And worship like a deity,
    And all things them allow;
The land and sea, and eke the air,
    And all that move therein,
Or is produc'd by human toil,
    To claim they think no sin.

You pray to God for daily bread,
    Why pray not to *my Lord?*
The ground is his to grow the corn,
    And all upon your board:
If God made all things for your use,
    That you might them enjoy,
My Lord is greater sure than he—
    That can His plan destroy.

By Satan they must be upheld,
    That seize on all the land,
And waste mankind with fire and sword,
    To get supreme command;
And with their Pagan laws to bind
    Their brethren to the clod,
In slav'ry, pain, and poverty,
    Spite of the laws of God.

To whomsoe'er the land belongs,
    To them you owe your breath;
They need no more than stop supplies,
    'Twill soon produce your death.
No one can give the smallest right,
    But those possess'd of land,
To hunt, or fish, or grow a plant,
    Without *my Lord's command*.

Nor may you trespasss on his ground,
    To nothing you can name,
To kip, nor haw, nor nul, nor sloe,
    Have you a *legal* claim:
If grass or nettles you could eat,
    The same would be denied;
For *my Lord's* land and herbage reach,
    Close to the highway side.

The Medusa

>   Now since 'tis clear you cannot live
>   On air or the highway,
>   Labour you must, on any terms
> 60   These *tyrants* choose to pay;
>   For they, *by law*, your wages stint,
>   Your strength you must not sell
>   At a *just* price—through industry,
>   Lest you should *live too well*.
>
>   And yet no laws were ever made,
>   The rich should you employ;
>   *But when of you they've serv'd their turn*,
>   You *starve*—while they enjoy.
>   Much *worse than cattle*, you perceive,
> 70   Is your unhappy lot,
>   For horse and oxen they maintain,
>   Whether they work or not.
>
>   But not so with their fields of blood,
>   Do they their av'rice bound,
>   As much as they can get's the rule,
>   By which they let the ground;
>   Like tygers lurking for their prey,
>   So on the watch they keep,
>   Lest *working men*, by any means,
> 80   *Their labour's fruit*—should reap.

Medusa (1819), 24. The author of this and the following poem could be E. J. Blandford, Allen Davenport, Robert Wedderburn, or some other Spencean poet. More so than Wedderburn, this poet has assimilated the agrarian socialism of Thomas Spence. The Spencean plan envisioned a republican form of government, a decentralized system of parish control, and the redistribution of land. Many Spenceans supported insurrectionary violence. For the Spencean poets, see Chase ch. 4 & 5; McCalman ch. 3, 7, 9; Hone ch. 6.

(*l. 51*): Kip, haw, nul, sloe: respectively, they mean the following: a hill or place to sleep; a hedge or small field or fruit of the hawthorn plant; land-title; wild plum.

THE RIGHTS OF MAN, OR, THINGS AS THEY WERE INTENDED TO BE BY DIVINE PROVIDENCE.

SPENCEAN PHILANTHROPIST

>   O, Heavenly Ruler, great and wise,
>   Creative Lord of all,

Rebirth of Radicalism

That meted out the universe,
   Ador'd by great and small,
'Twas thou ordain'st that men should be
   One family below,
And live in *peace* and *happiness*,
   To hunt, and fish, and sow.

Thou gav'st the *earth, one common farm*,
   For them to dress and till,
To make *this* globe a *paradise*;
   Such was thy HOLY WILL:
Thou gav'st them laws, and covenants,
   To regulate the whole,
One great *republic* to create,
   "From Indus to the pole."

Nor *kings*, nor *lords*, didst thou ordain,
   To seize on earth or sea,
But lotted out thine heritage
   In kind fraternity;
Commanding ALL should have *a part*,
   In freedom to rejoice:
"Thou shalt not covet"—was decreed
   By THY great heavenly voice.

Thou cursed'st [sic] him, *whose pride or power*
   Should, slily in the dark,
By any artifice whate'er,
   Remove the old land-mark;
Join *field to field*, or house to house,
   By heathen Pagan sway:
Forbidden is such wickedness
   From that time to this day.

And if, by chance, to poverty
   A family should fall,
No one should buy the heritage
   At any price at all;
But only lend a mortgage sum,
   To set his brother free;
For all must *have* their *land* again
   Upon the Jubilee.

Thus all the world BELONGS TO MAN,
   But NOT to kings and lords;

The Medusa

A country's land's the people's farm,
　　And all that it affords:
For why? divide it how you will,
　　'Tis all the people's still:
The people's country, parish, town;
　　They build, defend, and till.

Say, must the toil-worn, lab'ring herd,
50　　Produce the golden store,
To plough and sow, and reap and mow,
　　And thrash upon the floor;
And cattle tend,—the fleece prepare,
　　Nay, brave the foaming wave,
And from partaking be debarr'd,
　　From childhood to the grave?

Forbid it heaven! The Bible shows,
　　Since first the world began,
The earth should yield her full increase
60　　For the INDUSTRIOUS MAN;
But that the *idle* should not eat,
　　But held in lasting scorn,
His rights are far beneath the ox
　　That treadeth out the corn.

Whatever laws convey a right,
　　To any class of men,
To dispossess the multitude
　　Of upland, plain, and fen;
Then doom them, thro' their wretchedness,
70　　For *scraps* to *till the clod*;
Are such as hurl defiance at
　　The very name of GOD!

Let *lordly despots* show their right,
　　And title, to the ground;
But only in the HEATHEN LAWS
　　Can such a right be found:
The word of God rejects, with scorn,
　　To sanction such a plan,
But in *possession of the soil*
80　　Has fix'd the RIGHTS OF MAN!

Medusa (1819), 32. The poet articulates clearly the Spencean "plan" and provides a justification for the agrarian socialism. Cf. the section from Spence's *Pig's Meat*.

(l. 16): Pope, *Eloisa and Abelard* (1717), l. 58.
(l. 40): Jubilee—from Levitius 25: 10—was important in Spence's plan; see Spence's "Jubilee Song" (p. 63).
(l. 43): The "people's farm" expresses clearly the revaluation of landed property by Spencean socialism.

Nature's First, Last, and Only Will! Or a Hint to Mr. Bull.   E. J. B[landford].

When Nature her pure artless reign began,
She gave in entail all her stores to man;
The earth, the waters, eke the air and light,
And mines and springs, man held in equal right
For ever; the probate of her will declares,
Her boundless bounty fram'd in equal shares,
Alike to all, nor more to one or t' other,
That man on no pretence shall wrong his brother;
Or for encroachment urge exclusive claim,
10   But all in her abundance share the same,
Of what the elements combin'd produce,
By time and season for man's equal use,
Thus charging justice to chastise abuse!

   Awhile obedient to her sacred will,
Man did the office she assign'd him fill;
Rul'd by her just and salutary laws,
He made his equal rights a common cause;
Till lo! a lawless and marauding band
Of despots, rose and seiz'd the fertile land;
20   Snatch'd from the people ev'ry rightful due,
And robb'd the *many* to enrich the *few*!

   At first, by artful wiles of priestmen led,
The *many* starv'd,—the *few* were over-fed
In idle sloth, on that which fraud purloin'd,
Till power and force, with fraud and cunning join'd;
Then barefac'd pillage grasp'd the common soil,
And only poverty rewarded toil.

   Thus years roll'd on;—thus year succeeded year,
And suffering Nature shed her useless tear!
30   Thus heartless and cold-blooded knaves still view

The Medusa

Unmov'd, the murd'rous mischief they pursue!
Though they uncheck'd in their marauding pride,
Have Nature's will, and justice, set aside,
Yet, "by these presents," may it not be said,
Though Justice long hath slept,—*she is not dead*;
Soon shall her pulse in healthful music beat,
And REASON wake, this lesson to repeat,
"Let Nature rouse!—let courage give the word;—
"And let offended justice draw the sword!
40 "Thus from a band of tyrants to be freed,
"If courage give command, she must succeed!!!["]

Medusa (1819), 60. Blandford's emphasis in these pentameter couplets is on Enlightenment Reason and Nature, whereas the previous two Spencean poems were founded on biblical and religious authority. For Blandford, see Chase ch. 4; Hone ch. 6; McCalman ch. 7–9.

A REAL DREAM; OR, ANOTHER HINT FOR MR. BULL!   E. J. B[LANDFORD]

"If these be truths,
"Urg'd by the potent magic of a dream
"The dumb shall speak; and speak with voice so loud,
"That e'en the deaf shall hear and be advised!"

(The Powers of Fancy; a Poem. E. J. B.)

Last night, when Somnus' heavy hand had bound,
With leaden chain, and link'd in sleep profound
The active functions of the waking mind,
And all to dormant darkness were confin'd;
When reason clouded thus was mulct of light,
And judgment in the gloom deprived of sight;
When reminiscence in the trammels dozed,
And memory's tablets were to record closed;
Fancy, resisting all somnific power,
10 Then claim'd the sacred freedom of the hour;
And whilst 'gainst Somnus she defiance hurl'd,
She whisper'd, "come, let's forth and see the world;"
I took the hint; her offer I embrac'd,
And followed close in every path she trac'd.
    First, through some richly verdant fields we stray'd,
Where sportive plenty ruddy health display'd;
Where rustic swains and sylvan nymphs appear'd,
In sweet contentment, by the prospect cheer'd;

Rebirth of Radicalism

Where fruits and grain abundant round them grew,
Which all had care each season should renew;
Where equal toil the fertile soil prepar'd,
And all the equal gain of produce shar'd;
Where old and young an equal balance held,
And each with fruits an equal measure fill'd;
Where each had equal space for his abode,
With nature's equal laws their only code;
Where each in peace could prune and trim his vine,
To pluck the fruit none trod beyond his line;
Beyond his line, none inclination felt
To tread, or grasp;—for there Astrea dwelt!!!
Nor saw we there one proud presuming elf,—
In short, all seem'd beatitude itself!

    But on we passed, and soon the scene revers'd,
From those most blest, to those who seem most curs'd;
For here we find an idle few are fed,
To gluttony's excess;—while lacking bread
The slavish million starve, and seem to fear,
Lest wolves and vultures, their complaints should hear;
While to the daring, grinding fraud they yield
Of knaves with hearts 'gainst human sufferings steel'd,
Supine in apathy they still are tame,
And have no more of man, than just the name!
Disgraceful to themselves, in mean submission
They wear the galling yoke of imposition;
The pride of insolence they could suppress,
Yet take no measures to enforce redress!
    While I beheld this shameful degradation,
My quicken'd pulse beat high with indignation,
That such a grievous system should exist
Of crying wrongs, and men not dare resist,
The murderous band of plunderers, who unite,
To war 'gainst useful labour's common right;—
"Rouse men," cried I, "and for your freedom fight!"
    Scarce had I spoken thus, as so I dream'd,
When Fancy, in my vision as it seem'd
Turn'd short from these the sad abodes of woe,
To titled pomp's all-splendid raree-show,
Where herd the useless lumbers of the state,
I mean the mansions of the nick-named, *great!*

The Medusa

⁶⁰ This was a scene iniquitously base,
Here blood-stained vice assuming saintly grace,
With peculation, fraud, and falsehood stood
On tip-toe, boasting of their noble blood!
Were folly, pride, and guilt, together mix'd,
While on each face deceptious smiles were fix'd;
Here pimps and panders, punks and pious jilts,
And black-coat bugbears mounted on the stilts
Of class, and rank; who *rank* enough are found,
For on corruption's dung-hill they abound,
⁷⁰ Well-fed and fattened,—gross and over-grown
With waste of fruits and viands *not their own!*
   Methought insulted nature seemed amaz'd,
That proud profusion round these miscreants blaz'd,
And on *their* surface shed such brilliant light,
Whose hearts are black,—whose minds are dark as night!
O! monstrous guilt of blushless vice, cried I!—
Here Fancy cut me short with this reply.
   "Could these dumb guards, while they these dens surround,
"Be *moved* to action, and to sense of sound;
⁸⁰ "Could these dumb ranks of *iron-railing* speak,
"They'd from their stations start,—their yokes they'd break,
"And cry aloud, that e'en the deaf might hear,
"Quick let the PEOPLE for their RIGHTS prepare!
"In FREEDOM'S CAUSE we deprecate delay,
"When COURAGE shall command us,—we'll obey!!!"
   The tongueless IRON then in accent steady,
Replied, "when wanted you shall find us ready!"
   Here Fancy started at the sentence spoken,
And, by the shock, the cords of sleep were broken;
⁹⁰ When lo! I found 'twas real,—no mistake,
A REAL DREAM,—for I was wide awake!

Medusa (1819), 67–68. Blandford's dream allegory contrasts a pastoral utopia (ll. 15–32) with the corrupt status quo (ll. 33–46), and concludes with a call to rebellion (ll. 47–91), in much the same way as Shelley's *Queen Mab* (1813) and Volney's *Ruins* (1791). Pastoral conventions can be adapted readily to agrarian socialist ideology. As is typical of poetry promoting the most radical ideology, there is an especially emphatic stress on the potential courage and will-to-power of the oppressed, who are figured as degradingly passive.

   (l. 5): Mulct—deprived [should be *mulcted* for past tense].

   (l. 27): The allusion is to the image of peace and abundance in Solomon's reign (1 Kings 4: 25; echoed in Micah 4: 4).

(l. 30): Astrea is the Goddess of Justice; one of the last deities to leave the earth before the end of the Golden Age.

(l. 67): Punks and jilts were prostitutes, kept mistresses.

More Hints For Mr. Bull; With the last Hint, which at last Bull must take!!!

E. J. B[landford].

"Thrice is he arm'd who hath his quarrel just." Shakespear.

If Mister Bull be well inclin'd,
These useful hints to bear in mind,
To ACT, as well as think and speak,
He'll soon the YOKE of BONDAGE break!
   His strength is great would he but use it,
'Gainst knaves and rogues who now abuse it;
For though they strive with all their might,
To chouse him of his every right,
And on his shoulders place more weight
10   To keep his back from getting straight,
Than Bull has patient will to bear,
And patience he has none to spare,
Except that which, with coward mix'd,
Cries, *"John, don't stir,* the BAYONET's *fix'd!"*
Not thinking how (ere that was spoken)
Easily bayonets are broken,
When men resolv'd, with courage brac'd,
Against Corruption's force are plac'd,
And bravely daring take the field,
20   Whatever weapons they may wield,
Sure conquest on the action lies,
When Liberty's the golden prize!
When Freedom's flag waves high in air,
They'll find *no heart-sick* TREMBLERS there!
   If Bull, now for himself have love,
He will these glowing HINTS improve;
At once he'll rasise [*sic*] his mighty arm
To strike,—and break Corruption's charm!—
With Justice for his polar star
30   Amidst the struggle of the war,
If Reason prompt,—and Courage guide,

The Medusa

    Victory must for BULL decide!
    Be this LAST HINT, to set him right,—
    BULL *must at last for* FREEDOM FIGHT!!!

Medusa (1819), 78. Throughout 1819 there was increasing militance among especially laboring-class reformers, so that Blandford's wanting to push the militance further to insurrection was not implausible, even before Peterloo, as this poem was.
    Shakespeare quotation: Henry VI Part 2: act 3, scene 2, line 233.
    (l. 8): "Chouse" means to cheat.

INVOCATION TO BRITAIN   C. P.

    Sons of Albion, ye suff'rers of rapine and wrong,
    Arise from the slumbers yo[u]'ve lain in too long;
    Proclaim to the world, that by birth ye were free,
    And your watch word shall "FREEDOM and LIBERTY" be.
        Why should lords, or kings, or rulers,
            Bow ye down—your rights enslave?
        Freemen rise, and crush the spoilers,
            Or repose in Freedom's grave.
    We'll proclaim to the world, that by birth we are free,
10   And our watch word shall "FREEDOM and LIBERTY" be!

    The volume of hist'ry ye Britons behold,
    And study the truths that its pages unfold;
    There see how base monarchs from thrones were hurl'd down,
    How Charles lost his HEAD, and how James lost his CROWN.
        And shall we then our freedom barter,
            Sell our rights for chains of gold?
        No—bravely die—regain the charter,
            Tyrants long ago have sold.
    Let's proclaim to the world that by birth we are free,
20   And our watch word shall "FREEDOM and LIBERTY" be!

    Oh! Liberty's cause sure must warm ev'ry heart,
    And to each one a vital sensation impart,
    See slavery crouches—'tis hurl'd to the dust,
    And tyrants are torn from their rapine and lust.
        Reason now resumes dominion,
            King and priest-craft with their train,
        Fly away on rapid pinion,
            Never more to reign again.
    Let's proclaim to the world that by birth we were free,
30   And our watch word shall "FREEDOM and LIBERTY" be!

Medusa (1819), 87. C. P.'s insurrectionary rhetoric is not very remote from Shelley's "Rise like lions after slumber," in *The Mask of Anarchy* (1819; 1832), especially line 2 of this poem. The argument is from republican sources, as the poem evokes the Good Old Cause with references to regicide (l. 14—Charles I [1600–49]) and the Glorious Revolution of 1689 (James II [1633–1701]), and regaining "the charter" (l. 17).

An Ode, To Major Cartwright
A. D[avenport].

See CARTWRIGHT! though outworn with cares,
And quite o'erwhelm'd with length of years,
   Still writes his bold essays;
Though feeble, proud to brave the storm,
That strenuous Father of Reform
   Deserves his country's praise.

Though friends and foes have both combin'd,
To conquer his magnanimous mind,
   The soul of Freedom's cause;
10 But nothing shall that soul subdue,
He still is firm, he still is true,
   And fix'd as Nature's laws!

When Castlereagh, and satellites,
Shall sink into oblivious night,
   Or stand condemn'd in story,
CARTWRIGHT! shall burst from ev'ry tongue,
From male and female, old and young,
   From Patriot, Whig, and Tory!

Medusa (1819), 109. Major John Cartwright was a venerable proponent of universal manhood suffrage—radical parliamentary reform—from the 1760s until his death. The tribute to prominent reform figures like Cartwright was an important genre in the democratic periodicals, as it provided one further instance of countering the authority of established institutions. For Davenport, see p. 206.
   (l. 13): Castlereagh was the Foreign Secretary.

Man In Prospective, Or Things As They Are To Be!!!
[N.A.]

Hail, *glorious era, yet to come,*
   To bless the human race,

The Medusa

For peace on earth, good will to men
    Will surely then take place;
The golden age, so fam'd of yore,
    Will not a fable be,
But happiness will reign below
    To all eternity.

'Tis *christian policy*, alone,
    Will do the mighty deed,
Though pagan lords, and pagan laws,
    Still cause the world to bleed;
'Tis glorious Christianity
    That points you out the way,
In brotherhoods to form mankind,
    To give their reason sway.

Consider well from whence has sprung,
    That system called the church;
All corporations, parishes,
    Communities,—nay search
All records that can be produc'd,
    The wisdom of each sage,
Equality is no where found
    But in the sacred page.

There all mankind are brethren,
    The titled and the poor:
And when the system first began,
    That it might long endure,
Of all the wealth, that they could gain,
    They made a common stock,
Of house and land, and all things else,
    To feed the common flock.

This *policy*'s the corner stone
    On which the church is rais'd,
All christian clergy practice it,
    For ever be it prais'd.
Their lands and buildings to this day,
    Being property of all,
The rents of which they still divide
    Among them, great and small.

And are you not all christians,
    Except the pagan lords,

Rebirth of Radicalism

And members of the church of God,
    And all that it affords;
His policy extends to all,
    Who can deny your claim?
To hold the land in partnership,
    And all enjoy the same,

Thus, as the land and houses do
50   Compose the people's farm,
Each parish sure could let the same,
    Collect without alarm,
The parish rents,—as now the rates,
    The public dues discharge,
And what remain'd divide among
    Parishioners at large.

Thus O, ye suffering sons of men,
    Would you regain your right,
Consider well the scripture o'er,
60   And ponder day and night;
And all the laws of God you'll find,
    Are rules of property,
On which your happiness depends
    In every degree.

And when you're all convinc'd of this,
    The blessed time will come,
That saints and sages have foretold,
    Of the millenium;
When all the land, and houses too,
70   Are held by christian law,
Then pagan rights and tyranny,
    Must from this world withdraw.

Then read and teach, and sing and preach
    Of christian policy;
For till you do divide the rents,
    You never can be free.
To do as you'd be done unto,
    Is justice from on high,
No other system will admit,
80   But christianity.

Medusa (1819), 136. The poet here is probably the same "Spencean Philanthropist" who authored "The Wrongs of Man" and "The Rights of Man." Ideologically, the poem's taking Christianity and appropriating its established prestige for purposes counter to established power's own meaning follows Thomas Spence and is fairly typical of reformist revision of tradition.

A TERRIBLE OMEN TO GUILTY TYRANTS; OR THE SPIRIT OF LIBERTY!

E. J. B[LANDFORD].

"When the blast of war blows in our ears,
"Let us be tigers in our fierce deportment!" Shakespeare

Hail glorious epoch! Hour all bravely proud,
Now FREEDOM speaks in stern command aloud;
Bids bold RESISTANCE nobly dare the field,
And on the arm of courage brace the shield!
Bids Justice marshal all her mighty force,
And Victory shout, till Victory's self is hoarse,
With urging on the efforts of the brave,
Till conquest tramples on each tyrant's grave!!!
SPIRIT of LIBERTY, now 'midst the throng,
In awful grandeur dost thou move along;
From east to west, from north to south, behold
Thy power extended, moving uncontrol'd,
Tremendous rolling through the swelling tide,
Which shall the fate of despot power deride,
With still increasing numbers in its train,
While to oppose its march all strife is vain,
Vain and abortive in the tyrant's hand
No tyrant[']s strength now 'gainst its force can stand!
HAIL GLORIOUS EPOCH; Hail all glorious theme,
20   That by the sun of Freedom's brightest beam,
Each British breast is warmed; and all unite
In manly movement to assert their right,
With brave, collective, and o'erwhelming might!
Thus doth his heart with panting ardour glow,
Its too long smothered energies to show
In firm DECISIVE ACTIONS to the world,
Till every tyrant from the earth is hurl'd,
Each base impostor from its surface driven,
And EARTH shall be to MAN,—a PERFECT HEAVEN!!!

Medusa (1819), 160. The way time is figured in Shelley's *Prometheus Unbound* (1820) is not dissimilar to the way Blandford provides images for the utopian moment when "earth" becomes "heaven." There is also a Shelleyan image of the libertarian spirit as an uncontrollable force, although the poem makes clear the dependence of liberty on human will. For Blandford, see Chase ch. 4; Hone ch. 6; McCalman ch. 7–9.

Shakespeare inscription: *Henry V*: act 3, scene 1, line 5. The second line is a misquotation.

A Lord's Advice, and A Tradesman's Reply S. D.

My lord cried out, "While you've existence
Keep, son, plebeians at a distance;"
This speech a butcher over-heard,
And quick replied, "I wish my lord
You'd thus advis'd, before your son
So deeply in my debt had run."

Medusa (1819), 214.

On a Bloody Massacre [N.A.]

Who can pourtray the grief, the pangs acute,
The horrid agony; the bleeding mind,
Of those who on that fatal day have lost
Friends, Relatives, their dearest hopes in life;
Or saw them wounded! lacerated! torn!
Beneath the murd'rous arms of Ruffians fell?
Ruffians by cruel despot arm'd with power,
For which they would the tyrant[']s throne cement,
With E——n's best blood!
10   Can any brave free-born Sons endure the sight?
Oh! no—Perish the heart that does not *wish*,
That does not thirst for vengeance.
Rather in one yawning grave,
In one vast Charnel-house, let all be hurl'd;
Than to forget *this Deed*,
We wait the law—If justice flee the court
Not all the fears of loyal fools, not all
The whining *cant* of *cowards* shall prevail,
To keep us from our rights.
20   Upon the tomb of immolated innocence,
Of martyr'd patriots; we will sacrifice
The murderers! and eager snatch Revenge!

The Medusa

Medusa (1819), 240. For Peterloo, see the note on p. 219.
(l. 9): Englishmen's.

An Address to "The Rabble" [N.A.]

Ye English warriors, (glorious name)
Great heirs of freedom and of fame,
   Who bears [*sic*] the scars of war:
Ye great descendants from those men
Who shortened tyrant Stuart's reign,
   Oh! prove what yet ye dare.

To feed each starving family,
To rescue all from slavery,
   Now grasp th' avenging ———.
10 Methinks each infant thus complains,
E'er long we must in tyrant's chains
   The pangs of slavery feel.

Britons, be mindful of your fame.
Britons, (Oh! eternal shame,)
   The brave Lancastrians bleed.
See them, in peaceful council, lie
Slaughter'd by hell-hounds! see, they die,
   Englishmen, meed for meed.

Britons, now your voices join;
20 Britons, with your souls combine,
   T' avenge the infernal deed.
Let not th' adjacent nations view,
In Albion's Sons a dastard crew,
   That dare no slaves exceed.

Britons, can you tamely bear
The tyrants' insult? can you wear
   Degrading slavery's chains?
Can you, like Afric's injured sons,
Whose blood 'neath tyrant's lashes runs,
30   Live in perpetual pain?

With brazen throat Fame thund'ring cries,
"To deeds of glory, Britons, rise,
   And act a Briton's part;
Stand boldly forth upon that ground,

> Where fame eternal Hampden crown'd,
>   And bravest Patriots bled."
>
> And while collectively you stand,
> To free from slav'ry Britain's Land,
>   Let Union rule supreme;
> 40 Without her aid no strength can be,
> No brilliant crowns of victory
>   Can grace the Patriot's brow.
>
> O! England's primest flower, be firm, and hear—
> All, all's at stake that is to Britons dear;
> And soon will twine around the English name
> Eternal Glory, or Eternal Shame!

Medusa (1819), 292. For Peterloo, see the note on p. 219.

(*l. 5*): The Stuart kings, Charles I, and James II, were defeated in the Puritan Revolution and the Glorious Revolution.

(*l. 9*): Steel.

(*l. 15*): "Brave Lancastrians" were Manchester—Peterloo—demonstrators; Manchester is in Lancashire.

(*l. 18*): Recompense for recompense.

(*l. 35*): John Hampden, republican martyr.

Paddy Bull's Epistle to His Brother John [N.A.]

> Brother Johnny, my darling! faith, what is the matter,
> Why the duece [*sic*] dost keep up such a bother and clatter,
> Here's the big Whigs complaining they can't keep thee quiet,
> And say thou 'rt inclined for to kick up a Riot;
> By thy pranks thou has put 'em in such a sad fright
> That the hair of their wigs is all standing upright;
> By my soul they are making most woeful long faces
> And are chatt'ring like monkey's [*sic*] with monstrous grimaces;
> They are fearing lest thou, getting addled and crazy,
> 10 Should's [*sic*] knock the dust out of each well powder'd jazey,
> But I've known thee, my jewel, a good natur'd fellow.
> Yet, I own, rather humoursome when thou art mellow;
> Tho' I have known thee full oft take a frolicsome part,
> I never yet knew thee have malice at heart.
> But Johnny, they say thou dost jeer at thy betters,
> Art grown quite impatient and weary of fetters;
> That of passure [*sic*] obedience thou mak'st a meer scoff,

The Medusa

And hast said that thy shackles htou [sic] soon wilt knock of [f];
That thou hast in thy noddle [sic] a monstrous queer plan,
20   About Liberty, Freedom, and "Paine's Rights of Man."
Absurdly asserting how'er they treat
Thou 'st a soul, and hast feeling as well as the great.
Has said, howe'er humble and Lordly thy station,
That thou art the nerve and the soul of the Nation;
That Lords, Dukes and Descendants, and Princes and Kings,
Are vicious, expensive, and troublesome things;
Men baubles at best, but that often we find
The[y]'re the scourges, the curses, and pest of mankind—
That the[y]'re great carcase Butchers slaughtering in blood,
30   That the world but for them would be happy and good;
Hast a habit of swearing and say'st thou'lt be d——d.
If by their vile tricks thou wilt longer be sham'd.
But Johnny my darling do take my advice,
Thou shalt have it quite cheap, without money or price;
Oh! my dear, don[']t make use of one grain of thy reason,
Or, my honey, they'll hang thee—they call it rank treason;
Don[']t bother thy nob with affairs of the state,
But leave thou the whole swinish herd to their fate;
Is'n[']t better they all should in misery pine,
40   Shame Prince! leave off gaming, and whoring, and wine,
Oh! then, brother Johnny, my jewel, my honey,
Be easy, my love, now, and give 'em your money,
Or how can your Lords, Duke, and Princes, by scores
Keep Pavilions, Parks, Palaces, Panders, and Whores;
Then give thyself up to thy rulers['] discretion,
Be patient and humble, don't call it oppression,
Don't grumble what burthnes [sic] soever you bears [sic],
Let Sidmouth and Castlereagh mind thy affairs;
Nor dare those presume their merits to scan,
50   They'll govern thee, John, on a wonderous plan,
Of Castlereagh's kindness full well thou dost know—
I'd some very strong proofs but a short time ago.
Thou 'rt a hog and if grunting and grumbling thou goes,
Thy masters must put some cold steel in thy nose;
And this bit of cold metal when fix'd in thy snout,
Will keep thee from poking and muzzling about;
And by way of restraint, in thy nose let me tell ye,
Is better by far than if thrust in thy belly.
Here's Sam Straw, Harry Hobnail, Ben Buckskin, and more,

60 To quiet thee joins in a Yeomanry corps;
And like Manchester Heroes, with right and left buts,
If thou open'st thy mouth they will rip out thy guts;
Then an honest sensation I trow thou would feel,
To see thy guts dangling about at thy heel;
They say too, not having God's fear in thine eyes,
The Clergy so pure thou dost always despise—
Hast said they love hunting, and whoring, and drinking,
Much more than their books and the trouble of thinking.
That the story they tell thee is all a mere trick,
70 Just to keep off thine eyes while thy pockets they pick;
That unless thy guineas most freely are prid [*sic*],
There is no Pater Noster for thee to be said;
And altho' of their zeal they now make such a boast,
For just so much money there's so much Holy Ghost;
That unless they're well paid, for the story they tell,
They'd not preach a sermon to save thee from Hell.
That Mammon they worship like Judas of old,
And give 'em the money their God's to be sold,
That titles, and hnours [*sic*] and places, and pensions,
80 And to flatter rich rogues take up all their attention.
Now Johnny once more prythee take my advice,
About telling a thumper be not over nice,
Say thy Princes are virtuous, lovely, and kind,
And that malice itself not a blemish can find;—
That they all live in comfort at home with their wives,
And ne'er did commit a *faux paux* in their lives—
That they ne'er run in debt, head and ears, and then pray
For their whoring and gaming the nation would pay—
Say thy Statesmen are honest, and careful, and good,
90 And thy welfare and happiness well understood:
Say old England is flourishing, prosp'rous, and free,
And no nation on earth is so happy as we;
Say thy judges are learned, and wise, and upright,
And never judge any in malice or spite,
Say thy laws are impartial and free of expence,
That the rich and the poor get strict justice from thence;
Say the Parsons thou pays [*sic*] such large sums for to preach,
To the full always practice the doctrines they teach;
And no persecutors but hnmble [*sic*] and lowly,
100 Despising the world, self-denying, and holy;
All this my dear Johnny by thee may be said,

The Black Dwarf

Then of losing thy head, thou needs not be afraid;
There's Reform and Reason, two things thou must shun,
Or thou'lt have thy *quietus* with sword or with gun,
'Till some better times come, and together we pull,
I'm sincerely thy Brother and friend—PADDY BULL.

Medusa (1819), 327–28. These anapestic couplets read like a song although the poem is framed as an epistle, pointedly from an Irishman who is at least as oppressed as his English counterpart. In truth, there was not a great deal of emphasis in the radical culture on the commonality of the Irish and English. This poem, like others written after Peterloo, expresses an attitude of not being afraid of things getting any worse since the "worst"—Peterloo—seems to have already happened; therefore, extrapolating from the ironically "simple" attitude of the speaker, the time is ripe for bold action. The large number of misspellings and grammatical errors indicates an attempt to represent an unlettered Irishman, although the gesture is not consistent, as the persona uses and spells correctly *faux pas* (l. 86) and *quietus* (l. 104). For Peterloo, see the note on p. 219.

(l. 10): A jazey was a worsted wig.

(l. 20): Paine, *The Rights of Man* (1791–92).

(l. 40): George the Prince Regent (1762–1830) was a notoriously self-indulgent member of the royalty, with his mistresses, extravagent parties, and extraordinarily expensive Pavilion.

(l. 51): Castlereagh (1769–1822; *DNB*) led the bloody suppression of the Irish Rebellion of 1798.

(l. 82): Thumper—a big lie.

9. *The Black Dwarf* (1817–1824)

Edited by Thomas J. Wooler (1786?–1853; *DNB*), this four-pence (until the Six Acts, when the price became six pence) weekly periodical was an important radical voice for parliamentary reform and had a considerable following among laboring-class readers, probably second only to William Cobbett's *Political Register* in popular appeal. (According to Altick 326—citing Wickwar—circulation was 12,000 in 1819.) The periodical's title could have been inspired by *The Black Dwarf* (1816) of Walter Scott (1771–1832; *DNB*). According to the Border tale upon which the novel models itself to some extent, the black dwarf protected the wild creatures from hunters. After the success of Wooler's "Dwarf," other periodical dwarfs appeared, including *The Yellow Dwarf* (1818) by John Hunt and William Hazlitt (see Sullivan 1: 434–40).

Unlike Cobbett's journal, Wooler's contained a great deal of poetry, especially in the early volumes; Wooler, who was a professional printer not a man of letters, clearly loved literature. Indeed, the *Black Dwarf* had a special flair for satire, parodies, and comic representations of all sorts. Almost all the verse was topical, with only 13 percent of it not topical, and there was virtually no nonpolitical poetry (I counted one poem). The favored poetic forms were of course songs and ballads (34 percent), but perhaps taking the lead from Wooler himself, whose motto for each issue was from Alexander Pope's imitation of Horace's First Satire of the Second Book (ll. 69–72: "Satire's my weapon; but I'm too discreet / To run a-muck and tilt at all I meet. / I wear it in a land of Hectors, / Thieves, Super-cargoes, Sharpers, and Directors"), there was a considerable number of couplet poems, both in tetrameter and pentameter (25 percent). There were some sonnets (5 percent) and odes (4 percent), and a larger number of tribute poems or panegyrics (15 percent). The lattermost poetic form illustrates something important about the political culture of the time, namely, how closely related politics were to individual people. Thomas Paine, Algernon Sidney, Henry "Orator" Hunt (1773–1835; *DNB*), Major John Cartwright, and even Queen Caroline were so closely identified with certain ideals and positions as to have become symbols themselves. Radical culture, despite its occasional gestures towards a Godwinian allegiance to ideas alone rather than people, redefined and rearticulated—but could not dispense with—patriotism and loyalty.

The popularity of the *Black Dwarf* was strong enough to withstand the repression and stamp tax that were to follow Peterloo and that closed down so many other plebeian journals. Wooler also had his share of legal difficulty: in 1817 he successfully fought a seditious libel charge, but after Peterloo he was sentenced to eighteen months in prison, from which place he was able to edit the journal anyway. Wooler worked with Jeremy Bentham (1748–1832; *DNB*), Francis Place, Henry Hunt, and especially Major John Cartwright in promoting parliamentary reform. His literary allegiance was in part to the satirists like Pope and Samuel Butler (1612–80), but Wooler also made available to his readers the new poetry of Southey, Wordsworth, Burns, Coleridge, and Byron (1788–1824), mostly through extracts and reviews (indeed, the *Black Dwarf* is an unacknowledged early interpreter and popularizer of English Romanticism). The journal's prestige is apparent by the journal's publishing two of the best known radical poets, William Hone and Samuel Bamford (1788–1872; *DNB*).

For Wooler and the *Black Dwarf*, see Wickwar; Thompson 1963; Hone; Richard Hendrix, "Popular Humor and the *Black Dwarf*," *Journal of British Studies* 16 (1976): 108–28; Klancher 113–19.

THE PLOT.
A LETTER TO MY
BROTHER ROBERT IN
THE COUNTRY.   DICK (OF STEPNEY)

Dear Bob, I informed you full six months ago
Of the lads of Spitalfields, and the Skinner Street *row*;
That horrid rebellion! when twenty poor wretches,
Who muster'd among them scarce ten pair of breeches,
All armed *cap-a-pec*, fit for desperate work,
With (between them) a gun, two old swords, and a dirk;
Besides ammunition—Dear Bobby, how shocking—

The Black Dwarf

Maliciously cramn'd in *the foot of a stocking!*
Determin'd, like Despard, in villainous mood,
To deluge this palace of freedom with blood.
　　I was'nt [*sic*] aware when I wrote to you then,
Of half the designs of these blood-thirsty men;
How could I—unless like Lord Sidmouth, you know,
I had been in the secrets of *Castles and Co.?*
But his lordship's regard for the good of the people
Has made it as plain as a vane on a steeple.
　　Oh, Bobby, the ink that now flows from my pen,
Is whiter by far than the hearts of these men?
What men? Why the traitors—the traitors are—who?
Pshaw—nonsense—don't bother, I'll leave that to you.
　　The *Puritan Patriot Parkes* you remember,
Poked his nose in this horrible plot last December;
We did not believe what he said, but, alas!
The woeful *denouement* is since come to pass.
I cannot relate the details of the plan,
Or number the rebels exact to a man;
But I firmly believe, as I hinted before,
That (*Generals and all*) they were twenty or more!
This *army*, dear Bob, would have taken the Tower,
And the Bank, and the Bridges in less than an hour;
The soldiers were all to be murder'd or choak'd;
Or hung in their barracks, like herrings, and smok'd;
"The soldier's all murdered!" you cry with surprise;
"Now pr'ythee a truce with your London made lies:"
I know 'tis'nt [*sic*] likely, but still it is true,
And I'll tell you the plan that they meant to pursue.
　　The Manchester Blankets you haven't forgot;
Well, they were a part of this horrible plot;
Old women were hired, with the wicked design,
These blankets together with stitches to join,
And over the Barracks at Knightsbridge, 'tis said,
The blankets at midnight were all to be spread!
Some sulphur popp'd under, they'd manage with ease,
The soldiers would die just like grandmother's bees.
　　Now Bobby, if you've any doubts on your mind,
Of the truth of this story, pray just be so kind
As to turn to the Secret Committee's Report,
And those doubts in an instant will all be cut short.
But, can you believe it, these men have been tried?

50 And the Jury, it seems too, are all on their side!
    They've all been acquitted—Oh! Jurymen, oh!
    Where, where do you reckon *hereafter* to go?
    Not to Court I am sure——but I'll finish my letter,
    And when I am able I'll write you a better.

Postscript.

This letter, Dear Bob, would have reach'd you before,
But a smart looking *gemman*, one Oliver, swore
That it smelt so of powder, or ball, or old stocking,
It surely had something within that was shocking:
Like the rules of the Norwich Knight-errants 'twas sent
60 To the noble Lord S., who declar'd 'twas well meant,
Yet of Oliver said, as he'd serv'd the community,
Me'd dub him a Consul the first opportunity.

Black Dwarf (1817), 1: 415. These anapestic couplets were written while Habeas Corpus was suspended and political repression was bearing down on the reform movement, but as one can tell from the poem's tone, the movement was hardly cowed and was able to respond with buoyant humor and sarcasm. The strategy here is to ridicule the threat of violent revolution by portraying the Spa Fields rioters as a pathetic band of ill-equipped eccentrics and to concentrate attention on the government's well publicized use of spies and *agents provocateurs*. (For the reform movement after the Spa Fields riot and during 1817, see Thompson 1963, 631–69; Hone ch. 5–6.)

(l. 2): The Spa Fields riot of December, 1816, was led by Spenceans, was easily suppressed, and was the pretext for the repressive legislation of 1817.

(l. 5): Misspelling for *cap-á-pied*, from head to foot.

(l. 9): Colonel Despard (1751–1803; *DNB*), a revolutionary member of the LCS, United Irishmen, and United Englishmen, was executed for plotting violence against the government. (See Thompson 1963, 478–84.)

(l. 13): Lord Sidmouth was Home Secretary.

(l. 14): John Castle was a spy for the Home Office, and his role became public and notorious at the trial of the Spencean and Spa Fields rioter, Dr. Watson.

(l. 37): The protesters from Manchester who tried to walk to London in March, 1817 were called Blanketeers because so many were ill-clad and wore blankets in the bad weather.

(l. 56): Gemman: gentlemen; Oliver the Spy—W. J. Richards—was the most notorious informer and agent provocateur for his role in the Pentridge Rebellion of 1817. (See Thompson 1963, 649–71.)

(l. 60): Lord Sidmouth, Home Secretary.

Answer to the Threats of Corruption   T[homas]. J. W[ooler].

The tocsin sounds, and freedom's foes
  Again assert their impious power;
Defend the guilt by which they rose,
  And like vindictive demons lour.
Yet can their frowns appal the brave?
What terrors has the gloomy grave
  To him who fights for freedom[?].

Though wide the sanguine stream be spread,
  And seas of Patriot blood be spilt,
10 To save a venal statesman's head,
  Or wash away a monster's guilt.
Fearless will stand or fall the brave:—
Write, write but on the hero's grave
  He died, he died for freedom.

Should their fell vengeance sweep the land,
  And every son of freedom fall—
And tyrant rage but stay its hand
  When desolation buries all;
Sweetly will sleep the patriot brave:—
20 While the chain'd slave that treads his grave
  Envies a death for freedom.

Black Dwarf (1817), 1: 750. This is Wooler's tribute to the executed Pentridge rebels (see Thompson 1963, 659–69), memorialized also by Shelley in conjunction with the death of Princess Charlotte ("An Address to the People on the Death of the Princess Charlotte" 1817). Three laborers who participated in the unsuccessful insurrection, which was provoked to some extent by government agent provocateurs, were hanged.

A Tear   C. M. T.

There is, when day's last shadows fly,
  And no observers near;
'Neath mem'ry's retrospective eye,
A secret rapture in a sigh,
  A pleasure in a tear.

There is, when hush'd is ev'ry sound,
  The world absorb'd in sleep;

When peaceful silence reigns around,
A charm in pensive mood profound,
    To sit alone and weep.

Then come, now bustling day is o'er,
    And tranquil hours appear;
Peace to my wounded heart restore,
And let experience taste once more
    The pleasure of a tear.

Black Dwarf (1818), 2: 192. This poem's distinction is to be one of the very few nonpolitical poems ever published in the journal.

THE THREE BULLS AND THE JACKDAW. A FABLE.   PHILO TAURUS

Three English bulls, renown'd for Freedom's lore,
Reform's wide field had travers'd o'er and o'er,
Had toss'd or trod down every venal foe,
Who dar'd at Liberty to aim a blow;
When a pert jackdaw, from a western church,
On Lambeth's lofty belfry chose to perch:
Thence chatt'ring to his grace in courtly strain,
With senseless sophistry and witless brain,—
On me, he crows, depends old England's fate;
In me, behold the prop of Church and State;
Then feed me well, feather my nest, and I
For property, sans liberty, will cry.
By gabbling myst'ries none can understand,
From Bull asendancy I'll free the land;
Prove Cobbett, Cartwright, Bentham, driv'lers all,
For, spite of them, 'tis most political
To be but *moderately honest*, when
We reckon with high patron noblemen.
How good the great, how wise, how just, how kind,
How *mad* the mob, I'll ever keep in mind;
Forget that Jesus patroniz'd the poor,
And pray that Parliament will shut its door,
'Gainst justice, truth, benevolence, and right;
Reckless of ev'ry law, but that of might.
    Then saint Archbishop, religious "Lord of Trade,"*

*His Grace of Canterbury is a Lord of *Trade*.

> Let me a canon or dean be made,
> Archdeacon, prebendary, what you will,
> For my unrival'd controvers[i]al skill.

Black Dwarf (1818), 2: 347. This anticlerical poem was occasioned, according to the prefatory letter, by the poet's reading Robert Fellowes's (1771–1847; *DNB*) "The Rights of property Vindicated against the claims of Universal Suffrage." Fellowes was a philanthropist and moderate reformer who assisted Queen Caroline (1768–1821) during her battle with George IV (1762–1830). Fellowes was not a clergyman, according to the *DNB*, but he did graduate from Oxford and could have taken a church position had he wished; moreover, he authored a well-known attack on the English Jacobins, *A Picture of Christian Philosophy* (1798), which might have tied Fellowes's name to the church.

The poet contrasts Jesus's egalitarianism with the elitism of the church and protests against this institution that entailed welfare for the rich; moreover, Fellowes is portrayed as a propagandist (a jackdaw) for the church and against the theorists of radical reform—the three bulls. The poem reflects the conflict between the moderate reformers, centered in parliament, advocating a propertied franchise, and the radical reformers, in favor of universal manhood suffrage. The conflict plays itself out for decades until the 1867 Reform Bill.

Blake also uses a jackdaw-like bird as a figure for the clergy (for example, the raven in "The Human Abstract," in *Songs of Experience*—1794).

(l. 6): The Archbishop of Canterbury's residence in London was the Lambeth Palace.

(l. 15): William Cobbett, Major John Cartwright, Jeremy Bentham—all famous advocates of radical, not moderate reform.

(l. 25): The Archbishop of Canterbury then was Charles Manners-Sutton (1755–1828; *DNB*), father of the Speaker of the House of Commons, Charles Manners-Sutton (1780–1845; *DNB*).

INSOLENCE   F.[R. C. FAIR?]

"If you don't like the country—leave it."

> Your child is vicious, and would burn the rod.—
> So would the courtiers in this land of *Nod*.
> Complain of evils they create—they tell ye,
> "Leave it to us—elsewhere, and fill your belly."
> "No," I reply—"'tis you, curs'd spots must out—
> "Ye are the vermin—you, it is I'll rout."
> Who tills the land should of its fruits partake:
> The canker worm from out each root I'll shake—
> Reap where I sow, nor to the slothful give;
> Who'd millions starve, in luxury, to live.

Black Dwarf (1818), 2: 238. "F." could very well be Robert Charles Fair, Spencean shoemaker and poet who wrote a few other poems for this journal and whose participation in the *Theological Inquirer* was extensive. The emphasis here is radically anti-aristocratic, even to the point of laboring-class Spencean socialism. This poem is not unlike some of the radical songs Shelley wrote after Peterloo, such as "Song to the Men of England." For Fair, see p. 175.

(l. 2): Genesis, 4: 6: After Cain slew Abel, he "dwelt in the land of Nod, on the east of Eden."

Impromptu Reply to Impertinence   Clio

The sneaking COURTIER, and CORRUPTION's tool,
Thus speak the language, of both knave and fool.
"If you dislike the land you live in—leave it;["]
My answer is——(in metaphor receive it)
"If BUGS molest me as in BED I lie,
"I will not quit my BED for THEM,—not I;—
"But rout the VERMIN, every BUG destroy,
"*New make my* BED,—and all its sweets enjoy."

   Additional Lines.
New make your Bed!—You can't do that while in it—
Rouse, first, yourself and Bed—give air a minute—
Purge it of *all* its foulness—then, indeed
You *may* enjoy its sweets—You must succeed.

Black Dwarf (1818), 2: 256. This is a response to the previous poem. The additional lines were probably written by Wooler, the editor, who emphasizes activism, while Clio's own emphasis was comically sexual.

Ode to Major Cartwright   R. [C.] Fair

While virtue's charms can yet engage
   A few to tread the patriot's path,
Who 'mid corruption[']s hostile age
   Despise her gold, and dare her wrath:
Cartwright! so long thy honoured name
Shall hope to Britain's wrongs proclaim;
Shall scare the exalted robber's breast,
Shall cheer the multitude oppress'd,
To wise reform direct opinion's course,
10 And vanquish tyrant wrong by reason's force.

   Allured by every wanton wile
      That sports in pleasure's magic eye,

Alcides nobly scorned her smile,
  And climb'd renown's immortal sky.
So thou, disdaining to recline
In selfish ease, hast sought the shrine
Of patriot honour, and pursued
With steady aim thy country's good;
Unawed by public plunder's bloated train,
20 Who fling their venal obloquies in vain.

Apostacy's contagious pest,
  Of generous confidence the bane;
So oft has England's hope deprest;
  That doubt would hold his chilling reign.
Did not thy pure consistent course
Shame vile example's baneful force;
Changeless, as ever in thy place,
On universal freedom's base,
A pyramid of public truth sublime,
30 For age more valued, strengthened more by time.

Ye votaries of the dagon, Pitt,
  No more your lying rites perform,
Nor laud him as a "pilot fit,"
  Nor say he "weathered out the storm."
He was the *demon of its birth*;
And still it shakes our native earth;
Still all our energies must strive
To brave its fury, and survive;
Fixed through the gloom on that bright beacon flame,
40 Whose steady lustre glows round Cartwright's name.

Black Dwarf (1818), 2: 527. The poet is probably Robert Charles Fair, the "F." of the *Theological Inquirer* poems. One of the many tribute poems in the journal, Fair's panegyric to Major Cartwright is interestingly rooted in 1790s' categories, with William Pitt as the principal villain (l. 31). This indicates that Fair first became a radical during the Pitt era (radicals who came of age in the Regency period hardly ever mention Pitt). Fair's emphasis on apostasy versus integrity would also indicate his veteran status. For Fair, see p. 175.

  (l. 13): Alcides is Hercules, mythological hero.
  (l. 31): Dagon is a Philistine deity in Samson story; see Judges 16: 23.

To Belinda   Florio

  O say, lovely pleader, while thus you require,
    For your sex a political station,

Rebirth of Radicalism

What more can a *lady's* ambition desire,
   Than to *lord* o'er us lords of creation?

Enthroned in our hearts, you compel us to feel,
   The force of your regal dominion,
Can a soul-beaming glance be resisted by steel?
   What is reason to woman's opinion?

From our titular sway then why seek to remove us,
10   Not a jot would it boot ye, depend on 't;
Since like Princulo's kings, we have viceroy's above us,
   And woman still rules the ascendant.

Whatever taste, fancy, or science endears,
   All qualities rich and uncommon,
Nay Britannia herself, dear Britannia appears,
   In the form of a beautiful woman.

A word on your rights—while the principle guides,
   (And the gravest of sages confess it)
That the right most effective in *conquest* resides,
20   What heart but must feel YOU possess it?

In the sweet vale where innocence dwells, in the halls,
   Where fashion and luxury revel,
Still woman's legitimate power enthrals,
   So Wolstonecraft [*sic*]—go to the devil.

Black Dwarf (1818), 2: 592. Parliamentary reform was not the only political issue focused upon by the journal, which deals with feminism and anti-feminism. Although female suffrage was a marginal issue, the matter of women's rights, especially the nature of women's education, had been debated at least since the late sixteenth century. Mary Wollstonecraft in *A Vindication of the Rights of Woman* (1792) became the most prominent feminist of the age.

(l. 11): "Princulo" is probably a misprint for Trinculo, the jester in Shakespeare's *The Tempest*.

ODE TO THE LADIES ON THEIR ALLEDGED [*SIC*] RIGHTS   RODERICK RANDOM

Well done, fair votaries of ambition,
   Proclaim aloud your high commission,
Assume a voice in very public measure;
   Let not proud blustering man alarm ye,
   Be drilled and raise a standing army,
I will, for one[,] *yield to your arms with pleasure*.

The Black Dwarf

Yours is not quite a novel plan,
    For faith *old women* long have ruled us;
Such as dame Sid and mother Van,
    Who prettily indeed have school'd us;
Teaching with system a-la-Turk,
    Us tender babes to read and work;
That is, to read the *Courier's* lying pages,
And work, to pay the dirty knave his wages.

    'Tis time to "push 'em from their stools,"
        And dissipate delusion's bubble,
    Come then depose the brainless fools,
        And save creation's lord's the trouble.

Then with prompt Robespierrean parts,
    Dispose of *heads* as dextrously as *hearts*,
And kindly put an *end to all their pains;*
    Thus shall we all become your debtors,
    Gladly put on your Wisdom's fetters,
And glory in 'em as in Beauty's chains.

    Oh! happy era! when the busy fair,
        In courts of law through musty records wade,
    The pulpit mount, at Lloyd's assume the chair,
        Fib in the ring, and bluster on parade.

The rosy loves and graces round her sporting,
    See, rich *phenomenon*, a *fair* chief justice;
No slavish doctrines "false as hell" supporting,
    But that unbiassed course which Virtue's trust is.

Methinks I see in Lambeth Palace,
Some prim Right Reverend Kate or Alice,
    Beauty of *holiness* supreme in;
Or seated by Sir Will, an alderwoman,
Cracking dull jokes, aye, very coarse and common,
    Like Falstaff and Doll Tearsheet seeming.

Our gracious Regent too, whose relish
Is fond of all that can embellish,
    We'll find his taste exactly suited:
When from the proud bed-chamber rout,
Lady-like lords are all kicked out,
    And *lordly ladies* substituted.

> Lo! in your most *uncommon* House of Commons,
> Obedient to the lovely speaker's summons,
>   But hold—a mighty question here appears:
> One that will cause a most delightful squabble,
> And sadly agitate this charming rabble,
>   Setting the pretty vixens by the ears:—
> Among so many *admirable speakers*,
>   Who shall be *mistress* speaker in the farce;
> A question like to make ye all peace-breakers,
>   And render female *Manners* rather scarce.
>
> If rout, nor ball, nor concert court ye,
> You'll have no houses under forty.
>   Careless of public duties,
> But eager to assume dominion o'er us,
>   A rich divan of beauties,
> A perfect *hierarchy of angels glorious*
> St. Stephen's *graceless* chapel then will *grace*;—
> Blest change! for now th' *devil's in the place*.
>
> Over the gallery leaning, Admiration
>   Beholds a sparkling firmament of eyes,
>   And spite of privilege enraptured cries,—
> "England exult!" for never did a nation
> Boast such *bright prospects* in her legislature,
> Enough to change th' hardest despot's nature;
> From pride of empire absolute to shake him:
>   And, ('tis a paradox that somewhat odd is),
> Though they might *go against his stomach*, make him
>   Gladly *embrace* such legislative *bodies*.

Black Dwarf (1818), 2: 653. This anti-feminist satire tries to make jest of both the corrupt establishment and an imaginary female establishment. The poet's reliance on sexual puns and his choice of pseudonym—*Roderick Random* (1748), picaresque novel by Smollett—make clear his unequivocal defense of male prerogative. The poet uses Shakespeare (l. 38) and Tobias Smollett (1721–71) as signs for a particular kind of masculine sensibility that is threatened by both feminist women and the corrupt male establishment.

  (*ll. 9–12*): This refers to Sidmouth, Home Secretary, and Vansittart (1766–1851; *DNB*), Chancellor of the Exchequer, both enemies of democratic reform; Turkey was the proverbially repressive country.

  (*l. 13*): The *Courier* was the most prominent anti-Reform, pro-Tory newspaper.

  (*l. 19*): Robespierre (1758–94), Jacobin leader during Reign of Terror.

  (*l. 27*): Lloyd's is the insurance company.

  (*l. 28*): To fib in the ring is to fight with fists.

(l. 33): Lambeth Palace, London residence of Archbishop of Canterbury.
(l. 38): Falstaff and Doll Tearsheet, characters in Shakespeare's *Henry IV, Part 2*.
Regent (l. 39): The sexual promiscuity of the Prince Regent was notorious.
(l. 54): pun on the name of Charles Manners-Sutton, Speaker of the House of Commons (1817–35).
(l. 61): St. Stephen's is the locale for Parliament.

RIGHTS OF WOMEN.
ANSWER TO FLORIO. [N.A.]

Though the *rule of the sex* you so amply pourtray
   O'er the milder dominion of life:
We had rather, believe me, our characters play
   In the national drama of strife.

No more shall our masculine tyrants prevail,
   Or laugh at the slaves which they make us,
An army we'll raise, and the despots assail,
   With arms that will never forsake us.

Torn and mangled *your rights*, you have ours *betray'd*
10   Or usurped, what your pleasure had lent us;
But we will not repose in disgrace, nor degrade
   The free spirits that heaven hath sent us.

Ye traitors, ye cowards, *like you*, shall we see
   The birth-right, the freedom of all
Trampled down in the dust by corruption's decree,
   While knaves mock at liberty's fall!

No! fearless as free, to the field we advance,
   Our gauntlet is fairly thrown down;
To old honesty's pipe we'll make all *the rogues* dance,
20   And silence *the fools* with a frown.

Black Dwarf (1818), 2: 653. A poem like this would seem to indicate much more feminist insurgence within the reform movement than many historians have so far acknowledged. The feminist-anti-feminist exchange was to continue with "Roderick Random"'s "A Second Ode to the Ladies," 2: 704. The presence, then, of the feminist Cythna in Shelley's *The Revolt of Islam*, an 1817 poem, is not as idiosyncratic as one might have thought. Also, perhaps Byron's rather nasty satire on feminism, *The Blues* (1821), cannot be written off so easily as personal spite against his wife. For literary feminism and anti-feminism, see Marlon Ross, *The Contours of Masculine Desire. Romanticism and the Rise of Women's Poetry* (NY & Oxford: Oxford UP, 1989); and Donna Landry, *The Muses of Resistance. Laboring-Class Women's Poetry in Britain, 1739–1796* (Cambridge: UP, 1990).

Rebirth of Radicalism
Napoleon in Exile F. [R. C. Fair?]

Sun of Europe's horizon, immortal NAPOLEON,
  Though now thou hast left her to darkness and dole,
Where the mighty Atlantic's vast billows are rolling,
  In fancy I view thee, unconquered of soul.
No meanness hath sullied the tints of thy violet,
  The flag of thy glory shall never be furl'd;
Thy rays grow in splendour on you[r] lonely islet,
  Now lonely no more, for thy heart is a world.

The ramparts of Ocean thy exile maintaining,
  Exclude not the flight of thy country's desire;
And Science and Liberty hopelessly straining
  Their sight o'er thy course, claim thy genius of fire;
And, oh! if conjecture may grasp at thy vastness,
  May soar to the pitch of thy mind's eagle course,
And seek to explore the strong hold of its fastness,
  Sure thus it exults in the pride of its force:

"Oh; France, to thy shrine is my soul still devoted,
  In thine are my honour and happiness sought;
In midnight's lone musings thy weal I've promoted,
  In battle's red field for thy destinies fought.
When, thy principles pledged to the work of redeeming,
  In Italia thou gavest me the falchion of sway;
How I poured, like a torrent, the band of thy freemen,
  How Austria's slave-phalanx was chilled with dismay!

"Her dwelling by Nile long had science deserted,
  And barbarism scowl'd on her mouldering fane;
To its former effulgence thy fondness reverted,
  And languish'd to rear the proud fabric again;
Enlightenment's object to me was confided,
  I hail'd it with ardour, pursued it with joy;
And but left it to rescue, from counsels misguided,
  Thy honour, which traitors were sold to destroy.

"Ah! France, when thou gav'st me the purple of empire,
  And to all my life's energies strengthened thy claim,
My pride and my hope was to heal each distemper,
  Which faction's fierce jarring had left in thy frame.
The bright sun of Austerlitz gleamed on my fortune,
  The echoes of Jena resounded thy power;

The Black Dwarf

  In Moscovy's deserts thy weal still I thought on,
40   And cherish'd thy glories in peril's dark hour.

  "I failed—but my glory Time's breath cannot perish,
   Nor obloquy blast the immutable meed;
  Thou, Science, the theme wilt in gratitude cherish,
   And thy moisture the green of my laurels shall feed;
  For oft in thy portals I curs'd war's commotion,
   And the olive-wreath'd goddess invok'd to advance;
  But she who was free, though the tyrant of ocean,
   Saw her bane in the Peace and the freedom of France."

Black Dwarf (1818), 2: 782. This tribute to Napoleon by F.—possibly the *Theological Inquirer*'s Robert C. Fair—presents a very idealized picture of Bonaparte, who had been living in exile since 1815 and would die in 1821. Some English partisans of reform at the time, including the Romantic literary critic William Hazlitt, thought highly of Napoleon. See E. Tangye Lean, *The Napoleonists. A Study in Political Disaffection 1760–1960* (London, et al.: Oxford UP, 1970). For Fair, see the note on p. 175.

 (l. 5): Violet: probably a reference to the imperial color purple, but also Napoleon's blue eyes were often remarked upon.
 (l. 22): Napoleon's Italian campaign, 1796–97.
 (l. 25): Napoleon's Egyptian campaign, 1798–99.
 (l. 37): Austerlitz (Dec. 2, 1805), Napoleon's victory over the Third Coalition.
 (l. 38): Jena (Oct. 14, 1806), Napoleon's victory over Prussia.
 (l. 39): May, 1812, Napoleon began his ill-fated invasion of Russia.

TO BRITONS   CALEDONIUS

  Awake from your slumbers, ye true sons of freedom!
   Awake all the Patriots, ye bards of the lyre!
  Ye spirits of Washington, Wallace, and Hampden,
   Shed wide o'er their bosoms your generous fire!

  Britons, can ye see oppression
   Rolling like a mighty flood?
  Can ye see a band of wretches
   Draw the sword to shed your blood?

  Can ye see the aged father,
10   Groaning 'neath a load of years,
  Dragged to prison by the spoilers,
   Bound in chains, and drown'd in tears?

  Can ye see him, in his dungeon,
   Sighing o'er his reckless doom;

Hoping from his ruthless tyrants,
   Refuge only in the tomb?

Can ye see the tearful mother,
   Weeping o'er her hapless brood?
Destitute of house and raiment,
20   Vainly asking her for food?

Can ye see the foes to freedom
   Forging chains for us their slaves?
And withhold your purse and council
   To snatch thousands from the grave?

Mark the rose and thistle twining,
   Hark! their union calls on you,
Sons of Hampden and of Wallace,
   Join your hearts and hands—BE TRUE!

Spirits of your dread forefathers!
30   Spirit of the daring Tell!
Fill ye with their noble ardour!
   Bid them fall, as Hampden fell!

Say, shall freedom's soaring eagle,
   Leave for ever Britain's sky?
Mount upon her soaring pinion,
   Seize the wild nymph, liberty!

Then shall justice hold her balance,
   Snatched from *law* her sword shall be;
Then shall nature pour her gladness,
40   O'er the ransomed and the free!

Robbers of the rights of Britain,
   See a Charles upon his throne!
Mark him at the bar of reason,
   Stripped at once of life and crown.

Mark how James, a brother tyrant,
   Erring far from nature's lore,
Flies before a peoples' vengeance,
   From Britannia's rocky shore!

What a band of ruthless robbers
50   Could the muse of Scotia name!
Glittering in the present moment,
   Damned to everlasting shame!

Black Dwarf (1819), 3: 153. Caledonius emphasizes appropriately—given his name—the Scottish angle on radicalism, with the stock references to Wallace (d. 1305; *DNB*) and the thistle.

(l. 3): George Washington; John Hampden—republican heroes.

(l. 30): William Tell was a legendary thirteenth/fourteenth century Swiss hero who resisted Austrian oppression and who became a figure in nationalist ideologies. Schiller's 1804 play, *Wilhelm Tell*, was typical.

(l. 42): Charles I (1600–49) was beheaded during the Puritan Revolution.

(l. 45): James II (1633–1701), James I's son, was removed from power during the Glorious Revolution of 1688–89.

STANZAS OCCASIONED BY THE MANCHESTER MASSACRE!   HIBERNICUS

Oh, weep not for those who are freed
From bondage so frightful as ours!
Let *tyranny* mourn for the deed,
And howl o'er the prey she devours!

The mask for a century worn,
Has fallen from her visage at last;
Of all its sham attributes shorn,
Her reign of delusion is past.

In native deformity now
10   Behold her, how shatter'd and weak!
With *murder* impress'd on her brow,
And *cowardice* blanching her cheek.

With guilt's gloomy terrors bow'd down,
She scowls on the smile of the slave!
She shrinks at the patriot's frown;
She *dies* in the grasp of the brave.

Then brief be our wail for the dead,
Whose blood has seal'd tyranny's doom;
And the tears that affliction will shed,
20   Let vengeance, bright flashes illume.

And shame on the passionless thing
Whose soul can *now* slumber within him!
To slavery still let him cling,
For liberty scorns to win him.

Her manlier spirits arouse
At the summons so frightfully given!

And glory exults in their vows,
While virtue records them in Heaven.

Black Dwarf (1819), 3: 564. Dated August 21, this poem by the presumably Irish Hibernicus was written less than a week after Peterloo—August 16. In relation to Shelley's *Mask of Anarchy* (1819; 1832), the second stanza is most interesting in that the mask image comes to the poet's mind once the massacre has happened. For Peterloo, see the note on p. 219.

THE PETERLOO MAN [N.A.]

You have heard of the far-renown'd Waterloo plains,
    Where the sun, horror-struck at the slaughter, declin'd;
Where courage to frenzy abandoned the reins,
    And liberty fell 'midst the tears of mankind.

But a scene still more dreadful remains to the story,
    Where the blood of the helpless in wild torrents ran;
When women, and children, and grandsires hoary,
    Fell beneath the fierce sword of the *Peterloo Man*!

How brave were the heroes, what muse can relate;
10   On the breast of its mother, he bade the babe bleed!
And the mother herself would in vain shun the fate,
    That awaited her under the hoofs of his steed.

Stained deep with their gore, how he dashed along,
    Of banditti the first, since fell murder began;
How tremble the feeble among the scared throng,
    When they hear the fierce shout of the Peterloo Man!

What groups there assemble, what ferment prevails!
    'Tis a nation in search of the savages base;
And justice demands, in her still even scales,
20   To balance the wretches who Britain disgrace.

Whether Yeomen, or Magistrates, forth be they brought,
    Their deeds which a nation indignantly scan,
Well merit the doom to eternity fraught
    With the vengeance of God on the Peterloo Man.

Black Dwarf (1819), 3: 659–60. The poem was written so soon after the massacre that all the sarcasm of the name "Peterloo" is fresh. Recurrent in almost every Peterloo poem is the imagery of the violated family, a richly symbolic icon for the public revulsion towards the established powers. For Peterloo, see the note on p. 219.

STATE CONTRIVANCES!   W. F. L.

SCENE [1].—*A Parlour in Grosvener [sic] Square.*
Enter CASTLERAG, SIDEMOUTH AND SPYWARDS.

Side.—"Where hast thou been brother?"
Spy.—Making *Pikes!*
Cas.—"Brother, where thou?"
Side.—The filthy swine, that would our Lordships' *hang*,
   And cry Reform! Reform! throughout our land,
   Such rapid strides are making, far and wide,
   To stop the which, I've *made* us up a *plot!*
   For as they roar out "Liberty or Death!"
   We *won't* give *one*, but they *shall* have the other!
10   To make up which, the which—the which—you'll help.
Cas.—I'll give thee gold!
Spy.—My Lord, thou'rt kind!
Sid.—And I, t' insure thy escape will mind!
Spy.—I myself will get the other!—
   With hand-grenades we'll make a smother;
   I'll blow into their ears rebellion, loud!—
   I'll give them beer and pistols, bread and cheese;
   With gin, ball-cartridges, and pikes, and powder—
   And when they speak but *loud*—why, I'll speak *louder!*
20   I had forgot—*two bags* and 'tis compleat
   To put your *Lordships' heads in*—happy feat!
Sid.—Adieu!
Cas.—Success!
Sid.—The plot's to kill us *all!*
   At some great *dinner*, if it suit, or *ball!*

SCENE [2].—*Changes to a Tap Room.*

SPYWARDS *drinking.*
Spy.—I'll now off to the loft, which I have hired;
   Where all my victims meet, to meet their fates,
   To-morrow's dawn must see a little blood,
   If things turn out as I ordain they shall;
   The officers will first make their approach,
   The first man's luck to enter, is his death!
   For, when the lights are out, and hell lets loose,
   The blackest darkness it has got in store,
   Then, "thrive my sword;" as after, my escape!

10   When "mad for the slaughter, and confusion, *made*
Victims to vice, get halters—*Vice* gets *paid!*"

SCENE [3].—*Changes to the scaffold at the Old Bailey.*

Enter CASTLERAG, *ruminating on preparations—Time 8 o'clock.*

Cas.—"If it were done, when 'tis done, then 'twere well,"
That it is doing now:—"but in such case,
"We still have judgment here, that we but *teach*
"*Bloody instructions*; which, being *taught*, return
"To plague th' inventor! Perchance stern justice
"Returns th' ingredients of our poisoned chalice,
"To our own lips!" They were *incited* too,
By well paid *spies* to 'tempt the horrid deed!
And we, the guardians of this starving land,
10   Instead of list'ning to their strong complaints,
  See them urg'd on to deeds that must destroy them!
"This plead like angels, trumpet-tongued against
"The deep deception of their taking off!
"And pity like a naked new-born babe,
"Striding the blast, or heav'n's cherubim hors'd,
"Upon the sightless course[r]s of the air,
"Shall blow the horrid deed in ev'ry eye
"That tears shall drown the wind." "Conscience avaunt!"
They dying shout, *Reform!* which through my brain
20   Flies, and expels all sense, but to revenge!
Which, (cordial antidote for rebel men)
Stops their foul mouths from bullying damn'd truths,
Which, swell—Ah! hear! 'tis "LIBERTY," they cry!
Rabble—but—see—I'm satisfied, they die.

SCENE [4].—*A street in London*—CASTLERAG *walking home.*

Cas.—Our spy now safe, *Juries* have our consent
That he for treason should indicted be:
Thus *good men*, seeing "Reform," the mere watch-word
Of foul conspiratiors, and such like herd,
Will Loyal turn, and join us, as we sing,
Tax all the Radicals "God save the King!"

Black Dwarf (1820), 4: 795–96. This satirical burlesque of the Cato Street Conspiracy is a good example of radical popular art at its best. On February 23, 1820, the group of Spenceans and government-paid provocateurs, who were supposedly ready to overthrow the government violently, and who wanted to kill the Home

The Black Dwarf

Secretary, Sidmouth, and the Foreign Secretary, Castlereagh, and then to display their heads on the ends of pikes, were arrested after a violent exchange during which one Bow Street runner was killed. Shortly thereafter it became public knowledge that the main conspirator in this attempted coup was George Edwards, Home Office agent, who was kept hidden by the government even after the pro-reform Middlesex Grand Jury indicted him for high treason. *Black Dwarf*'s Wooler was a leader in the defense committee for the "conspirators," and the defense consisted entirely of pointing out the degree to which the acts of treason had been contrived by the government itself. The trial took place in mid-April and six men were hanged on May 1, and another six Spenceans were transported. For the history, see David Johnson, *Regency Revolution. The Case of Arthur Thistlewood* (London: Compton Russell, 1974); Thompson 1963, 702–6; Hone 305–6; 347–48.

(Scene 3): From the first line to line 18 there are quotations from *Macbeth* act 1, scene 7, lines 1–25.

The poem's last line had a special, reactionary resonance because of the Queen Caroline Affair that was raging at the time, during which Tories supported King George IV in his attempt to get rid of Caroline, who was defended by the Whigs and the reform movement.

SONNET TO REASON   WILLIAM STURCH

"There is a spirit in man, and the inspiration of the Almighty giveth them understanding."

Thou noblest gift of heaven to human kind,
    To guide the generous purpose, to control
    The waves that o'er the tortur'd bosom roll,
And check the heart to lawless joys inclin'd,—
Bright emanation of that wond'rous mind
    That governs all! By thee, the aspiring soul
    Pervades all space, and sees throughout the whole—
8 One mighty plan by boundless love design'd!
Thrice happy he who owns thy sovereign sway;
    Who, reckless what the sons of priestcraft teach,
And firmly trusting nature's friendly ray,
Amid the storm right onward wends his way
    Through this dim vale of sorrow, till he reach
The peaceful mansions of eternal day!

Black Dwarf (1820), 5: 376. William Sturch (1753?–1838; *DNB*) was an ironmonger and Unitarian intellectual who was active in Westminster Reform politics and who wrote in 1799 "Apeleutherus; or an Effort to attain Intellectual Freedom." Sturch's Unitarianism seems like deism, which encompassed a broad spectrum of belief, and this particular version of the creed is remarkably devout at least in tone and structure. Only the phrase "sons of priestcraft" seems to be as rhetorically militant as was typical in the Carlile-Painite tradition of English deism. For information on Sturch's politics, see Hone.

The Queen's Triumph   J. W. Dalby

O, let the bells of England
    Ring a right merry peal,
For our wronged royal lady,
    And for the common-weal!

No more shall petty greatness
    O'er tortured virtue reign—
The day of such dishonor
    May ne'er return again.

Sink, ye heartless Parasites!
10   Sink low into the earth,
For little is your portion
    Of a glad people's mirth.

Go, court your wretched master,
    And teach him, if ye can,
To turn from crimes and folly,
    And be at last—a man,

And thou—accursed slanderer—
    The brand upon thy brow—
Where all are mean, the meanest—
20   How beats thy base heart now?

Think not thy rank and title,
    Will guard thee from the hate,
The scorn and indignation
    Thy baseness must create.

Go, seek—some desert cavern,
    And waste thy life away;
From mortal vengeance hidden,
    And from the light of day!

Rejoice! ye happy millions,
30   Who took the wronged one's part—
Let boundless joy and revelry
    Lighten each manly heart.

The Black Dwarf

Your's is the noble triumph,
    As much as it is hers,
On whom the people's blessing
    Her greatest right confers.

To you—her first defenders
    That royal heart will turn,
In which the light of gratitude
40   Will ever brightly burn.

On you—the brave and honest—
    The firm, altho' opprest,
Praise from all posterity
    Eternally shall rest!

Since crushed are the conspirers,
    The lofty and the low,
And since this hellish project
    Has met its mortal blow;

Since truth and justice conquer—
50   The injured and opprest—
And since the base and mighty,
    No more the field contest;

O, let the bells of England
    Ring a right merry peal,
For our victorious lady,
    And for the common-weal.

Black Dwarf (1820), 5: 715–16. Dated November 11, Dalby's was one of many poems on the Queen Caroline Affair. For an interesting New Historical approach to the political controversy over the Queen, see Thomas Laqueur, "The Queen Caroline Affair: Politics as Art in the Reign of George IV," *Journal of Modern History* 54 (1982): 417–66. The Queen's victory which is here celebrated was short-lived, as she died in 1821 without assuming any royal position. The Whigs and the reform movement defended the Queen as the new King George IV tried to divorce her. Although at the time many reform leaders were in jail and the Six Acts crippled the radical press, the reform movement exploited the Queen Caroline Affair and was able to work around the repression.

    Between 1818 and 1820, John Watson Dalby—of Suffolk Street—wrote fourteen other poems for *Black Dwarf*, making him the most frequently published poet in the periodical. The British Library records *Poems* (1822) (and a second edition), a memoir of Charles Lamb (1837), and *Tales, Songs, and Sonnets* (1866).

Jeremy Bentham B.

I have travell'd the world, and that old man's fame
    Wherever I went—shone brightly;
To his country alone belongs the shame—
    To think of his labours lightly.

The words of wisdom I oft have heard
    From that old man's bosom falling,
And ne'er to my soul had wisdom appear'd
    So lovely, and so enthralling.

No halo was round that old man's head,
10   But his locks—as the rime-frost hoary,
While the wind with the snowy relics play'd,
    Seem'd fairer than crowns of glory.

In him I have seen—what a joy to see!
    In divinest union blended,
An infant child's simplicity,
    By a sage's strength attended.

He dwells like a Sun the world above,
    Tho' by folly and envy shrouded;
But soon shall emerge in light of love,
20   And pursue his path unclouded.

That Sun shall the mists of night disperse,
    Whose fetters so long have bound it;
The centre of its own universe,—
    Ten thousand planets around it!—

Black Dwarf (1821), 6: 340. Reprinted from *The Examiner* (Feb. 18, 1821), this sentimental and lyrical tribute to Bentham contrasts with Bentham's unsentimental, dismissive view of poetry. Nevertheless, he was one of the prominent theorists of the radical reform movement.

The Banished Printer to his Trade J. W. B.

Compositor of PRINTING fame!
Quit, oh! quit, your wooden frame!
Working, starving, idling, drinking;
Oh, the gain, the loss of PRINTING!
Cease fond *Printer*, cease your trade,
And shun *the laws* for *Printers* made.

The Black Dwarf

    Hark! thy sentence:—Judges say,
    "*Libel Printers*, go away!"
    What is this embitters life?
10   Starve my children—kills my wife;
    Send me abroad for punishment;
    Tell me, my trade—'tis banishment!

    England recedes;—it disappears;
    France opens to my eyes, my ears;
    With foreign accents ring:—
    Lend, lend, your ships! I said—I fly!—
    Oh, Judge! where is thy victory?
    Oh, Law! where is thy sting?

Black Dwarf (1821), 7: 276. In the repressive atmosphere after the Six Acts, the radical press was severely hampered, one symptom being illustrated here.
  (ll. 17–18): Variation on 1 Corinthians 15: 54–55.

TRIBUTE TO THE MEMORY OF AN INJURED QUEEN
                                    F. G.

    Hark! the death-bell's solemn toll
    Speaks the freedom of a soul,
    Just escaped from foes malign,
    'Tis our much lov'd Caroline.

    Hapless Princess! doom'd to know
    Each extreme of poignant woe;
    Fraud and cruelty combine
    'Gainst thee, injur'd Caroline.

    Many a sympathetic heart
10   In thy sorrows claim'd a part,
    And shall cypress wreaths entwine
    Round the tomb of Caroline.

    Yet forbear to mourn the dead,
    From the scene of suff'ring fled;—
    For the Almighty—power benign—
    Saw the griefs of Caroline.

    He, of innocence the friend,
    Did his gracious mandate send,
    And from ev'ry base design,
20   Hath deliver'd Caroline.

'Tho' denied a seat on earth,
Due to her illustrious birth;
Crown'd on high in Courts Divine,
Reigns the Royal Caroline.

With contempt she views below
Short liv'd pageantry and show;
Whilst eternal splendors shine
Round the throne of Caroline.

When time presents the future page,
30   And prejudice hath spent its rage,
Then shall the world to truth incline,
And learn to pity Caroline.

Hence with shame ye hireling crew,
Your detested falsehoods view'd,
And your blunted shafts resign,
Aim'd in vain at Caroline.

Black Dwarf (1821), 7: 348. The poet from Maidstone composed this shortly after the queen's death in August. For the Queen Caroline Affair, see the note on p. 271.

ODE TO A PLOTTING PARSON. WRITTEN JAN. 1820.   S. BAMFORD

Come over the hills out of York, H——
Thy living is goodly, thy mansion is gay:
Thy flock will be scattered, if longer thou stay,
Our shepherd, our vicar, the *good* Parson H——.
Oh! fear not, for thou shalt have plenty indeed,
Far more than a shepherd so humble will need,
Thy wage shall be ample, two thousand or more,
Which tythes and exactions shall bring to thy store.
And if thou *should'st* wish for a *little encrease*,
10   The lambs thou mayst *sell*, and the flock thou mayst *fleece*.
The market is good, and the prices are high,
And the butchers are ready with money to buy.

Thy dwelling-house pleasantly stands on a hill,
And the town lies below it so quiet and still;
With a church at thine elbow for preaching and prayer,
And a rich congregation to slaver and stare.
And here like a good loyal priest shalt thou reign,

The Black Dwarf

The cause of thy patrons with zeal to maintain;
And the poor and the hungry shall faint at thy word,
As thou doom'st them to h——! in the name of the Lord!

And here is a barrack with soldiers enow,
The deed which thou willest all ready to do;
They will rush on the people in martial array,
If thou but thy blood-d[r]ipping cassock display,
And Meagher shall ever be close by thy side,
With a brave troop of yeomanry ready to ride;
For the steed shall be saddled, the sword shall be bare,
And there shall be none the defenceless to spare.

Then the joys which thou felt upon St. Peter's-field
Each week, or each month, some new outrage shall yield:
And thine eye which is failing, shall brighten again,
And pitiless gaze on the wounded and slain.
Thy Prince then shall thank thee, and add to thy wealth,
Thou shalt preach down sedition, and pray for his health;
And Sidmouth, and Canning, and sweet Castlereagh,
Shall write pleasant letters to dear cousin H——!

Each dungeon now silent shall sound with a groan,
For the captive shall mourn in its darkness alone;
And the chain shall be polish'd which now hangs in rust,
And brighten'd the bar which is mouldering to dust.
And the tears of the virgin in torrents shall flow,
Unheeded her tears, and unpitied her woe;
And the blush of her cheek like a rose-bush shall fade,
For the youth whom thy villainous arts have betray'd.

For thy spies they shall lurk by the window at night,
Like bloodhounds to smell out the prey of thy spite;
And the laugh shall be hush'd, and when townsmen do meet,
None even his neighbour shall venture to greet!

And when gloomy famine doth stalk through the land,
No comfort the poor shall receive at thy hand;
And the widow shall curse thee while life doth remain,
And the orphan shall lisp back her curses again.
And the night wind shall sound as a scream in thine ear,
And the tempest shall shake thee with terrible fear;
And the zephyr that fans thee shall bring thee *no cure*,
It will whisper a tale which thou canst not endure.
And the day shall arise, but its joys will be fled,

And the season of darkness shall add to thy dread;
And a mark of affliction thou ever shalt be,
60   And none shall partake of thy troubles with thee.

Black Dwarf (1821), 7: 670–72. Samuel Bamford was the reform movement's best-known poet, whose work acquired additional interest because of his imprisonment after Peterloo. Between 1818 and 1822 the *Black Dwarf* published numerous Bamford poems. For information on Bamford and his poetry, see Martha Vicinus, *The Industrial Muse* (NY: Barnes & Noble, 1974); and Brian Maidment, *The Poorhouse Fugitives. Self-Taught Poets and Poetry in Victorian Britain* (NY: Carcanet, 1987). For Bamford's life, see *Autobiography of Samuel Bamford*, ed. W. H. Chaloner, 2 vols. (NY: Augustus M. Kelley, 1967).

The object of Bamford's satire is Rev. William Robert Hay (1761–1839; *DNB*), one of the three important Manchester magistrates (ll. 1, 4, 36). For Peterloo, see the note on p. 219.

(l. 25): Edward Meagher, the yeomanry's trumpeter, was blamed publicly for killing people at Peterloo (see Marlow).

(l. 35): Lord Sidmouth, Home Secretary; George Canning (1770–1827; *DNB*), Tory leader, to become Foreign Secretary after the suicide of Lord Castlereagh.

THE LATE HONOURABLE CONDUCT OF THE RADICALS JUSTIFIED   RADIX

When Mordecai, and Israel's suff'ring tribes,
Were made t' endure the scoffing Courtier's gibes,
They cried to Israel's God for quick relief,
And Haman's gallows bore the treach'rous chief.
The retribution just made them rejoice,
And blameless was their welkin-ringing voice:—
So Londonderry's Lord revil'd our cause,
Abridg'd our rights, conspir'd against our laws;
Foul Spies engender'd, foster'd, and caress'd,
10   Till dread of Spies alarm'd his raging breast:—
He seiz'd the knife, the laws of heav'n defied,
And England's foe lay breathless at our side:—
How great our triumph! and how just our pride!

Black Dwarf (1822), 9: 432. This is one of many poems celebrating the suicide of the Foreign Secretary, Lord Castlereagh. The number and intensity of these poems illustrate the degree to which Castlereagh was passionately hated by the reform movement. The analogy with the Book of Esther is not quite precise because Haman did not commit suicide, but indeed the gallows he built for Mordecai were used to hang not Mordecai but Haman. The reform movement did not typically draw upon

Jewish tradition to figure its own concerns, but here the poet depicts the Purim-like glee in the defeat of a hated oppressor.

A NEW LOYAL SONG, MEANT TO PLEASE MR. MURRAY. [N.A.]

Great George the Third was England's King,
His praises, therefore, I will sing,
   Lest Murray be offended;
The good he did I do not know;
But good he was, for all allow,
   He never could be mended.

There never was a man more chaste;
'Tis said he never had a taste
   Of female charms but Charlotte's;—
10 He ne'er seduced the Quaker maid,
Nor after fruit forbidden stray'd,
   Nor played with naughty harlots.

He never let a minion rule;
He never was a favourite's tool;
   Is honest Murray swears;
And all that history lets drop,
Is not worth half the wooden prop,
   That half of Murray bears.

To war he never was inclin'd;
20 To all his subjects faults was blind;
   Not one did ever fall,
In battle-field, or on the main—
Indeed I don't think in his reign,
   That any died at all.

And then (oh! naughty Byron, blush!)
He valued money not a rush,
   But freely gave his pelf:
To whom—for what—is not so clear—
But the poor King, for many a year,
30   Was forced to *beg* himself.

His reign was always fortunate;
Of debt we have not got a groat;
   The taxes have been *lower*
By many millions every quarter,

Than they had been since Charles the Martyr,
   Or ever were before.

He never did lose sight of wit;
There never was a man call'd Pitt
   To forge, and lie, and cheat
40 A silly bumpkin, called John Bull,
With open heart, and solid skull,
   Oft seen about the street.

But all was right as right should be,
And all should praise the Majesty
   That pleases Mr. Murray:
And those that won't must have a care,
Or tread-mill-law, and prison fare,
   Awaits them in a hurry.

Black Dwarf (1824), 12: 187–88. This satire is not on John Murray (1778–1843; *DNB*), Lord Byron's publisher, but on Charles Murray, lawyer for the Constitutional Association, which initiated the prosecution of Byron's *The Vision of Judgment* (1822). There were considerable legal problems encountered by Byron's poem, published first in the *Liberal* (1822), a satire ostensibly on George III after his death but also on the poet laureate, Robert Southey. To make matters confusing, John Murray in fact altered the text of the poem and the Hunts—Leigh and John—later restored the original, so that John Murray was indeed associated with repression and the poem. The *Black Dwarf* followed John Hunt's trial, which took place in January, 1824; Hunt was sentenced June 19, 1824, with a one-hundred pound fine. The journal took considerable interest in Byron, reviewing *The Age of Bronze* in (1823), 10: 465–70, and publishing a number of extracts from his work (six in total: *Marino Falerio*, act 2, scene 2, lines 93–107, in [1821], 6: 627; "Sonnet on Chillon," in [1821], 7: 54; *Don Juan*, canto 3: stanza 86, lines 1–16, in [1821], 7: 797–99; *The Giaour*, lines 68–141, in [1822], 8: 127–28; *Childe Harold*, canto 2, stanzas 73–74, in [1822], 8: 414–15; *Don Juan*, canto 8: stanzas 50–51, in [1824], 12: 113).

(*ll. 9–10*): Although the king was faithful to his wife Charlotte Sophia, before he married her he was romantically linked with a Quaker woman.

(*l. 12*): The sexual promiscuity of the Prince Regent, later George IV, was notorious.

(*l. 35*): Charles I was executed during the Puritan Revolution.

(*l. 39*): William Pitt was the prime minister during the 1790s.

An Ode, Written by G. Dyer, Esq. on reading Major Cartwright's Appeal, &c.

Originally published in 1799.

Ah, why should song, enchanting song,
Her votaries lose in error's maze;

The Black Dwarf

    Why flattery, poisoning future days,
Give pride those laurels that to truth belong?
    Avaunt, thou bard of ancient time,
    I hate the base insidious lyre,
    That bids the gazing croud retire,
    While tyrants sit as Gods sublime.

    I hail the man of generous frame,
    Who beams with love of human kind,
Who leaves the vulgar great behind,
And scorns the splendid treacheries of a name.
    Patriots, the touch-stone page explore,
    The wily statesman's craft it shews,
    And blood-stain'd heroes to expose,
    Unfolds lov'd freedom's sacred lore.

    When discord hurl'd her torch on high,
    Recount the warrior-Romans dead,
    The blood of gallant Britons shed,
Her vassal'd sons hear humbled Gallia sigh?
    How stream'd the Rhine with German gore!
    Let Caesar mount the victor's car,
    And Rome, amid the spoils of war,
    Her Conqueror, and the world's, adore.

    Ah, vain the pomp, th' imperial sway,
    When justice takes her watchful stand;
    Actions she weighs, with patient hand,
Nor dares she rashly give her palms away.
    She spurns the mad heroic race;
    And oft while Poeans rend the skies,
    While altars breathing incense rise,
    The conqueror marks for long disgrace.

    Lift high to Catherine's name the strain,
    O, Russia, deck thy monarch's brow—
    But, first, survey that form of woe,
Stalk ghastly over Warsaw's fated plain;
    And hear the groans from Ismael's tower,
    The pond'rous groans of thousands rise;
    And women's screams, and infant's cries,
    Attended conquest's baneful hour.

    Then hail thy Catherine wise and great,
       Then proudly wave thy banners round,
       And spread the trump's parade of sound,
The pomp of robes, and all the monarch state.
       But see her day of glory flown—
       Europe has cursed her baneful name,
       And nature veils herself in shame,
       To think what ruffians wear a crown.

       Yet fame shall her elysium raise,
       While genius culls his wreathe of flowers,
       And seated in unfading bowers,
Alfred, ennobled, shine through endless days.
       And circle high the mount sublime,
       Fancy has hailed the visioned sight,
       Round living streams of sapphire bright,
       The bards, who raise the lofty rhyme.

    "Blest, Alfred, be thy honored name;
       A people's voice of praise is sweet—
       And sweet the songs, his ears that greet,
The Prince, whose bosom glows with freedom's flame.
       Still blossom, 'midst the lapse of years,
       The laurels wreath'd on virtue's brow,
       In richer pride their honours blow,
       And age their memory but endears.

    "See Britain rising from her seat,
       Proud of her rights, and equal laws,
       Ardent in freedom's sacred cause,
Proclaims thee, Alfred, wise and good and great.
       'Twas thine each citizen to fire,
       They pant the thirsty lance to wield,
       They rush impetuous to the field,
       And Freedom sees her foes expire."

    They ceas'd—and cease the lyric strain—
       For Alfred lives to bless no more:
       Though still, it's [*sic*] day of splendour o'er,
Downward the sun but sinks to rise again.
       Thus Alfred shines, a glorious name,
       And darting golden glories high,
       Still marches stately through the sky,
       While nations bless the sacred flame.

The Black Dwarf

Black Dwarf (1824), 12: 529–32. This poem, upon the death of Major Cartwright—who financially backed the *Black Dwarf*—concluded the periodical. Appropriately the poet was George Dyer, a poet active in the 1790s. For Dyer, see Reiman 1979.

(ll. 18–23): Allusions to the Roman imperial conquest of Britain, Gaul and Germany.

(l. 33): Catherine II (1729–96) of Russia attacked and partitioned Poland in 1793 and 1795 (l. 36), and in warring with the Ottoman Empire, her armies captured and massacred people at Izmail—a town on the Rumanian-Ukrainian border—on December 22, 1789 (l. 37).

(l. 52): King Alfred was a libertarian figure in reformist writing, in part because he fit well into a native Anglo-Saxon tradition of constitutional monarchy that preceded the "Norman yoke," and in part because he was a patriotic warrior against the Viking invaders.

BIBLIOGRAPHY

Abrams, M. H. "Structure and Style in the Greater Romantic Lyric." *From Sensibility to Romanticism.* Ed. Frederick W. Hilles & Harold Bloom. Oxford: UP, 1965.
Allen, B. Sprague. "William Godwin's Influence on John Thelwall." *PMLA* 37 (1922): 662–82.
Altick, Richard. *The English Common Reader. A Social History of the Mass Reading Public 1800–1900.* Chicago & London: U of Chicago P, 1957.
Aspinall, Arthur. *Lord Brougham and the Whig Party.* Manchester: UP, 1927.
———. *Politics and the Press, c. 1780–1850.* London: Home & Van Thal, 1949.
Bamford, Samuel. *Autobiography of Samuel Bamford.* Ed. W. H. Chaloner. 2 vols. NY: Augustus M. Kelley, 1967.
Bartel, Roland. "Shelley and Burke's Swinish Multitude." *Keats-Shelley Journal* 18 (1969): 4–9.
Baylen, John O., & Norbert J. Gossman, ed. *Biographical Dictionary of Modern British Radicals, vol. I: 1770–1830.* Sussex & New Jersey: Harvester P & Humanities P, 1979.
Bennett, Betty T., ed. *British War Poetry in the Age of Romanticism: 1793–1815.* NY & London: Garland, 1976.
Binns, John. *Recollections of the Life of John Binns.* Philadelphia: Parry & M' Millan, 1854.
Blechem, John. *"Orator" Hunt. Henry Hunt and English Working-Class Radicalism.* Oxford: Clarendon P, 1985.
Bloomfield, Robert. *Collected Poems (1800–1822).* Ed. Jonathan N. Lawson. Gainesville: Scholars' Facsimiles & Reprints, 1971.
———. *The Remains of Robert Bloomfield.* 2 vols. Ed. Joseph Weston. London: Baldwin, Cradock, & Joy, 1824.
———. *Selections from the Correspondence of Robert Bloomfield.* Ed. W. H. Hart. 1870. Walton-on-Thames: Robert F. Ashby, 1968.
Boas, Louise. "'Erasmus Perkins' and Shelley." *Modern Language Notes* 70 (1955): 408–13.
Bourne, H. R. Fox. *English Newspapers.* Vol. I. 1887. NY: Russell & Russell, 1966.
Burke, Edmund. *Reflections on the Revolution in France.* Ed. Conor Cruise O'Brien. 1790. Harmondsworth et al.: Penquin, 1969.
Burke, Redmond, & Burton Pollin. "John Thelwall's Marginalia in a Copy of

Bibliography

Coleridge's *Biographia Literaria.*" *Bulletin of the New York Public Library* 74 (1970): 73–94.

Butler, Marilyn. *Jane Austen and the War of Ideas.* Oxford: Clarendon P, 1975.

———. *Romantics, Rebels and Reactionaries.* Oxford: UP, 1981.

———, ed. *Burke, Paine, Godwin, and the Revolution Controversy.* Cambridge: UP, 1984.

Carnall, Geoffrey. "The *Monthly Magazine.*" *Review of English Studies* n. s. 5 (1954): 158–64.

Cestre, Charles. *John Thelwall, A Pioneer of Democracy in England.* London: Swann Sonnenschein; NY: Charles Scribner's Sons, 1906.

Chase, Malcolm. *"The People's Farm." English Radical Agrarianism 1775–1840.* Oxford: Clarendon P, 1988.

Claeys, Gregory. *Citizens and Saints. Politics and Anti-Politics in Early British Socialism.* Cambridge: UP, 1989.

Coleridge, E. H., ed. *Coleridge. Poetical Works.* Vol. 1. Oxford: UP, 1912.

Cone, Carl. *The English Jacobins. Reformers in Late Eighteenth-Century England.* NY: Charles Scribner's Sons, 1968.

Cookson, J. E. *The Friends of Peace. Anti-War Liberalism in England.* Cambridge: UP, 1982.

Curran, Stuart. "The I Altered." *Romanticism and Feminism.* Ed. Anne K. Mellor. Bloomington & Indianapolis: Indiana UP, 1988.

Davenport, Allen. *The Life and Literary Pursuits of Allen Davenport.* London: G. Hancock, 1845. NY & London: Garland, 1986.

Dickinson, H. T. *British Radicalism and the French Revolution 1789–1815.* London: Basil Blackwell, 1985.

———, ed. *The Political Works of Thomas Spence.* Newcastle-upon-Tyne: Aero, 1982.

Dinwiddy, J. R. "William Cobbett, George Houston and Free Thought." *Notes and Queries* 222 (1977): 325–29.

Erdman, David V. *Blake: Prophet Against Empire.* Rev. ed. Garden City: Anchor Books, 1969.

———. "Citizen Stanhope and the French Revolution." *Wordsworth Circle* 15 (1984): 8–17.

———. *Commerce des Lumières. John Oswald and the British in Paris, 1790–1793.* Columbia: U of Missouri P, 1986.

Fawcett, Trevor. "Measuring the Provincial Enlightenment: The Case of Norwich." *Eighteenth Century Life* 8 (1982): 13–27.

Friedman, Albert B. *The Ballad Revival. Studies in the Influence of Popular on Sophisticated Poetry.* Chicago: UP, 1961.

Gallop, G. I. *"Pig's Meat": The Selected Writings of Thomas Spence, Radical and Pioneer Land Reformer.* Nottingham: UP, 1982.

George, M. Dorothy. *English Political Caricature. 1793–1832. A Study of Opinion and Propaganda.* Oxford: Clarendon P, 1959.

Goodwin, Albert. *The Friends of Liberty. The English Democratic Movement in the Age of the French Revolution.* Cambridge: Harvard UP, 1979.

Gossman, Norbert J., & John O. Baylen, ed. *Biographical Dictionary of Modern British*

Radicals, Vol. 1: 1770–1830. Sussex & New Jersey: Harvester P & Humanities P, 1979.

Graham, Walter. "The Authorship of the Norwich *Cabinet*, 1794–5." *Notes and Queries* 162 (1932): 294–95.

———. *English Literary Journals*. NY: Thomas Nelson & Sons, 1930.

Griggs, Earl Leslie, ed. *Collected Letters of Samuel Taylor Coleridge*. 4 vols. Oxford: Clarendon P, 1956–72.

Grumbling, Vernon O. "John Thelwall: Romantick and Revolutionist." Diss. U of New Hampshire, 1977.

Harvey, Arnold D. *English Poetry in a Changing Society, 1780–1825*. NY: St. Martin's P, 1980.

Hearn, Francis. *Domination, Legitimation, and Resistance. The Incorporation of the Nineteenth-Century English Working Class*. Westport: Greenwood P, 1978.

Hendrix, Richard. "Popular Humor and the *Black Dwarf*." *Journal of British Studies* 16 (1976): 108–28.

Hone, J. Ann. *For the Cause of Truth. Radicalism in London 1796–1821*. Oxford: Clarendon P, 1982.

Howell, T. B., ed. *A Complete Collection of State Trials*. Vol. 22. London: Hansard, 1817.

Jewson, C. B. *The Jacobin City: A Portrait of Norwich in its Reaction to the French Revolution 1788–1802*. Glasgow: Blackie & Son, 1975.

Johnson, David. *Regency Revolution. The Case of Arthur Thistlewood*. London: Compton Russell, 1974.

Johnston, Kenneth R. "The Politics of 'Tintern Abbey.'" *Wordsworth Circle* 14 (1983): 6–14.

———. *Wordsworth and "The Recluse."* New Haven & London: Yale UP, 1984.

Klancher, Jon. *The Making of the English Reading Audiences, 1790–1832*. Madison & London: U of Wisconsin P, 1987.

Kovalev, Y. V. *An Anthology of Chartist Writing*. Moscow: International, 1956.

Landry, Donna. *The Muses of Resistance: Laboring-Class Women's Poetry in Britain, 1739–1796*. Cambridge: UP, 1990.

Laqueur, Thomas W. "The Queen Caroline Affair: Politics as Art in the Reign of George IV." *Journal of Modern History* 54 (1982): 417–66.

———. *Religion and Respectability. Sunday Schools and Working Class Culture, 1780–1850*. New Haven & London: Yale UP, 1976.

Lean, E. Tangye. *The Napoleonists. A Study in Political Disaffection 1760–1960*. London, et al.: Oxford UP, 1970.

Little, Geoffrey. "Tintern Abbey and Llyswen Farm." *Wordsworth Circle* 8 (1977): 80–83.

Lonsdale, Roger. *Eighteenth-Century Women Poets. An Oxford Anthology*. NY & London: Oxford UP, 1989.

Low, Donald A., ed. *Robert Burns. The Critical Heritage*. London & Boston: Rutledge & Kegan Paul, 1974.

Maidment, Brian. *The Poorhouse Fugitives. Self-Taught Poets and Poetry in Victorian Britain*. NY: Carcanet, 1987.

Bibliography

Marlow, Joyce. *The Peterloo Massacre.* London: Rapp and Whiting, 1969.

Mayo, Robert. "The Contemporaneity of the *Lyrical Ballads.*" *PMLA* 69 (1954): 486–522.

McCalman, Iain. *Radical Underworld. Prophets, Revolutionaries and Pornographers in London, 1795–1840.* Cambridge: UP, 1988.

McCue, Jr., Daniel L. "Daniel Isaac Eaton and *Politics for the People.*" Diss. Columbia U, 1974.

———. "The Pamphleteer Pitt's Government Couldn't Silence." *Eighteenth-Century Life* 5 (1978): 38–49.

McGuire, Richard L. "The *Monthly Magazine* (1796–1843): Politics and Literature in Transition." Diss. Rice U , 1968.

Mellor, Anne K. "On Romanticism and Feminism." *Romanticism and Feminism.* Ed. Anne K. Mellor. Bloomington & Indianapolis: Indiana UP, 1988.

Murphy, Michael J. *Cambridge Newspapers and Opinion, 1780–1850.* Cambridge: Oleander P, 1977.

Parssinen, T. M. "Thomas Spence and the Origins of English Land Nationalization." *Journal of the History of Ideas* 34 (1973): 135–41.

Pollin, Burton, & Redmond Burke. "John Thelwall's Marginalia in a Copy of Coleridge's *Biographia Literaria.*" *Bulletin of the New York Public Library* 74 (1970): 73–94.

Porter, Dale H. *The Abolition of the Slave Trade in England, 1784–1807.* NY: Archon Books, 1970.

Prothero, Iorwerth. *Artisans and Politics in Early Nineteenth-Century London. John Gast and His Times.* Folkestone: William Dawson & Son, 1979.

Reiman, Donald H. Introduction. *Ode to Science by John Thelwall.* NY & London: Garland, 1978.

———. Introduction. *George Dyer's Odes and The Poet's Fate.* NY & London: Garland, 1979.

Reinitz, Neil Robert. "The French Revolution in London Newspaper Verse of the Seventeen-Nineties." Diss. U of California, 1958.

Rickword, Edgell, ed. *Radical Squibs and Loyal Ripostes.* NY: Barnes & Noble, 1971.

Roberts, Michael. *The Whig Party 1807–1812.* 1939; London: Frank Cass, 1965.

Roe, Nicholas. *Wordsworth and Coleridge: The Radical Years.* Oxford: UP, 1988.

Ross, Marlon. *The Contours of Masculine Desire. Romanticism and the Rise of Women's Poetry.* NY & Oxford: Oxford UP, 1989.

Rudkin, Olive. *Thomas Spence and His Connections.* London: George Allen & Unwin, 1927.

Scheckner, Peter. *An Anthology of Chartist Poetry. Poetry of the British Working Class, 1830s–1850s.* Rutherford et al.: Fairleigh Dickinson & Associated UP, 1989.

Scrivener, Michael. *Radical Shelley.* Princeton: UP, 1982.

———. "The Rhetoric and Context of John Thelwall's 'Memoir.'" *The Spirits of Fire.* Ed. G. A. Rosso & Daniel P. Watkins. Rutherford et al.: Fairleigh Dickinson & Associated UP, 1990.

Selincourt, Ernest de, & Chester L. Shaver, ed. *Letters of William and Dorothy Wordsworth. The Early Years 1787–1805.* 2nd ed. Oxford: Clarendon P, 1967.

Shelley, Percy Bysshe. *Shelley. Poetical Works*. Ed. Thomas Hutchinson & G. M. Matthews. Oxford: UP, 1969.
Smith, Olivia. *The Politics of Language 1791–1819*. Oxford: Clarendon P, 1984.
Sullivan, Alvin, ed. *British Literary Magazines. The Romantic Age, 1789–1836*. Westport & London: Greenwood P, 1983.
Thale, Mary. *Selections from the Papers of the London Corresponding Society, 1792–1799*. Cambridge: UP, 1983.
———, ed. *The Autobiography of Francis Place*. Cambridge: UP, 1972.
Thelwall, Mrs. [Cecil]. *The Life of John Thelwall*. London: John Macrone, 1837.
Thompson, E. P. "Disenchantment or Default? A Lay Sermon." *Power and Consciousness*. Ed. Conor Cruise O'Brien & William Dean Vanech. London & NY: U of London P & New York UP, 1969.
———. *The Making of the English Working Class*. NY: Vintage P, 1963.
Vicinus, Martha. *The Industrial Muse: A Study of Nineteenth-Century British Working Class Culture*. NY: Barnes & Noble, 1974.
Vincent, David. *Bread, Knowledge and Freedom. A Study of Nineteenth-Century Working Class Autobiography*. London & NY: Methuen, 1981.
Walvin, James. *Black and White. The Negro and English Society, 1555–1945*. London: Allen Lane, 1973.
Werkmeister, Lucyle. *A Newspaper History of England 1792–1793*. Lincoln: U of Nebraska P, 1967.
White, Newman I. *Shelley*. Vol. 1. NY: Alfred A. Knopf, 1940.
Wiener, Joel. *Radicalism and Freethought in Nineteenth-Century Britain. The Life of Richard Carlile*. Westport & London: Greenwood P, 1983.
Williams, Raymond. *Keywords. A Vocabulary of Culture and Society*. NY: Oxford UP, 1976.
———. *The Long Revolution*. London: Chatto & Windus, 1961.

Author Index

A. R.: "A Picture and a Prophecy," 160
Aikin, John: "To Gilbert Wakefield, A. B. on his Liberation from Prison," 155; "To Liberty," 40
Aikin, Lucy: "On Miss Linwood's Admirable Pictures in Needle-work," 145; "To the Memory of the Rev. G. Wakefield," 158
Alderson, Amelia: "Sonnet to Winter," 124
Alfred: "Monopoly," 203
Anthocles: [Burdett!], 162

B.: Jeremy Bentham, 272
Bamford, Samuel: "Ode to a Plotting Parson . . . ," 274
Best, Thomas: "Song," 95
Blandford, Edward J.: "More Hints for Mr. Bull; With the last Hint, which at last Bull must take!" 238; "Nature's First, Last, and Only Will! Or a hint to Mr. Bull," 234; "A Real Dream; Or, Another Hint for Mr. Bull!" 235; "A Terrible Omen to Guilty Tyrants; or The Spirit of Liberty!" 243

C. M. T.: "A Tear," 253
C. P.: "Invocation to Britain," 239
C. V. L.: "Domestic Felicity," 58
Caledonius: "To Britons," 263
Citizen of World, A: "On Sugar," 47
CLIO: "Impromptu Reply to Impertinence," 256

Coleridge, Samuel T.: "The Devil's Thoughts," 215

Dalby, J. W.: "The Queen's Triumph," 270
Davenport, Allen: "A Hint to the Congress," 213; "An Ode, to Major Cartwright," 240; "Saint Ethelstone's Day," 224; "The Topic," 205
Davison, T.: "Majesty in the Shades," 228
Dick: "The Plot. A Letter to my Brother Robert in the Country," 250
Dyer, George: "Hymn on the Fast," 44; "An Ode . . . ," 278; "Song," 127

Emigrant, An: "An Ode to Kentucky," 98

F. A. C.: "Invocation to the Genius of Britain," 129; "Lines Written by a Female Citizen!" 122
F. G.: "Tribute to the Memory of an Injured Queen," 273
Fair, Robert C.: "Insolence," 255; "Napoleon in Exile," 262; "Ode to Major Cartwright," 256; "Ode to Religion," 175; "The Ruined City," 179; "Scripture Soliloquies. Our Blessed Saviour on Mount Calvary," 177
Florio: "To Belinda," 257

Author Index

Grant, W. D.: "Tribute to Liberty," 69

Green, W. H.: "The Attributes of Liberty," 100; "Cato's Soliloquy Parodied," 93; "Political Conundrums," 96; "The Republican Crop. A New Song," 103

H. W.: "On the New and Unconstitutional Legislative Acts . . . ," 200

Hibernicus: "Stanzas Occasioned by the Manchester Massacre!" 265

Holcroft, Fanny: "The Condemned Sailor," 159; "Conscience the Worst of Tortures," 143

J. W. B.: "The Banished Printer to His Trade," 272

Joshua: "Sonnet: The Lion," 128

L.: "Address to Poverty," 131

Lady, A: "Sedition Act," 45

M.: "To Englishmen," 209

No Work: "Two Ways . . . ," 76

P. F. P———: "Spontaneous Verse," 185

Philanthropos: "Effects of War," 84

Philo Taurus: "The Three Bulls and the Jackdaw. A Fable," 254

Pindar, Tommy: "A Tale," 87

R. M.: "Every Inch a Patriot, A New Song," 104

Radix: "The Late Honourable Conduct of Radicals Justified," 276

Renege: "The Wish," 57

Rickman, Clio: "Ode on the Anniversary of T. Paine's Birth-Day . . . ," 206; "Sonnet. Written with a Pencil . . . ," 212

Roderick Random: "Ode to the Ladies on Their Alledged [sic] Rights," 258

Rutt, John T.: "Part of an Inscription Designed for a Garden," 160; "Stanzas to Thomas Paine," 41; "The Wrongs of Poverty," 54

S.: "On Sectarian Persecution," 179

S. D.: "A Lord's Advice, and a Tradesman's Reply," 244

S. R.: "Appeal to Englishmen," 204

S. W.: "Ode to Terror," 140; "To the Memory of the Right Honourable Charles James Fox," 168

Scott, Mr.: "A Song Composed for the Anniversary of the French Revolution . . . ," 50

Shorter, Robert: "The Bloody Field of Peterloo! A New Song," 218; [Let Preachers waste their breath . . .], 217; "On seeing in a List of New Music *The Waterloo Waltz,*" 201; "A Psalm, to the Praise and Honor of Liberty," 219; "The Wanton Wife of Bath," 220; [When Babylon's Notorious Wh———re . . .], 217

Sly, Sam: "Epigram," 52

Spence, Thomas: "Alteration," 67; "Burke's Address to the 'Swinish Multitude!'" 65; "The Downfall of Feudal Tyranny," 73; "Edmund Burke's Address to the Swinish Multitude," 69; "Examples of Safe Printing," 68; "[Jubilee Hymn] From Spence's Rights of Man . . . ," 63; "The Rights of Man for Me . . . ," 72

Spencean Philanthropist: "The Rights of Man, Or, Things as they were intended to be by Divine Providence," 231; "The Wrongs of Man. Or, Things as they Are," 229

Sturch, William: "Sonnet to Reason," 269

Sylvanus Amicus: "Sonnet," 93

T. A. T.: "It is Lovely to Die for Our Country," 227

T. P.: "Monday's News at Bath . . . ," 165

T. R.: "Soliloquy," 57

T. S. S.: "Effusion on the Approaching Fast-Day," 139

Author Index

Taylor, G.: "Distress of the Poor; A New Song," 212
Tell: "The Present War," 61
Thelwall, John: "Glee (*Glorious Apollo*)," 134; "News from Toulon . . . ," 113; "Ode on the Destruction of the Bastille," 109; "A Patriot's Feeling; or the Call of Duty," 119; "A Sheepsheering Song," 115; "To Stella, On her Birth-day . . . ", 138

W. F. L.: "State Contrivances!," 267
Wakefield, Gilbert: "Horace, Book i. Epist. 18 Verse 96. to the End," 154; "To John Aikin, M.D.," 157

Wedderburn, Robert: "The African[']s Complaint on board a Slave Ship!" 196; [Britons!], 198; "The Desponding Negro," 195; "An Englishman's Domestic View of his Political Situation . . . ," 190; "The Negro Boy sold for a Watch," 196
Wooler, Thomas J.: "Answer to the Threats of Corruption," 253

Z.: "The Cottage. A Competence and not Riches the Source of Happiness," 125

SUBJECT INDEX

Periodical abbreviations:

Athen. = *Athenaeum*
BD = *Black Dwarf*
CI = *Cambridge Intelligencer*
FH/ALttR = *Forlorn Hope/Axe Laid to the Root*
FPR = *Flower's Political Review*
M = *Medusa*
MC = *Morning Chronicle*
MH = *Manchester Herald*
MM = *Monthly Magazine*

MPM = *Moral and Political Magazine*
Oec. = *Oeconomist*
Phil. = *Philanthropist*
PM = *Pig's Meat*
PP = *Politics for the People*
SPR = *Sherwin's Political Register*
TI = *Theological Inquirer*
TPC = *Theological and Political Comet*
Trib. = *Tribune*
WH = *White Hat*

Poem's title	Periodical	Author	Pg.#
English Politics			
Burke's Address	*PM* (1793)	T. Spence	65
E. Burke's Address	*PM* (1794)	T. Spence	69
Devil's Thoughts	*Mirror* (1817)	S. T. Coleridge	215
Effusion on the Fast-Day	*MM* (1797)	T. S. S.	139
Epigram	*MH* (7-28-1792)	S. Sly	52
Hymn for the Fast Day	*PP* (1794)	n. a.	88
Hymn on the Fast	*MC* (4-18-1793)	G. Dyer	44
Impromptu	*BD* (1818)	CLIO	256
Monday's News at Bath	*FPR* (1807)	T. P.	165
New Song	*Phil.* (1795)	n. a.	94
On Abuses	*PP* (1794)	n. a.	90
Patriot's Feeling	*Trib.* (1795)	J. Thelwall	119
Political Conundrums	*Phil.* (1795)	W. H. Green	96
Queen's Triumph	*BD* (1820)	J. W. Dalby	270
Radicals Justified	*BD* (1822)	Radix	276
Reform	*MH* (5-1792)	n. a.	48
Sheepsheering Song	*Trib.* (1795)	J. Thelwall	115
Song	*Phil.* (1795)	T. Best	95

Subject Index

Poem's title	Periodical	Author	Pg.#
Sonnet: Westminster	*SPR* (1818)	C. Rickman	212
Sonnet: Who loves	*Phil.* (1795)	Sylvanus Amicus	93

French Revolution/War

Anniversary of French Rev.	*MH* (7-21-1792)	Mr. Scott	50
Caramagnole	*Phil.* (1795)	n. a.	97
Effects of War	*PP* (1794)	Philanthropos	84
For the Tenth of Aug., 1795	*Phil.* (1795)	n. a.	102
Friends of French Freedom	*MH* (7-7-1792)	n. a.	49
Genius of France	*MC* (11-30-1792)	n. a.	43
Hint to the Congress	*SPR* (1818)	A. Davenport	213
Napoleon in Exile	*BD* (1818)	R. Fair	262
News from Toulon	*Trib.* (1795)	J. Thelwall	113
Ode on Liberty	*MC* (7-17-1792)	n. a.	37
Ode on the Bastille	*Trib.* (1795)	J. Thelwall	109
Ode to Terror	*MM* (1797)	S. W.	140
On seeing . . . *Waterloo Waltz*	*SPR* (1817)	R. Shorter	201
Present War	*Patriot* (2-1793)	Tell	61
1694	*PP* (1794)	n. a.	77
Sonnet	*Phil.* (1795)	Sylvanus Amicus	93
To Liberty	*MC* (9-14-1792)	J. A.	40

Liberty

Attributes of Liberty	*Phil.* (1795)	W. H. Green	100
Englishman's View	*People* (1817)	R. Wedderburn	190
Glee	*MM* (1796)	J. Thelwall	134
Hymn to Liberty	*PP* (1794)	n. a.	82
Ode to Freedom	*Phil.* (1796)	n. a.	105
Song	*MPM* (1796)	G. Dyer	127
Song . . . to Liberty	*CI* (10-19-1793)	n. a.	56
Song. The Fire of Liberty.	*MH* (12-8-1792)	n. a.	52
Tribute to Liberty	*PM* (1794)	W. D. Grant	69

Peterloo Massacre

Address to "The Rabble"	*M* (1819)	n. a.	245
Blood Field of Peterloo!	*TPC* (1819)	R. Shorter	218
Manchester Massacre	*BD* (1819)	Hibernicus	265
New Song	*TPC* (1819)	n. a.	225
Ode to Plotting Parson	*BD* (1821)	S. Bamford	274
On a Bloody Massacre	*M* (1819)	n. a.	244
Paddy Bull's Epistle	*M* (1819)	n. a.	246
Peterloo Man	*BD* (1819)	n. a.	266
Saint Ethelstone's Day	*TPC* (1819)	A. Davenport	224

Subject Index

Poem's title	Periodical	Author	Pg.#

Philosophy/Religion

[Blush, Christian]	TPC (1819)	n. a.	222
[Let preachers]	TPC (1819)	R. Shorter	217
[When Babylon's]	TPC (1819)	R. Shorter	217
Holy Anticipation	FPR (1808)	n. a.	171
Majesty in the Shades	M (1819)	T. Davison	228
Man in Prospective	M (1819)	n. a.	240
Necessity	Athen. (1808)	n. a.	163
Ode to Religion	TI (1815)	R. C. Fair	175
On Sectarian Persecution	TI (1815)	S.	179
Psalm	TPC (1819)	R. Shorter	219
Ruined City	TI (1815)	R. C. Fair	179
Scripture Soliloquies	TI (1815)	R. C. Fair	177
Sonnet to Reason	BD (1820)	W. Sturch	269
Three Bulls & the Jackdaw	BD (1818)	Philo Taurus	254

Poetry/Poet

Independence	PP (1794)	n. a.	83
Song: While Venal Bards	MPM (1796)	G. Dyer	127
To Robert Burns	MM (1797)	n. a.	134

Poverty/Economic Protest

Address to Poverty	Phil. (1795)	n. a.	92
Distress of the Poor	SPR (1818)	G. Taylor	212
England	SPR (1818)	n. a.	210
Fable. The Ass & the Driver.	MPM (1797)	n. a.	130
Insolence	BD (1818)	F.	255
Lord's Advice	M (1819)	S. D.	244
Monopoly	SPR (1817)	Alfred	203
Nature's . . . Will	M (1819)	E. J. Blandford	234
On Abuses	PP (1794)	n. a.	90
Parallel	PP (1794)	n. a.	86
Rights of Man	M (1819)	Spencean	231
Sonnet: Go place	MPM (1797)	n. a.	130
Tale	PP (1794)	T. Pindar	87
Topic	SPR (1817)	A. Davenport	205
Two Ways	PP (1793–94)	No Work	76
Wrongs of Man	M (1819)	Spencean	229
Wrongs of Poverty	CI (8-31-1793)	J. T. Rutt	54

Repression

Banished Printer	BD (1821)	J. W. B.	272
Every Inch a Patriot	Phil. (1796)	R. M.	104

Subject Index

Poem's title	Periodical	Author	Pg.#
Examples of Safe Printing	*PM* (1794)	T. Spence	68
New Loyal Song	*BD* (1824)	n. a.	277
On the Unconstitutional	*SPR* (1817)	H. W.	200
Plot	*BD* (1817)	Dick	250
Rights of Man For Me	*PM* (1795)	T. Spence	72
Sedition Act	*MC* (1-5-1796)	A Lady	45
Soliloquy	*CI* (4-5-1794)	T. R.	57
State Contrivances!	*BD* (1820)	W. F. L.	267
To G. Wakefield	*MM* (1800)	J. Aikin	155
To J. Aikin	*MM* (1801)	G. Wakefield	157
To the Memory of G.W.	*MM* (1801)	L. Aikin	158
What Makes a Libel?	*PP* (1793)	n. a.	76

Republicanism

Genius of Britain	*MPM* (1796)	F. A. C.	122
Goitre	*PP* (1794)	n. a.	79
Logs, Storks, and Asses	*PP* (1794)	n. a.	78
Republican Crop	*Phil.* (1795)	W. H. Green	103
Sonnet. The Lion	*MPM* (1796)	Joshua	128
Tale	*PP* (1794)	T. Pindar	87

Revolution

[Britons!]	*FH/ALttR* (1817)	R. Wedderburn	198
Alteration	*PM* (1794)	T. Spence	67
By a Female Citizen	*Trib.* (1795)	F. A. C.	122
Feudal Tyranny	*PM* (1795)	T. Spence	73
Genius of Britain	*MPM* (1796)	F. A. C.	129
Invocation to Britain	*M* (1819)	C. P.	239
It is Lovely to Die	*WH* (1819)	T. A. T.	227
[Jubilee Hymn]	*PM* (1793)	T. Spence	63
More Hints for Mr. Bull	*M* (1819)	E. J. Blandford	238
Sonnet: Muse	*WH* (1819)	n. a.	226
To Britons	*BD* (1819)	Caledonius	263
To Englishmen	*SPR* (1818)	M.	209

Slavery

African's Complaint	*FH/ALttR* (1817)	R. Wedderburn	196
Desponding Negro	*FH/ALttR* (1817)	R. Wedderburn	195
Negro Boy Sold	*FH/ALttR* (1817)	R. Wedderburn	196
On Sugar	*MH* (4-7-1792)	Citizen of World	47
Song . . . to Liberty	*CI* (10-19-1793)	n. a.	56

Tributes

[Burdett!]	*MM* (1809)	Anthocles	162
Answer to . . . Corruption	*BD* (1817)	T. J. Wooler	253

Subject Index

Poem's title	Periodical	Author	Pg.#
Cato's Soliloquy Parodied	*Phil.* (1795)	W. H. Green	93
Jeremy Bentham	*BD* (1821)	B.	272
Ode	*BD* (1824)	G. Dyer	278
Ode . . . Paine	*SPR* (1818)	C. Rickman	206
Ode to Maj. Cartwright	*BD* (1818)	R. C. Fair	256
Ode, to Maj. Cartwright	*M* (1819)	A. Davenport	240
Part of an Inscription	*MM* (1801)	J. T. Rutt	160
Spontaneous Verse	*People* (1817)	P. F. P——	185
Stanzas to Thomas Paine	*MC* (9-28-1792)	J. T. Rutt	41
To Charles J. Fox	*FPR* (1807)	S. W.	168
To Robert Burns	*MM* (1797)	n. a.	134

Utopia/Nature/Pastoral

Ballad	*MM* (1796)	n. a.	132
Cottage	*Oec.* (1798)	Z.	125
Domestic Felicity	*CI* (3-21-1795)	C. V. L.	58
Harvest Moon	*Oec.* (1798)	n. a.	126
Horace	*MM* (1800)	G. Wakefield	154
Ode to Kentucky	*Phil.* (1795)	An Emigrant	98
Owen Parfet	*MM* (1799)	n. a.	146
Picture and a Prophecy	*MM* (1803)	A. R.	160
Real Dream	*M* (1819)	E. J. Blandford	235
Soliloquy	*CI* (4-5-1794)	T. R.	57
Sonnet to Winter	*Cabinet* (1795)	A. Alderson	124
Sonnet: O! Thou	*CI* (6-5-1799)	n. a.	60
Sonnet: Ye woods	*CI* (3-30-1799)	n. a.	59
Tear	*BD* (1818)	C. M. T.	253
To Stella	*MM* (1797)	J. Thelwall	138
Wish	*CL* (7-19-1794)	Renege	57

Women

By a Female Citizen	*Trib.* (1795)	F. A. C.	122
Condemned Sailor	*MM* (1801)	F. Holcroft	159
Conscience	*MM* (1798)	F. Holcroft	143
Female Ed. at Two Periods	*MM* (1799)	n. a.	150
Genius of Britain	*MPM* (1796)	F. A. C.	129
Maid's Enigma	*MC* (10-13-1792)	n. a.	42
Ode to the Ladies	*BD* (1818)	R. Random	258
On Miss Linwood's	*MM* (1798)	L. Aikin	145
Rights of Women	*BD* (1818)	n. a.	261
Sedition Act	*MC* (1-5-1796)	A Lady	45
Sensibility	*MC* (1-6-1792)	n. a.	37
To Belinda	*BD* (1818)	Florio	257
Wanton Wife of Bath	*TPC* (1819)	R. Shorter	220